Turia Pitt has written three bes
shoulders with the royals (securi
shared the stage with Tony Robbins, and finished the Hawaiian Ironman.

Oh! And she has a crocodile named after her.

She likes to make cool stuff that helps people get happy (like this book!), and has coached more than 40,000 people via her digital courses.

She also likes looking at rocks, running, licorice and spending time with her family on the south coast of New South Wales (Yuin country).

She writes a weekly letter; in fact, it's her favourite thing to do.

Visit her at www.turiapitt.com/letter.

Nice stuff people have said

Turia wholeheartedly sets out to do good, then does even better. She's a national treasure and an astonishing inspiration. I'm genuinely considering a 'What would Turia do?' tattoo.
Zoë Foster Blake, author and founder of Go-To

Turia is a strong and determined woman. Inspirational in every sense of the word! Put simply, a role model for people of all ages.
Mick Fanning, three-times surfing World Champion

Turia Pitt has taught so many of us so much about resilience, persistence and finding joy amid life's challenges.
Leigh Sales, anchor of ABC's *7.30*

Turia Pitt's perspective on happiness is like a refreshing splash of cold water to the face.
Michelle Andrews and Zara McDonald, co-hosts of the *Shameless* podcast

Turia Pitt is an unstoppable force of positivity. She has so much to teach us.
Mia Freedman, co-founder and creative director of the Mamamia Women's Network

Turia is an incredible woman. Forthright, fierce, resilient, bold, strong & oozing courage. She has so much to teach us about life, challenges and cultivating confidence.
Sandra Sully, journalist and senior editor, Ten News

This is what the world needs right now! A self-help book with just the right amount of sass – this is your manual for finding happiness and hanging on to it.
Edwina Bartholomew, journalist

We should all take a leaf out of Turia's life (and this book!) and use the strategies she suggests to get ahead and enjoy our lives even more.
Emma Isaacs, founder and global CEO, Business Chicks

I absolutely LOVE Turia. If there was someone to write about happiness it is this all-star crazy go-getter, who embraces life with everything she has. It's a big fat YES from me to anything she does. This book will not disappoint!
Lisa Messenger, founder, Collective Hub

More nice stuff people have said

Turia, you always make me happier and uplifted! – Dorise

Turia's tips are like nuggets of gold. From a made bed (goal achieved) to a cold shower, they remind me that life is good and to get on with my day – Fiona

Turia makes me laugh, cry, think, and feel inspired – Jess

I love when my mailbox goes 'ding' on a Thursday with your weekly email. There is always something in there that makes me smile, laugh or just gives me a little pick-me-up. Thanks for the simple reminders that this life we have is pretty damn good! – Maz

Every time I read something Turia's written it literally makes my day. It's like a one-on-one therapy session with her! – Nigar

Turia makes me feel refreshed, invigorated and happy to be alive! – Lucy

Your writing helps me to focus on the brighter side of things that so often gets overlooked when we're in doubt or going through a tough time. Thank you! – Caitlin

It's like you can read my mind: you seem to know exactly when I need a little pep-me-up. Thanks for making me happier! – Kat

I love what Turia does and what she's about. She empowers us all to make a difference – Zoe

Turia, you make me happy at times by giving me a giggle. Your down-to-earth yet hilarious personality comes through in every sentence – Jamie

Other cool stuff that Turia has made

Good Selfie

Unmasked (with Bryce Corbett)

Unmasked Young Readers Edition (with Bryce Corbett)

Everything to Live For (with Libby Harkness)

TURIA PITT

EBURY
PRESS

EBURY PRESS

UK | USA | Canada | Ireland | Australia
India | New Zealand | South Africa | China

Ebury Press is part of the Penguin Random House group of companies whose addresses can be found at global.penguinrandomhouse.com

First published by Ebury Press in 2020

Copyright © Turia Pitt 2020

The moral right of the author has been asserted.

All rights reserved. No part of this publication may be reproduced, published, performed in public or communicated to the public in any form or by any means without prior written permission from Penguin Random House Australia Pty Ltd or its authorised licensees.

While the utmost care has been taken in researching and compiling *Happy*, the information contained in this book is not intended as a substitute for professional medical advice. You should obtain professional advice from a medical or mental health practitioner before making lifestyle changes relating to your health.

Cover photography by Elizabeth Allnutt Photographer
Cover design by Adam Laszczuk © Penguin Random House Australia Pty Ltd
Internal design by Midland Typesetters, Australia
Typeset in 12.5/17.5 Minion by Midland Typesetters

Printed and bound in Australia by Griffin Press, part of Ovato, an accredited ISO AS/NZS 14001 Environmental Management Systems printer

A catalogue record for this book is available from the National Library of Australia

ISBN 978 1 76089 288 3

penguin.com.au

Imagine the dismay. You've picked up a book, frantically danced your fingers through the pages until you find the dedication page . . . only to find that *once again* you haven't been mentioned.

Not this time!

This book, dear reader, is dedicated to *you*! Fallible, flawed and perfectly imperfect you.

You're welcome :)

I would like to acknowledge the traditional custodians
of the Australian lands on which I live and work,
and on which I learn. I pay my respects to
all Elders, past and present.

This book was written on Yuin country.

Contents

Letter to the reader (that's you!)

When I was first asked by my publishers to write this book, I screamed to them in my best Jerry Maguire voice: '*Show me the money!*'

Then I felt weird and embarrassed because no one laughed. Anyway, I signed on the dotted line, and promptly forgot all about any book and carried on with my life, which mostly involves me fawning over images of myself dressed up in front of a wind machine.

I got a few friendly reminders from my publishers – one even threatening legal action unless I showed them I was doing something, which gave me the kind of heart palpitations you get when you're really scared because you've definitely over-committed and *why, oh why did you tell everyone you liked writing about confidence and happiness?*

•

Yes, indeed, I had a lot of self-doubt when I was writing this book (and thinking about this book, and researching for this book, and dreaming about this book). Why? Well, hasn't everything on happiness already been . . . done? The subject's been studied for thousands of years. There are more than thirteen billion search results when you type 'happy' in to Google. I'm not a scholar or a psychologist; the only academic qualifications I have are for mining engineering (so if ya need any rock excavations . . .). I felt at times as though I didn't have value or insight to add to the conversation and I didn't feel like a 'real writer'.

When I envisage a real writer, I think of a crazed intellectual staying up till three in the morning, with a bottle of whisky on their desk (a desk plastered with reams of paper and ancient texts and original works by Voltaire and Oscar Wilde) frantically scribbling down their thoughts with a quill, creative genius gushing from their mind – until they burst forth into their publisher's office on the day of the deadline, slap the manuscript down on the publisher's desk and light a cigar, *inside.*

That wasn't me.

I worked out how long it would take me to write each chapter. Then I created a Gantt chart that ensured I had ample time to incorporate revisions and feedback. Then I downloaded all sorts of useful software, colour-coded to my heart's content, and then . . . realised I still actually had to do the writing. And I was getting paid so I had to deliver, y'know?

So, with no 'organising' left to procrastinate with, I started to write. And these words you're reading right now? Well, they were written for you. Not in a creepy, staring at you through a window in the dead of night kind of way. But you were on my mind as I wrote. Late at night, and early in the morning, bleary-eyed and over-caffeinated. I gave you a lot of thought. Because I wanted this book to genuinely speak to you.

But, of course, it was written without knowing the intricacies and idiosyncrasies that make you, YOU. Because you are special. There's never been and is no one else on the planet who has your life circumstances, your personality, your upbringing and your hair. That makes you unique, and it also makes it very hard to write a *personalised* book just for you. So this book is mainly about me (haha!). Okay, not 'about me', but about what I believe to be true about happiness.

This is my take, my spin on it, having been through something pretty hectic, rebuilt my life from the ground up and, in the process, done some really cool shit.

Now, I don't know your exact personal circumstances: you may have experienced something extremely traumatic, you may be going through something distressing right now (and if this is you, please make sure you're getting some professional support: there are some awesome services listed in the Resources section).

You may have a different belief system to me, or a different moral compass, or you might just think differently to me. This book was written from my perspective – and my perspective is that of a straight woman in a long-term relationship, who's had a good upbringing in a largely white, small coastal town. And while I've travelled, and tried to educate myself on a wider set of perspectives, of course mine has been skewed by my personal circumstances. So, as with anything that you read (my books included), take what works for you, and leave the rest.

I've tried not to rely on conventional wisdom about happiness, and since being a smartarse is my default state, I've found that pretty easy. I've also tried hard to use evidence-based theories, and when I couldn't find any that were satisfactory, I just got drunk with my friends and asked them. Joking! I made them up.

Some of the strategies I share are easy to master (to boost your happiness, literally all you need to do is hug someone). Some of them, are, um, a bit more challenging (to boost your happiness, you must have a purpose in life. Righto, then).

Enjoy these words. I enjoyed writing them for you!

Lots of love,

Turia

Introduction (start here plz)

I wrote most of this book in 2019, while I was pregnant with my second son. I'd set out to discover whether happiness was an aspiration worth pursuing. See, for almost a decade, people have asked me a lot of questions about happiness. Thousands of emails, hundreds of questions. People wanting to know how I was so goddamn happy, damn it, and how they could get some of it too.

What they were really asking was: how can you survive a grassfire, suffer burns to 65 per cent of your body, have your life and appearance fundamentally changed, and still, um, be happy? And how could they get through their fucked-up divorce/cancer diagnosis/crippling self-doubt, and be happy as well?

For the most part, I knew how to answer them – in the sense that I knew what happiness meant for me. But, as you'll discover in this book, I have what we'll call a high regard for the facts. I'm a mining engineer by trade. I value research-driven data. I like systems. I wanted to know, beyond a shadow of doubt (*because it's been rigorously tested in peer-reviewed research*) what does, actually, make you happy.

I liked what I uncovered. And, if you'll allow me to say it, I liked what I'd written. I had a sassy little introduction. My chapters felt fun, well researched, my claims backed by science. I shared strategies that I believed (and science demonstrated) could actually improve your happiness.

This little book on happiness had made me, yes, happy.

And then, in late 2019, my hometown almost burnt down.

Bushfires had surrounded towns up and down the coastline I called home, raining embers and ash on our streets and beaches, destroying homes and livelihoods, wreaking immense, wide-scale devastation.

It was a shit summer, but as the weeks went on, life began to return to some semblance of 'normal'. And something extremely lovely happened for my family. Four weeks after the worst of the fires, I gave birth to the sweetest little baby boy. We named him Rahiti, meaning 'sunrise' in Tahitian.

But then, when Rahiti was four weeks old, rumours of a coronavirus started to percolate. By the time Rahiti was seven weeks old, Australia was in lockdown, non-essential businesses were forced to close, mates and family members had lost their jobs. Like so many people around the world, I had to quickly pivot and grapple with an ever-changing reality. I restructured my business, and restructured again, and then started to let employees go as my work dried up and an uncertain future was just about the only real certainty we could rely on.

I looked at the positives: I got more family time. More time at home. More time to cook. More time with my new baby. But when I turned on the news it was hard not to be sucked into the fear-inducing vortex that it created.

In short, it was hard to be happy at times. (Haha! Just like regular life!)

Not really knowing how else to focus my time, and what to give back to my audience, I started writing emails under the guise of 'Fourteen days of happiness'. They were simple, zippy, speedy little notes, based on the strategies I share in this book. And you know what? Every day hundreds of people replied to those emails. Their words were a demonstration that, *yes*, this shit really helps, and really works.

When I explained how breathing could help us manage our emotions, Ann-Maree wrote back: 'Thank you so much for this breathing exercise. It was like you were next to me on the day I was freaking out and melting down. It helped!'

When I talked about how showing kindness to others helps us to be happier, Linda replied: 'Thanks for this! It's a beautiful start to the day!'

When I shared the one question I ask myself every day to put myself in a good mood, Brad wrote: 'Love this. Started to feel sorry for myself today so I made it great by enjoying some simple pleasures. Good workout, hiked, ordered lasagne for dinner (a real treat) and made sure I told my wife how much I love her. Thank you, Turia.'

So, yes. This book can teach you how to be happier.

But, I want to be very, very clear: the constant and never-ending quest for happiness is not only exhausting but unattainable. I'm not saying that *improving* your happiness is unattainable because it's very much attainable, and that's exactly why I've written this book. But I am saying that there's no endpoint. The journey's a continuum, with ample space for improvement along the way.

In fact, it's a wiggle line. It's dependent on and impacted by life events that are often out of our control (although most of these events, whether they're winning the lottery or getting divorced, don't have as big an impact on our happiness levels as we might imagine). It's how we deal with both the events we didn't see coming, and the ones that *are* in our control, that's key to our ability to enjoy our lives.

In this book, I'll show you how to handle the external elements that impact our happiness, such as making sure that you're set up for the best day possible, investing in your relationships, looking after your money and staying healthy.

I'm also going to show you how to get the most out of your emotions. In other words, I'll help you to platform more of your lighter emotions, such as joy, contentment and humour, as well as to recognise that darker emotions like guilt and shame are, at their essence, just emotions and there's absolutely nothing wrong with experiencing them from time to time. Indeed, in some circumstances they are the only possible emotions we can feel, so we should let them in and accept them; they are valid and necessary for the human experience.

So, the premise of this book? Forget about being happier. As an endpoint or goal, 'happy' is arbitrary, highly subjective, hard to measure and what does it even mean?

Instead, focus on amplifying happy moments. Practise gratitude, be present with your loved ones, savour the good times, learn to love yourself, try to have fun, enjoy your friends and family, and be kind.

Will this lead you down the path of hedonistic mania?

Yes, to an extent.

You'll make time for indulgences, family and loved ones. You'll stop being so 'busy' and start spending your days in a more meaningful way on stuff you enjoy. You'll spend money, but on things that will actually make you happy (as opposed to things that'll gather dust), and you'll appreciate yourself.

While I've been writing this book I've also been speaking to cool people whose perspectives on the subject of attaining bliss and enjoying life I thought would be valuable. And they were! So you, lucky reader, also get to download the pearls of the brilliant Meik Wiking, CEO of the Happiness Research Institute and author of many books including *The Key to Happiness*; Marie Forleo, entrepreneur and author of the number one *New York Times* bestseller *Everything Is Figureoutable*; incredible surfer and all-round amazing person Mick Fanning; the wonderful author and entrepreneur Zoë Foster Blake; and many others, who will light up the following pages with their insights.

Do I – and the people I spoke to, and lots of v. clever researchers – think it's possible to become happier?[1]

YES! A resounding YES shouted from the clifftops.

Do I think it's possible to become happier without working on it?

Nope. Sorry. You don't get something for nothing. As with everything in life: you get out what you put in.

So brace yourselves for a joyful ride and let's crack this happiness thing together.

1 Gratitude, savouring, anticipation

In our first chapter together, I want to give you, dear reader, a quick win. I call it GSA.

According to the plethora of research out there, employing GSA in your life will more than likely increase your happiness levels. It's not *guaranteed*, though. Why?

Well, nothing is guaranteed in this life, sweet cheeks. You might not meet the right person. You might find out you can't have kids. You might be running in an ultramarathon and get caught in a fire. Even that age-old adage 'If you work hard, you'll succeed' is, in its essence, an exaggeration. It should really be changed to 'If you work hard, you'll most probably succeed.'

But I'll tell you one thing – if you don't practise GSA, I can guarantee that you won't get any happier.

So, what is GSA? Top marks if you spotted that it's an acronym.

No, it's not Good Sex Always! (That's how my randy mind remembers it.)

It's: Gratitude, Savouring, Anticipation.

Let's break these three babies down. You can *anticipate* or look forward to the moment. You can be *grateful* for the moment. And you can *savour* the moment after it's gone.

But gratitude comes first because it's the big momma. Anticipation and savouring are the kids. Or you can think of gratitude as the tree, and anticipation and savouring as its leaves. Whichever metaphor you want to use, if you actively and consciously practise gratitude, savouring and anticipation, your happiness levels are very likely to increase.

So without further ado, we'll jump into the big dawg: gratitude.

Gratitude

Let's talk a little about my favourite topic. Me!

When I was twenty-four, I was killing it. I'd graduated from my Mining Engineering and Environmental Science degrees, and Michael and I had moved to the remote mining town of Kununurra, in Western Australia. We were living our dream. I'd landed a fantastic job at the prestigious Argyle diamond mine and we spent our weekends fishing, rock climbing, camping and swimming in waterholes – fully exploring Australia's beautiful outback. Every few months we'd fly home to the south coast of New South Wales to surf and hang with our friends and family. Michael and I were completely in love, we had a wide circle of friends, and we knew we had a bright future together.

So, I was happy, but . . . often I still felt as though my life wasn't good enough. It's not like I was *ungrateful* for my life (just as I know you're not), and I'd done enough travelling and volunteering in developing countries to know how much I 'should' be grateful for, but I was stuck in that trap of focusing on things that weren't going right for me. And because I'm one of those high-achiever types, I thought it was a good thing to focus on the areas of my life that seemed to need improvement.

Doing that, however, meant I wasn't operating from a state of contentment.

This brings me to the biggest myth about showing gratitude: that it might lead us to become complacent. Because if you're content with your life, doesn't that mean there's no room for improvement?

No! Gratitude inspires compassion. It makes you want to give, which forces you to grow. Gratitude is part of growth.

Fast forward seven years. I'm at home recovering from an operation. I've had a really bad night's sleep next to Hakavai. He's teething and has obviously decided that if he can't sleep, I shouldn't be able to either. (Yes, I sleep next to him, still haven't figured out how to put him down by himself #nojudgementsplease.) In the morning, my eyes are so gritty it feels like I've rolled down a sand dune on them.

I stumble out of bed carrying Hakavai, and feel my neck go. Oww, owww, owwww! In my haste to put him down, I stumble over his building blocks and stub my toe on the corner of his change table. I hop out into the kitchen and the mess from last night's dinner is still there – there's crap everywhere. Michael slept on the couch and has left its big cushions strewn over the floor like a pile of giant marshmallows. 'How bloody hard is it to tidy up?' I think to myself.

I hear the garbage trucks on the street and realise that he also didn't take the bins out last night. (Yes, I hear you, I could've taken the bins out last night, but in our household

I have 'my' jobs and Michael has 'his' jobs. You can call me sexist, but I prefer the term 'innovative' because there's a system behind having our jobs so clearly demarcated! And, usually, the system works.)

Fuck.

I contemplate hobbling out there myself, but I'm only wearing an old pair of beige knickers and the thought of putting on a t-shirt is too hard.

Fuck, again.

I am most definitely now in a bad mood; I feel like screaming.

But, first: coffee.

I put a pod into my coffee machine and inhale the delectable aroma as it streams out like a trickle of golden nectar. Then I scull a large glass of water and turn on my diffuser. I scull another glass (for good measure) and take my coffee over to where Hakavai is playing on the floor. Sunlight is flooding through the living room windows, and I marvel at my boy's tiny fingers as he concentrates deeply. I do my deep breathing to reset me (more on this on page 66).

Then I start my gratitude practice. As soon as I start focusing on what I'm grateful for, I can feel my body respond. I'm more conscious of my heart beating, of the way my breath fills and expands my lungs. Positive images flood my brain, of when Hakavai was one week old; sitting next to Michael in the car as he's driving me to another operation; going surfing with my brothers when they were here last week; getting *Taurumi** from my mum.

The feeling of gratitude is so intense that tears start flowing. I welcome them – they're happy tears, after all.

---

* Tahitian massage

Now I feel 100 per cent grateful to be alive, to be here, to have so many opportunities (like writing this book for you); for my family, my friends, my loved ones; and on top of everything else in the infinite universe, most of all for my beautiful son. I remind myself that life is a gift, not a given, that we're not here forever, that our lives are made up of myriad fleeting moments that we can't catch and stall, but which we can be grateful for, appreciate and savour.

Showing gratitude has got to be the easiest and quickest way to diminish negative feelings. It's an antidote to envy, bitterness, anger, hostility, boredom, fear, shame, humiliation ... the list goes on.

But just because something is the 'antidote' to negative emotion, that doesn't mean it actually makes you happier. Right?

Wrong.

There have been far too many studies on gratitude and its benefits for me to list them all here, though if you're interested, as a start you could read Janice Kaplan's *The Gratitude Diaries* and *Thanks!* by Robert Emmons. What we can take from them is that grateful people have stronger social connections and relationships, are less stressed, sleep better, have higher self-esteem, are more trusting and altruistic, and in general more satisfied with life.[1]

Practising gratitude stops that stream of constant comparison with the Joneses (and the other billion people whose lives you watch on Instagram). Gratitude allows us to celebrate the present. It magnifies positive emotions. It helps us to be more resilient, particularly in the face of adversity. It's even been shown to reduce the frequency and duration of episodes of depression.[2]

Okay, so you get it. It's good shit.

So, umm, what is it, exactly? What really is gratitude?

You know when you say 'thank you' to your Aunt Violet for your knitted sweater which fits like . . . well, not like a glove, cos it's a sweater, but it's really nice and cosy. Or after a great meal when you say 'thank you' to the waiter, and you really mean it. Or that moment when one of your kids stops terrorising you, your house and your family pet long enough to lean against you, look up and say 'I love you', and you wonder how you got so lucky.

That's gratitude.

According to some clever researchers, 'gratitude is typically defined as a state that requires us to endorse two facts: that a positive outcome has been achieved, and that this positive outcome came from an external source'.[3]

Let's break this down into layman's terms. You are grateful to your barista (external source) for making a delicious almond latte (positive outcome). You are grateful to your new joggers (external source) for making your walk to work so enjoyable (positive outcome).

Now here's where it gets even more interesting. You don't necessarily need 'good events' in your life to feel gratitude. According to Robert Emmons, a maestro on all things gratitude, grateful people are good at reframing.[4] For example, you are grateful to the sun (external source) because it's a beautiful, sunny day (positive outcome). But if it's raining (external source) you are still grateful because your plants are pretty thirsty right now (positive outcome).

On top of all that, here's a crucial point about gratitude. You know how if you practise tennis a lot, and you go to tennis camps, and you get tennis coaching, you'll most probably get better at tennis? Well, if you're practising gratitude every day, you get better at it. You reinforce the brain pathways that generate more positive feelings. So thought of in this way, gratitude is a type of mental exercise that primes you for positivity.

Just so you know, my default position on most things is highly sceptical with a dash of cynicism, a sprinkle of incredulity, all topped off with garnish of apprehension. And when gratitude was first suggested to me years ago by my psychologist, I had a few reservations. I mean, I'd just been trapped by a grassfire, 65 per cent of my body was burnt, I'd been made redundant from my job, lost seven fingers and couldn't walk more than 100 metres in one go.

So what the hell did I have to be grateful for? Below are my reservations. And the way my psych rebutted every single one of them.

Reservation	Rebuttal
If I'm grateful with my life as it is now, that means I'm satisfied with 'my lot' and therefore I'll have zero motivation to make any changes. I'll be a lazy lethargic lizard who never sees the world beyond her own street.	No, you won't be a lazy lethargic lizard. Research has shown that gratitude can be really motivating, especially because it makes you want to give back some of the goodness you've received.
Mmmm, gratitude is just a bit naïve and clichéd, isn't it? I'm not really into all that woo-woo crystals and yoga stuff.	You don't have to wear flowing robes and crystals around your neck to practise gratitude. Anyone can do it, anywhere and anytime, and with as much or as little spiritual attachment as they like.

Reservation	Rebuttal
I know everything is not about me, but . . . it kind of is, isn't it? I'm the one who's doing the work. I'm the one with the injury.	Even if your life is about you right now, it doesn't have to be. Gratitude will give you a different perspective.
It's hard for me to be grateful right now, with everything I've been through and everything I'm dealing with. I mean, what could I possibly be grateful for?	This one is real. And there's power in being real with yourself, owning your emotions and accepting that you feel shit/angry/frustrated/annoyed and so on, but gratitude will give you the perspective you'll need to find a way out of this. The more you do it, the more you'll see how much goodness surrounds you right now.

Now it's over to you, dear reader. You're an adult, after all, or at least a fully independent guinea pig. So that means you can practise gratitude in a way that suits you. Below are strategies and things for you to try. Give them a go and see which methods work best for you.

This is how I practise gratitude:

- In my head. I don't write things down. Yes, yes, I know that handwriting creates way more neural pathways and you're more likely to remember something you handwrote as opposed to typing or just thinking of things. But I still don't write this stuff down.
- I try to pick things from different categories, these ones in particular:
  - A person who really helped you in the past.

  - An opportunity you have today. Maybe that's an opportunity to see a friend, or an opportunity to go to work. It doesn't have to be something grandiose!
  - Something great that happened yesterday.
  - Something simple near you.
- I'm specific. Note that the more specific you are, the easier it is to connect with the feeling of gratitude. So I won't think, 'I'm grateful to Michael,' I'll think, 'Wow. Michael caught a kingfish yesterday. That's really hard to do. And now we've got heaps of fish, and Michael's a nice person and he's given a lot of them to my mum and my brother, and our son loves the taste of fish.' More details, more imagery = easier to anchor in the feeling of gratitude. Also, I've got some prompts for these categories to freshen things up a bit if you're feeling stale. Check 'em out in the Resources section.
- With music. I like to listen to my gratitude playlist. You can get the link by going to the Resources section. If you want. But, like, you do want to, don't you?

Additional gratitude exercises

- Practise daily but note that it's important to really feel grateful as opposed to rushing through the list on autopilot. You can buy a gratitude journal, you can use your Notes app on your phone, you can simply ruminate on the things you're grateful for.
- Nightly practice: a list of three thanks, or three things that made your day good. Writing a list of three makes it easier to focus on the day's positives and go to sleep in a better mood.

- Writing a thank-you letter to someone. Anyone. Even yourself. John Kralik wrote a beautiful memoir about writing a thank-you letter every day for a year.[5] The act of writing a thank-you letter is a poignant reminder that you do indeed have a lot to be grateful for. I rarely send a thank-you card in the post (I'm not great at handwriting). But I do send a thank-you card using Paperless Post, or if I don't have someone's email details I'll send a note via text. It's not a perfect way to say thank you, but in my opinion it's better to do things imperfectly rather than not do them because you're waiting to do them perfectly.

Savouring

I'm in the Abel Tasman National Park in New Zealand. I wake up and feel my beautiful baby boy in my arms. Instinctively, I curl my arms around him. He's still small enough that he fits against me like a babushka doll. I feel his little toes, squishing them individually between my fingers. It's like crushing little rosebuds in a garlic press, but not quite as hectic. I can hear the Foo Fighters album that Michael has on in the background. To be honest, it's a little too loud for me this early in the morning, but I'm happy. I'm savouring the knowledge that I've just achieved something important to me – the Mountain Run at the Kathmandu Coast to Coast.

No, it wasn't the furthest I've run, or the hardest or the longest race I've done (probably the most scenic, though, if that sort of thing counts?). For months, I'd fielded questions from presumably well-intentioned people about why I wasn't doing the whole thing. 'It's not that long, is it?' 'You've run heaps further than that before, right?' 'I thought you would have done another Ironman or something more challenging.'

But you know what? It was my first race after having a baby. I was proud of myself for committing to it, and for training for it. For running through the black mornings with a head-torch strapped on, trying to fit in a three-hour session before Hakavai woke up and Michael left for work. And for the 'bitch-of-a-run' when, with no other option, I'd put Hakavai in the pram and take him with me to do hill sprints (Hakavai + pram = heavy to push up an incline). And I was proud of myself for the days when, shock horror, I just didn't want to go for a run but I sucked it up and did it anyway.

But so often we do really cool things and then immediately move on from them. And when we receive a compliment about doing our first triathlon, or for finally hitting 10,000 followers on our business Instagram account, or for how nice our hair is looking after doing a 'thirty days of hair nourishment' course, we are audaciously nonchalant and act as though it was nothing, when in reality, to us, it was *something*.

•

Let me introduce to you the art of savouring. According to Laurie Santos, Professor of Psychology and Cognitive Science at Yale University, savouring is 'the act of stepping outside of an experience to review and appreciate it'.[6] Any experience (positive or negative) can be amplified or diminished, depending on how much you think about it. So savouring an experience might mean you eat your chocolate chip cookie mindfully, thinking about the contrast between the dark chocolate chips and the buttery crumbs of the cookie. It might be the sensation of getting into a hot shower after hitting a gym class you didn't feel like doing. Or it might mean you're reflecting on a past experience, like running through a mountain range in New Zealand, and being proud of your achievement.

One of the massive benefits of savouring is that it can thwart *hedonic adaptation*.

Hedgy adap-ta-shon. That old chestnut, hey?

So, what exactly is Hedgy? It's a fancy term to describe the rapid way we humans become accustomed to our surroundings. For example, when you first get a new car, how do you treat it? Everyone who travels with you must hose and dry their shoes before entering, have washed their hair, undergone a health check to look for signs of possible motion sickness, and must wear only white, so specks of dust are clearly visible. Even then you don't take the plastic off the seats!

Fast forward six months: are you still taking the same precautions with the car?

Yeah, I see that dirty KeepCup with three-day-old coffee in it. That car is anyone's game now.

This is hedonic adaptation at play. You become used to something and begin to take it for granted. It applies to everything: our job, career, house – and to some extent even our relationships.

I'll give you an example. A couple of years ago I had yet another nose operation. This operation resulted in me being able to breathe through my nose for the first time in seven years. Kind of a big fucking deal.

What were those first few nostrils full of oxygenated air like? You know how on a hot day, you take a sip of ice-cold fizzy drink through a jumbo party straw and it is invigorating, intoxicating, energising and pacifying all at the same time?

Yeah, it felt like that, but a billion times better.

Each time I breathed in, I marvelled at my nostrils. 'I can't believe how much air is getting in through these bad boys!', 'It's like a wind tunnel there!', 'Holy smokes, here comes another rush of oxygen!'

How do you reckon I felt less than a week later?

'Oh yeah, I can breathe through my nostrils now. It's pretty awesome!'

A month later?

'Yeah, I've been able to breathe through my nostrils for a while now.'

A year later?

'What nostril surgery?'

What happened to me? I adapted to my circumstances. I got used to my nostrils. I even began to take them for granted.

But what helped me stop this very natural tendency to take shit for granted was to *savour* it. Relish it. Reflect on it. Ruminate on it. Stop and enjoy the experience.

How else do you put the brakes on Hedgy?

1. **Be grateful**

   This makes sense, yeah? Showing gratitude for positive experiences puts our focus on positive things in our life. And appreciating our lives, *as they are now*, is key to thwarting hedonic adaptation.

2. **Acknowledge and accept**

   Yes, buying a BMW will make you happier. Initially. Then you'll just get used to it. Hedonic adaptation happens. Buying a new iPhone will make you happier. Initially. And then, you'll get used to it. Hedonic adaptation happens. And if something is *inevitable*, in my experience it's far better to acknowledge and accept it rather than resist and deny it.

3. **Magical relationships**

   We adapt to pretty much everything in our lives – with one exception: our intimate relationships. Yes, we still adapt to them to a certain extent, but nowhere near as rapidly or as easily as we adapt to stuff.

   To delay adaptation to our relationships, we need to intentionally put effort into them, to keep them loving, meaningful and vibrant.[7]

4. **Novelty**

   The more easily people can understand and explain an event, the quicker they adapt to it. This applies to good stuff as well as bad stuff (we'll talk more about the bad stuff in the 'Hard times' chapter). Using this logic, if something is harder to make sense of, you'll adapt to it less quickly. The variables include novelty, surprise, uncertainty and inconsistency. So, let's say, for example, that out of the blue you're gifted a fancy high-tech hairdryer, a device you didn't know existed. Its various features provide you with hours of satisfaction (and, perhaps, entertainment). You might be surprised and impressed by the results it produces. But after doing your hair with it every day for two weeks, you're likely to get used to the fancy high-tech hairdryer and take its efficiency for granted. If, however, you meet a good friend you haven't seen for ages in a new Japanese restaurant, it's an experience you aren't likely to be repeating time after time, you can savour the evening and practise gratitude for your fortune in having such a lovely friend and being able to enjoy their company for an evening. That way, ole' Hedgy won't get a look-in.

Right, back to savouring. How exactly do you jump on board the savour-y train? It's surprisingly easy. When you take part in a positive experience (eating a chocolate chip cookie, jumping into the ocean, participating in a fun run, making a garden gnome, etc.), simply savour the experience. You could share it with another person (go to a café and eat the cookies together and notice out loud how bloody delicious they are). Keep a souvenir of the activity, such as the participation medal you got at the end of the fun run. Take a photo of the finished garden gnome. And try to stay in the present moment the entire time (if you're like most people and you struggle with being mindful, go to page 67).

I like to take photos. But Michael hates it when I take photos. That's difficult since I'm a massive fan of documenting my entire life, but I also know that Michael loves *looking* at photos of the surf, fish he's caught and our son (not necessarily in that order). So I take the photos anyway, knowing that while he'll dislike waiting for me to take another picture of the morning surf, he'll enjoy it later on. In fact, sometimes we put Hakavai to bed and then Michael and I will grab my phone and start watching videos of him. We're sickos like that.

What's the difference between savouring an experience and simply recording it? Go back to the definition of savouring. You're not on autopilot, sculling your coffee and rushing to work. You're consciously appreciating the subtle earthy notes of your mushroom latte and noticing how beautiful the frangipanis are in summer.

Some people savour by writing in a diary every day. Others share positive moments in conversations with friends and loved ones. Some meditate on them quietly. Some get up early in the morning to drink a cup of tea as the sun rises and think about all the cool elements of their life.

Find a way to savour the big stuff, and the little stuff. Pay attention to the fab things you do. Enjoy the feeling of having done them. It'll make you happier.

Anticipation

Imagine standing by the water's edge on a baking day. Think of staring at a slice of cake when you're starving. Think of that feeling before a first date with someone really hot. You're *anticipating* a positive experience.

We need stuff to look forward to. If we're looking forward to something (as opposed to dreading it) it must be something that

- we enjoy
- makes us feel good, or . . .
- is both of these things

Anticipatory joy is a thing. I'm a bit of a robot, or, to use a superior phrase, a 'master of efficiency', which means I don't like 'wasting' time. I don't extensively research the best coffee shops at my holiday destination (I've already chosen my accommodations and selected the optimal activities within the brief window of time I used to book the holiday) or potential clothes and outfits (I know what I'll be wearing to that wedding in two weeks, any additional online shopping or browsing will only confuse me).

But as Hakavai's first birthday loomed (I started planning six months out) I massively leant into anticipatory joy. I wanted to make him a cake from the classic *Australian Women's Weekly* cookbook. I oscillated between cakes. Should I go with the cricket one, in deference to Michael's youth as a cricketer? What about the little pig, or will guests take offence? At first, my indecision frustrated me. I got annoyed at myself for my inefficiency but then reminded myself to enjoy the process.

Eventually I selected the shark cake. I was so excited about it. I googled construction ideas. Our oven was broken but I worked out a way to overcome that barrier by buying premade cakes from the supermarket. I ordered triple quantities of icing sugar and food colouring, trimmed the cakes while they were still frozen and spent hours constructing the shark cake. And when it came together, it looked magical and delicious and delightful, and I had a belly ache from the vast quantities of sugar I'd consumed. To say I got a lot of joy out of anticipating and savouring the making of the cake would be an understatement.

And what did the cake taste like? Look, it was a kid's birthday cake. Full of sugar and not bad. But with so much focus on GSD (Good Sex D— wait, sorry, I mean Getting Shit Done) and being efficient and super-productive, we can lose sight of simply enjoying ourselves before and as we do something.

And while we can't always be jetting off to the south of France with Bey and Jay-Z, there's still plenty of stuff we can look forward to. I like to have a Small Anticipation, Medium Anticipation and Big Anticipation in my future. Small is, rather obviously, the small things (there's that marketing genius just firing away). A mid-week clothes swap that I have with my mates. A new episode of my new favourite show that's about to drop. Taking my baby for a walk in the morning. Y'know, that type of stuff.

Medium is – *you got it* – the medium things. For me, that's going for a big-ass run in a couple of weeks. Taking a mate on a bushwalk. Launching a new campaign in my business. For you it might be the copywriting seminar you've signed up for in six weeks, or going mountain biking, or cooking for friends at the weekend.

And big things are even bigger than that. Like going away with Michael for our ten-year anniversary (we only travelled 40 minutes from where we live. But it still felt like a holiday, y'know?).

When we have things in our life to look forward to, we experience anticipatory joy. That boosts our happiness, gives our days meaning and purpose and, yes, very often what we anticipate become the things we can savour once they're over. And that's all stuff to be grateful for.

That little circle of life right there: GSA.

To sum up, in order to squeeze the most life and joy and happiness from our experiences, we can anticipate them, savour them, and express gratitude for them for years to come.

Eddie Jaku

Eddie Jaku was born Abraham Jakubowicz in 1920. In 1938 he was captured by the Nazis and taken to Germany's Buchenwald concentration camp. Over the following seven years he survived three periods of imprisonment, two in Auschwitz. He lost 150 family members in the Holocaust. He now lives in Sydney and calls himself 'the happiest man on earth'.

What is key to your happiness?
Be happy with what you have. This is the most important aspect to being happy.

How has your understanding of happiness changed over the years?
As you get older you acquire more wisdom and become more flexible in your attitude.

I'm interested in the effect adversity has on a person's happiness. Many people who go through incredibly challenging times tend to come out with a different view of the world, and a deeper appreciation for life. Was choosing to be happy after your experiences a difficult decision, and how long did it take for you to be able to feel happy again?
It took me about two years after I came back from the concentration camps; losing my parents and lots of uncles, aunties and cousins was very difficult to swallow. I was always asking *why?* But when my first son was born, that all changed. I had new responsibilities, a new life and a beautiful outlook. I was happy.

Having hope for the future can help people get through hard times. During your time at Auschwitz, did you have a sense of hope for your future? What did you think about to keep your mind strong?

Giving up hope brings the end to your life. I survived Auschwitz through friendship and hope. I never gave up hope. One flower is my garden. One good friend is my world. Don't walk in front of me, I may not be able to follow. Don't walk behind me, I may not be able to lead. Just walk beside me, and be my friend.

•

What's a TL;DR?

Now, I know you're probably young and hip and already know what a TL;DR is, but just in case you don't, it's internet-speak for 'too long; didn't read'.

I also realise you are an extremely diligent student, and that you're planning to add flags and tabs and sticky notes and highlighters throughout the book, but just in case, I'm including a TL;DR section at the end of each chapter as a summary. How thoughtful of me!

TL;DR

- Gratitude is being thankful and showing appreciation for our lives.
- The antidote to feeling bitter, envious, resentful, angry and so on is gratitude.

- How do you practise gratitude? There are lots of different ways. I like to think of people I'm grateful for, an opportunity I have, and something tangible.
- Savouring is the act of stepping outside of an experience to consciously appreciate it.
- When we have things in our life to look forward to, we experience anticipatory joy. That boosts our happiness, gives our days meaning and purpose and, yes, very often things we anticipate become those we can savour once they're over. And that's all stuff to be grateful for.

2
The very best morning routine

I know what you're thinking. You're wondering how I have such long and luxurious hair (Tahitian genetics and a quarterly keratin treatment).

I know what else you're thinking (and it's not that I'm a creepy mind reader). You're wondering how exactly having a 'morning routine' is going to help you get happier. Well, it's not like one of those boring morning routines of washing your face with pearl extract and brushing your teeth with cashmere fibres. This routine is for your mindset – to ensure you're feeling strong and positive for your day ahead.

Now, when I talk about your 'mindset', I really just mean your state of mind. It's a mental framework of how you respond to both good and bad things in your life. It's your attitude towards yourself, towards others and towards life itself.

You, dear reader, might not be as fit as you'd like, have the career you feel you deserve, have the family you want, have the intimate relationships you crave. The way to start creating a better life for yourself is to start using your mindset to your advantage. Strengthening it, fortifying it and working on it. And personally? I think mornings are the best time of day to do this. Why mornings? Let me count the ways . . .

1. You could die tomorrow, yo

I know with every fibre of my being that life is way too short for most of us. That we're only here for a short, finite period of time and *we are all going to be dead at some point in the (hopefully) distant future.*

Yes, I know, I'm super fun to be around! But the whole 'life is short' shebang – this is firsthand shit. Maybe you know it firsthand, too. Maybe you've lost someone important to you, had a close call with cancer, or been through an awful divorce that made you reassess your life. Or maybe you know this *intellectually*, but the idea that 'you could get hit by a bus tomorrow' doesn't feel real to you.

Now, look, I don't necessarily think it's healthy to walk around with thoughts of our imminent mortality front and centre of our minds. That would be a terrible (and um, rather stressful) way to live. But I do think it's a good idea, on occasion, to hit pause, slow down, and view each day as an extraordinary opportunity in your life.

Mornings are *perfect for this*. Think about it: each morning is like a whiteboard that's been expunged of all the whiteboard marker, fresh and clean and beseeching you to scribble all over it.

In the words of Maya Angelou: 'This is a beautiful day. I've never seen this one before.'

2. Mornings are sacred

Early in the morning, the world is quiet. The only living things awake other than you are the kookaburras in the gum trees (and on Mondays, the garbage men). Mornings provide you with a rare, precious gift. No, not frankincense or myrrh.

Time.

If you don't have small delightful children, it might even be 'me time'. Selfish time. Fill-up-your-bucket-first time. Time to do something just for you, whether that's creating a delicious breakfast. Writing. Working out. Spending time with your partner.

For those of you who do have small delightful children... you may need to shift your mentality on your mornings. I used to exercise and write and 'set my intentions' and make wholesome smoothies for myself in the early morning. That's not possible anymore.

So I changed how I see my mornings. Now mornings are uninterrupted time with my family. I can drink my coffee as I watch Hakavai play with his blocks; I can read to him; I can watch his dad push him around the house on his balance bike; we can water the garden.

If you wait until the end of the day to do stuff that's important to you (exercise, read, give your family your uninterrupted attention, wash your Tahitian hair) it's highly likely *not* to happen. As the end of the day approaches, plans to go to the gym will get replaced by a glass of wine on the couch; your boss will decide another round of changes to that presentation is vital to the company's success; your mum will call you for one of her impromptu chats (read: hour-long monologue).

If it has to happen, it has to happen first.

3. You've got a full tank

Hopefully of petrol (or a fully charged solar-powered battery), but also of willpower! If you've had a good sleep and you're well rested, your willpower tank is refreshed, renewed and raring to go.

Roy Baumeister is one of the world's most influential and prolific psychologists (I mean, the man has published more than thirty books and authored hundreds of scientific papers). He researches willpower and self-control, and points out that the 'age-old adage "things will seem better in the morning" has nothing to do with daylight and everything to do with depletion. A rested will is a stronger will'.[1]

Deciding which caviar to eat for breakfast, navigating the traffic on your tricycle, listening to your boss drone on about his new drone, sitting in a two-hour sales meeting, forcing yourself to order a salad rather than hot chips with gravy at lunch. All of these seemingly inconsequential decisions weaken your willpower. Think about how you usually feel at the end of the day. Does your willpower tank overfloweth to the level where you could challenge *Dodgeball*'s White Goodman and taunt yourself with doughnuts?* Or are you completely wrecked, and incapable of making a choice between Indian from Uber Eats or Italian from Deliveroo?†

I talk a lot about willpower and how to make the most of it in my digital course, School of Champions. Since this is a

* You know – that scene where Ben Stiller's character White Goodman is hooked up to the electrocution machine, and every time he reaches for a doughnut, he electrocutes himself?

† This is me. Not implying it's you.

book ostensibly about happiness, and not willpower, I'll save you the lecture and succinctly say this:

You need a good night's sleep for a full tank of willpower.

Your willpower is strongest in the morning.

Decision-making weakens your willpower.

4. Research says so

Research has shown that how we start our day has a massive impact on how the rest of our day flows. You run the day or the day runs you, yeah? Morning people have been shown to be happier, more productive and more content with their lives.[2] It seems even our brains are bigger when we first wake up.[3]

•

The gist of all that? Mornings are good. Enjoying a serene morning in whatever way you see fit (exercising, spending time with progeny, tweezing toe hairs) correlates with a happier and more productive life.

But . . . what if you're not a 'morning person'?

Most people reckon the world can be broadly segmented into two different avian categories: larks or owls.[4] Larks are those annoyingly cheerful morning people. And, given we're now a few pages into my rant on Why Mornings Are Great, you'd be forgiven for thinking I'm a lark.

And you'd be right! I am. But I used to be an owl. When I was younger, I hated going to sleep. There was so much I wanted to do that I'd try to stay up all day and night. I used to fantasise about what I'd do with my sleeping hours. I could learn another language! I could master the violin! I could crack the relative meaning of the universe!

At uni I'd pull all-nighters (fuelled by the holy trinity of caffeine, nicotine and sugar) madly finishing an assignment on time. Alas, my body would inevitably fail me and I'd fall asleep at seven in the morning, not waking up until three in the afternoon. Sure, if my friends and I had planned a camping trip or a sunrise bushwalk I'd be up, no problem.* But in my day-to-day life? Yeah, nah. A lack of sleep was glorified.

I was an owl for longer than I've been a lark. So I understand that we may have an inherent tendency to be one of these birds, but we *can change our tendencies.*

My species change came a few years ago. At half past eight in the morning, I was in bed, and I was reading Laura Vanderkam's brilliant book, *What the Most Successful People Do Before Breakfast.* I was intrigued by this revelation of waking up earlier. So some people get up far earlier than they need to, I pondered to myself. And it makes them more productive and happier? Fascinating!

Eager to see if I too could become a happier little lark, I took on Laura's advice and started getting up earlier. Her idea is to start slow. No big, cataclysmic changes overnight (Laura's my kind of gal). Set your alarm clock fifteen minutes earlier each morning (going to bed fifteen minutes earlier each night too – smart!). And in this training phase, you use the new morning time for something you really enjoy. Now I know you can't really get *that* much done in fifteen minutes. But you can still make a delicious bulletproof coffee, plan to read a book, or listen to the start of a podcast. Because if you're gonna do something uncomfortable like waking up earlier

---

* I'd literally just stay awake.

than you need to, why not reward the act with something to look forward to.

Two weeks in, the habit had stuck. I was waking up one whole hour earlier. And I used that hour to make a coffee, and drink it, snuggled up with a blanket on the couch, reading a book. I'd made it as easy as possible to get up earlier, and it was working.

As I got used to the earlier starts, I found other things I wanted to do. I love crunching numbers, so I'd use that time to get my bookkeeping done. When my alarm went off, I would be so excited at this whole hour to do something I loved, uninterrupted.

According to one research paper, sun time is the dominant zeitgeber* for entraining the human clock.[5] In normal English: sunlight wakes us up.

If you can, try to get some sun on you in the morning. Morning sun has more of a wakey-wakey effect on your body than any other sun.[6] Artificial lights (um, like that Mickey Mouse-shaped lamp you have next to your bed) have no effect. So if you live in a cold, dark apartment building, and the sun is on vaycay, you can try getting a sun lamp.

---

* A zeitgeber is something that helps us maintain our circadian rhythms. So the sun is a very good zeitgeber, in that it helps wake us up, and makes it feel 'natural' for us to be awake during the day.

Sunlight reduces stress, boosts productivity and helps you sleep better at night.[7]

Anyway, all of that is to say: sunlight is cool (or actually, warm. Haha!). Get it into your mornings.

Now I love my mornings so much I'm tempted to hop back into bed with them. And while I think it's ridiculous to tell someone all about your morning routine (as if you are the authority on a time of day), it turns out I'm exactly that kind of ridiculous person. Cos I'm gonna tell you what I do, every morning.

You can laugh at it, laugh at me, use some of the tips or not use any of them. Up to you.

Every morning, I start the day in the same way (or, note: I try to start the day in the same way – I am, alas, a mere human, and thus flawed and fallible).

Step 1: A morning routine starts at, um, night!

Yep. A good morning always starts the night before. A good night's sleep is key. Like I said earlier, I used to glorify a lack of sleep. These days? That shit is precious. Commodified. Necessary to our survival.

We all know how you feel after a good night's sleep – as if your whole body has been soaked in a feel-good solution. And the day? The whole day goes your way! You exceed your instructor's expectations at your morning Zumba class. Your fresh juice at breakfast is tantalisingly delicious. You benevolently allow the car in front of you to nudge into your lane. Your creativity is through the roof. You blast everyone with a radiant smile. You have time to ensure you're wearing matching socks.

Sleep, man. It's a drug. One that we should all get happily addicted to. Read more about it in the 'Zest' chapter.

These days, I sleep next to my progeny (I'm scared of the dark, and it really helps alleviate that). Hakavai is usually asleep, god and all the deities willing, by 7.30 pm. If I'm all out of sleeping tablets and red wine (JK, JK! I prefer vodka) I go to bed at around nine. Even if I'm not tired. And once I'm in bed, I read. Sometimes, I'll get an hour of reading time to myself (my bliss) and sometimes I'll fall asleep immediately.

No pillow for this armadillo

It started in hospital, not long after the fire. The skin on my neck had been grafted, so using a pillow would have caused it to contract (get tighter). So, I wasn't allowed to use a pillow. Literally. The nurses and doctors refused to give me one and confiscated it whenever I was able to manipulate my mum into finding me one.

So now I don't use a pillow, which I think is phenomenal for my neck and back. According to biomechanist Katy Bowman, a pillow acts as an orthotic – it keeps your neck overly supported, and immobilised.[8] She suggests that sleeping without a pillow helps your neck and shoulders to get stronger from all the tiny little patterns of movement created as you sleep.

Step 2: Waking

The peacock calls (Hakavai sits up in bed and woofs like a dog), I glide out of my gossamer sheets (untangle the doona), slip on my finest silk slippers (hiking socks) and drink a cup of the rarest opium tea (head blindly for the coffee machine).

After that's done, I *don't* do something.

What's that something? I don't look at my phone. Because what happens when you look at that magic little rectangle, dear reader? Well, if you're anything like me, you get sucked into a digital vortex of (mostly bad) news stories, emails and calendar notifications, Instagram stories, your Twitter and Facebook feeds, and all of a sudden you're thinking about what everyone else is doing before you've even considered what *you* would like from your day, thank you very much.

Looking at your phone first thing has also been shown to make you feel anxious and stressed, and already 'behind', *even though it's the goddamn first thing in the morning*. Look, there's plenty of time to feel like that later in the day. No need to drag those feelings into the day so early on.[9]

The mornings are sacred and special. And most importantly, they're *yours*. Don't clog them up looking at other people's shit.

Step 3: Making the bed

A boring and mundane task?

I used to be one of those people who leapt out of bed in the morning and failed to revisit the scene of the crime until night (because, y'know, busy-ness). I could see my messy, unmade bed from the kitchen table where I worked, complete with random socks dispersed all over the floor.

Then one day Michael bought me a book called *Make Your Bed* by a former US Navy SEAL, Admiral William McRaven. I was affronted by Michael's implication that I was untidy person who needed instructions for the most basic of household tasks (which, let's be honest, I probably did) so there it sat, forlorn and uncared for, on my shelves for months.

And *then* I was sent a link to McRaven giving a speech. A friend sent it to me. (Michael! Michael had the audacity to send it to me.) The video link landed in my inbox on a day when I really did not feel like writing. So I watched it.

In a word (or two!)? Mind-blowing. Life-changing. And yes, we're still talking about making your bed.

Why is making your bed important? And how does it lead to making you happier? Well, if you make your bed in the morning, you start off with a win. True, it's a minuscule win, but it's a win nonetheless, and that propels you forward. Making your bed, says McRaven, reinforces the fact that the little things in life matter, 'and if you can't do the little things right, you'll never be able to do the big things right.' And if you have a shit day? 'You will come home to a bed that is made – that you made – and a made bed gives you encouragement that tomorrow will be better. So if you want to change the world, start off by making your bed.'[10]

Word, McRaven, word.

Indeed, research shows that making your bed correlates with better productivity and emotional well-being.[11] Now, pay attention to this. *Correlation, not causation.* It's not that making your bed all of a sudden makes you excessively cheery, but as a 'keystone habit' it can start a chain reaction that helps other good habits (exercise, healthy eating, meditation) stick. When I first read this, I was a bit confused. How does it start a chain reaction? Well, according to the dictionary, a chain reaction is: 'a series of events, each caused by the previous one'. In a nutshell: tiny consistent steps that propel you forward. If you can make your bed, maybe you can keep your room tidy.

If you can keep your room tidy, maybe you can muster up the discipline not to look at your phone. If you can stop looking at your phone, maybe you can spend ten minutes meditating.

I'm not suggesting you do all of these things all at once and straight away. That's mental.

Remember, it's a chain reaction. Making your bed may just be the catalyst for progress in other areas.

So, just make your damn bed already.

Step 4: Gratitude

Once I've made a coffee, I put Hakavai on the floor with his toys, open the blinds to let the sunlight in, and practise gratitude. This isn't a lengthy task. Three minutes tops. But if you read the first chapter, you'll know by now that it *changes everything*.

Step 5: Q&A

Next, I ask myself one question: 'What would make today great?' As in, what's the one thing I could do today that would make it a brilliant day?

Note: it's not 'What do I have to do today?' It's not 'What shit do I have to do for other people today?' (Give Hakavai his daily massage, shampoo Michael's chest hair, send off a hectic email, run fifty kilometres.) It's 'What would make today great?' (Yep, you've already read that sentence.)

For me, it might be taking Hakavai to the beach. Catching up with mates for a pizza. Working on my collection of garden gnomes. Watching a new episode of *Veep*.

You've already learnt in the last chapter about the power of anticipation. It kind of comes into play here. Focusing on what 'great' thing you can do has three outcomes:

1. It forces you to filter out the noise of daily life and focus on something positive. More on this below.
2. It gives you a happiness boost through the power of GSA: you're able to look forward to (*anticipate*) drinks with your friends, *savour* the moment and the time with your friends, and then feel *grateful* for that moment when you're riding your bike on the way home.
3. It gives you permission to make time for yourself. And that's a damn good thing to do.

Why you should use your filters

We are constantly bombarded by information. Think of a crowded store with noise and music blaring through the PA. Or of a noisy cinema, with people crunching their popcorn and rustling in their seats and the sound of the air conditioning whirring.

Even though there's lots going on all around us all the time, our brains can only process so much data (estimated by some clever researchers to be 120 bits per second).[12]

In other words, there's more information than we can handle.

And so our brain is very good at filtering this information. This is why you probably don't find the store overwhelming and you're able to pick up bread and milk, and why once the movie starts, you're fully engrossed in it.

The cool thing is, we get to decide what the filter should be. For example, you know when you decide you like the look of a red Mitsubishi Mirage and suddenly you're spotting them all over the highway? You've stuck a big Post-It note on the Mitsubishi Mirage, which lets your mind know to filter information appropriately. Your filter is the reason why you suddenly pay attention when someone says your name, or the reason you can learn a new word and then start hearing it everywhere.

You can call this the frequency illusion, you can say it's your RAS (reticular activating system) at work, you could say it's selective attention, you can attribute it to your powers of manifestation, or you can simply say: whatever you search for, you find.

So if you ask yourself 'What would make today great?' instead of 'What do I have to do today?' you're training your brain to seek out the positive experiences in your future.

Step 6: Doing important stuff

This is the part that's really good. The time for doing the stuff that matters to you. For me, this used to be quiet, reflective writing time. When I was training for Ironman I used the early mornings to get a head start at the pool, or I'd strap on a head-torch and go running.

Now, as a mum, that 'important stuff' has shifted, along with just about everything else in my life. So from six to eight each morning Michael, Hakavai and I are hanging out. This is the time we have as a family. It's important, so (let's recall Laura's words here!) it has to happen first.

Step 7: Cold water

I try to go for a swim, and if that's not possible, I jump in a cold shower. Cold water has a weird ability to 'reset' how you're feeling and give you a blank template. It can enhance your immunity[13] and some studies have found cold showers to be mood boosting.[14]

A cold shower also improves mental alertness, boosts your energy and is an all-round invigorator. If you've ever been thrown into a cold shower, or had cold water thrown at you, then you'll know it wakes you the fuck up.

Step 8: Deep-thinking work

I work for myself, and while I'm a domineering boss, I'm lucky in that I can structure my time in a way that makes me most productive. That means in the morning I do my deep-thinking work. Writing, strategy – the stuff that requires my mental energy the most.

Remember what I said earlier about willpower? This comes into play here. I don't use early-morning willpower to answer emails. They have to be answered (people just keep emailing – I can't seem to stop them) so I'll get that done. What does require my willpower is to stay focused on that deep-thinking stuff. And it doesn't bug me the way those pesky email-sending people do. So, if I don't prioritise it, it won't get done.

Use your willpower where it's really needed. And remember – if it's important, it has to happen first.

•

So, dear reader, that was my morning routine. You're a special and unique person, so it would make sense that you would have your *own* morning routine. It might look a little something like this:

1. Wake up.
2. DON'T LOOK AT PHONE. CAPITALS ARE FOR EMPHASIS.
3. Something for yourself (coffee, gratitude practice, watching the sunrise, doing an at-home Zumba workout, spend meaningful time with your menagerie of Shetland ponies and chow-chows).
4. Asking yourself, 'What would make today great?'
5. Cold swim or shower to wake you the fuck up for your day.
6. Start your day in a good mood (for me, that's doing some deep-thinking work, for you that might be doing your warm-up as a parkour instructor).

An important note: your morning routine isn't always going to be perfect. While I was writing this chapter, my team and I went away for three days to strategise for the year ahead. I went without Michael and Hakavai. In the morning, I'd wake up at five to do 'deep-thinking work' (writing this chapter). Then I'd go down to the beach for a run, my olfactory nerves going into overdrive with the heady mix of salt and surf. I'd come back to our meticulously restored sanctuary set among opulent palms and grass that didn't dare grow over the smooth stepping stones. I'd plunge myself into the cold pool, emerging feeling like I'd taken a shot of energy intravenously. I'd have a warm outside shower and set my intentions for the day. At the close of each day, I'd sink into my warm, soft nest of a bed, dreaming sweetly of fields of lavender and inky blue butterflies.

And then I drove home.

Stepping across the threshold, I noticed a cornucopia of shoes, spades, buckets, Hakavai's pram and old coins all over the tiles. There was a rancid lamb chop in our bathroom. Hakavai (or Michael?) had eaten something (chocolate? Tahini?) on our bed, smudging it across the doona.

You're not always going to be capable of crafting the perfect routine. Life can and will get in the way. Keep it simple, focus on what makes you feel good and the rest will follow.

•

TL;DR

- Your mornings are precious and sacred; your willpower tank is full. It's a chance for you to do something for yourself.
- A good morning starts at night. Get a good night's sleep in order to make the most of your mornings.
- Don't look at your phone first thing. You'll be sucked into a digital vortex before you can even think about what *you* would like from your day.
- Ask yourself: what would make today great?
- Focus on big-picture stuff in the morning.

3

Zest (energy, not citrus)

Life is better when you're filled with energy. I mean, think about it. If you have more energy, are you a better parent? Yep. If you have more energy, are you a better partner? Yep. If you have more energy, are you more motivated, more caring, more invested in the stuff that matters? Triple yep.

If you have more energy, are you a purple unicorn? (Just checking you're still awake!)

And taking into account all those kind-of-rhetorical questions, are you *happier* if you have more energy?

Yes! And, vice versa, the happier you are, the more *energy* you'll have. On top of that, higher energy levels help boost your self-esteem.[1] Anecdotally you know this to be true. Think of a morning when you woke up bursting with energy. You might have bounced out of bed, tickled your partner, farted like an elephant, sung in the shower, high-fived your colleagues, and felt like an all-round legend.

Now, think of waking up after a night when you didn't get enough sleep. You may have snarled at your kids, skipped your morning workout, lectured your partner for not making your smoked salmon smokey enough, got annoyed by the traffic on your commute, and walked into work feeling exhausted AF.

Energy energy energy. Say it with me! Energy! I mean, how much BETTER is life when you're overflowing with zest and brimming with *joie de vivre*! It's incredible! Ecstatic! Three levels above whatever ecstatic is!

I mean, it's sort of obvious, right? When you have more energy, you can do more of what makes you happy!

Now, this doesn't mean you have to be bouncing off the walls. But it does mean you need to be taking care of yourself. If you want healthy energy levels, energy levels that will heighten your sense of wellbeing, you need to put some strong foundations in place.

I bet you know what these consist of, but, this being a book, 'n' all, I'm going to run through them anyway. The three most important elements for happy energy, as far as I (and many others) am concerned are:

1. Moving your body
2. Eating well
3. Getting enough sleep

And once you've got a body like Beyoncé, you eat like Gwyneth Paltrow and you sleep like a koala, we should also tackle the old grey matter – your mind! Cos how you *feel* and how you *think* affects how much *energy* you have and thus affects how much happiness you're building.

I like to think of my energy levels as a house. A beautiful house, with solid foundations, old stone walls and a lovely wide verandah; inside, an old-fashioned wood-fired stove roaring away, a pot of soup bubbling on the top. A fresh breeze rolling through verandah doors and big windows to let in the light.

For me, eating well, exercising and getting a good night's sleep are the foundations of the house.

The old stone bricks? Those are your mental and emotional patterns – how you think and how you feel. The thoughts you have, the way you think about the experiences and interactions that make up your days, massively impact your energy.

(Note to reader: don't sweat it, I'll cover this stuff thoroughly in 'Self-talk'.)

I'm not saying that it's realistic to hope that every day we'll jump out of bed brimming with the energy to take on any challenge, but if you look after your foundations and work on adjusting your thought patterns, in my experience, your ability to do just that will be greatly increased.

Getting back to our house, finally there are the quick fixes, which I compare to opening the windows and verandah doors to let the light and a breeze float through the house, or putting that pot of soup on the stove and enjoying its aromas, or washing the sheets on your bed – energy refreshers. These can be things like jumping in a cold shower, or doing some deep breathing.

So, let's get your house in order, yeah?

Eating well

After the fire, I went from being a fit, healthy woman, to a pale stick insect. I needed to put on weight, and quickly, so I was told to eat more, and even to eat fast food. And I obliged. Boy, did I oblige. I ate McDonald's, KFC, Red Rooster – whatever I could get my hands on. Sure, all that stuff was delicious, in a fast-foody way. But I was on so many different types of medication – sleeping pills, antidepressants, pain medication – that quite quickly the combo made me feel sick and exhausted.

It was a really shit time; I needed life to be considerably less shit.

So, I started with food. I ate the beautiful meals my mum provided. I drank fresh juices, flooded my body with good stuff. I started cooking more meals from scratch for myself. And, whadda ya know, I began to feel better.

You probably know that after you eat foods like a triple deep-fried mountain burger, you can feel pretty average. And research shows that on days when you eat more fruit and vegetables, you feel calmer, happier and more energetic than usual.[2]

Now, I'm not gonna prescribe a certain diet or way of eating. I'm no food purist (I just ate a brownie with lashings of cream). But what you put into your body affects what your body and your mind are able to do.

There are a million cookbooks and programs out there that will help you eat better – I've listed some of my favourites in the Resources section. At its core, my philosophy on food is basic. Just eat (mostly) real food.[3] A banana is real food. Eggs are real food. Milk is real food. Fish is real food. Almonds are . . . Okay, sorry, you get the picture. I'll move on. (But before I do: Pop-Tarts are *not* real food. A deep-fried Mars Bar is not real food. Plastic cheese is not real food.)

Some advice on eating makes healthy food sound expensive, unattainable and complicated. But it doesn't have to be. There are loads of chefs and cookbooks out there that emphasise this (think Jamie Oliver, and the 3/4/5 Ingredient recipe books). And when you think about it, food is meant to be enjoyed. Sharing meals with friends and family amplifies the experience. Eating *should* be fun and it should be yum. Why not savour the sweet glory of a tomato, or take delight in the crisp tartness of an apple, or relish in the exquisite pleasure of slathering creamy and salty butter over a freshly baked croissant?

Now, I got lucky in life – I had a mum who was a wizard in the kitchen and who prioritised home cooking: she would make the most incredible concoctions from tofu and sesame seeds and bok choy and fish. And sometimes, when cash was low, we'd eat red beans and rice, but it was still that magical combination of delicious yet nutritious.

I'm also lucky because Michael is a fisherman, so we eat fish and shellfish on the reg. We grow veggies and herbs, we compost, we make our own honey.

Wow, we sound like one of those annoying healthy-earthy-wanky couples. I promise you we're not. But I do make a concerted effort to eat fresh, healthy foods. This doesn't mean it always happens. But I know I don't have a complicated relationship with food. If I'm hungry, I eat. If I feel like eating raspberries, I eat them. If I feel like eating hot chips, I eat them. I don't eat to reward myself or to punish myself but *to go on a culinary adventure.*

For example, this is what I fed my body yesterday:

- On waking: water. And a strong coffee. And a banana.
- Breakfast: peanut butter on toast.
- Lunch: steak with roast veggies (potato, sweet potato, beetroot) and broccolini, which I fried up with some sesame seeds and olive tapenade.

- Afternoon: about a million seaweed crackers with a kilo of hummus.
- Dinner: pumpkin and chickpea coconut curry. (I love meals from the slow cooker. I make a big batch and we'll eat them for three consecutive nights.)
- Dessert: um, I felt like a peach so I ate that. And a Ferrero Rocher. And, oh yeah, I also had a glass of red wine (it was a veryyyy large glass, but was one glass nonetheless).

So my advice? Explore with your food. Nurture your relationship with food. Trial certain foods to see how they make you feel. What we eat influences our biochemistry. And our biochemistry is fundamental to our mental health and how we feel.

When I spoke to Dr Libby Weaver, a highly respected nutritional biochemist and author, she gave me some more fascinating insights into the effects our food can have on our sense of wellbeing. Here they are for you to chew on . . .

Dr Libby Weaver

What makes you happy?

Waking up each day. Being alive. Having my senses so I can appreciate Nature. Reading. The magpie who flies in and sits on my leg each morning, while I sit outside in the early morning light, and has a good old sing. Growing vegetables. Supporting people to live with better health and energy and understand the biochemical, nutritional and emotional aspects of their own health picture. And the ripple effect of this can generate to others and the planet.

How does eating well affect our happiness levels?

The way we nourish ourselves can have a profound impact on how content and happy we feel, as food can influence our mood through a variety of different pathways. In a more acute sense, it can affect our blood glucose levels, which then influence our energy and mood. When we eat in a way that supports steady blood glucose levels, we tend to experience steadier energy and a more even mood. When we eat in a way that contributes to peaks and troughs in our blood glucose levels, our energy also peaks and troughs, and when our blood glucose dips low we can feel agitated, irritated, anxious or even angry.

Studies have also shown that the quality of our overall dietary pattern can influence our mental health, with a way of eating that is predominantly based on whole-foods having the potential even to assist in managing depression. There are likely numerous mechanisms through which a nutrient-dense way of eating can benefit our mood. Some examples include improved intake of specific nutrients that go on to help create neurotransmitters and hormones and keep our body functioning properly, as well as alterations in the gut microbiome, which may then influence the messages sent via the gut–brain axis.

And remember that eating predominantly whole-foods (reducing highly processed foods), particularly including a variety of different plant foods, can go a long way towards supporting better physical and mental health.

Put simply, yes, we are what we eat. And yes, we can boost our mood by what we eat. For example, dark chocolate (the strong shit, like more than 70 per cent cacao) raises endorphin levels.[4] But it's not as easy as just eating chocolate to make ourselves feel happier. As Drew Ramsey explains in his book *Eat Complete*, the amount of serotonin in our brain helps to regulate our mood. And for our brain to be able to produce this chemical, 'You must eat foods that contain the amino acid tryptophan (such as pumpkin seeds, cod and beef) as well as foods high in iron, folate and vitamin B12 (such as lentils, mussels, and kale).'[5]

In short, the relationship between how we feel and what we eat is complex but one we can manage by making judicious adjustments to our diets. And *you*, dear reader, are the best judge of what foods make you feel good, and what foods make you feel shit.

Sometimes eating badly can make us feel like shit because certain foods are bad for our gut health. There's been a swathe of research over the past decade or so on the gut–brain axis.[6] Turns out that our gut can influence our moods, our emotions and even how we cope with stress. A few years back German scientist Giulia Enders wrote the gangbusters bestseller *Gut: The Inside Story of Our Body's Most Underrated Organ*, unpacking the ins and outs of our guts. It's a fascinating read that I'd highly recommend. Here are Giulia's gut-centric answers to my questions on happiness.

Giulia Enders

What makes you happy?

Symbiosis. This is a term that refers to bacteria helping trees or the gut to be healthier, but it translates to many things. For example, my body and mind working together well, creating something or simply agreeing to have a good rest. Or in terms of other people – when my sister and I have a good conversation or can help each other with our different perspectives. A good symbiosis creates, improves. It essentially says: I see the good and I can do something with it. For a good life, sometimes this is what's needed.

How has your understanding of happiness changed over the years?

When I was younger it was much more influenced by attainment. I wanted to have good grades, have friends, have a partner, achieve something in life. Like things on a list. I have achieved something in life now and I was really surprised at how little this changes the basic feeling you have during the day. I'm actually much more passive nowadays than I used to be. I think that is because knowing the feeling of doing something that feels very purposeful and right made me lose interest in many things that don't really give me a feeling of attraction or meaning.

There is so much incredible research and knowledge shared in your book about the gut and how its health can affect our ongoing happiness. What are the three key things you wished people knew about their gut, and what are the three key steps people can take to improve their gut health as it relates to their happiness?

I think number one is to be considerate with your body. Many people told me that they had had diarrhoea regularly or stomach pains and just kept going, or they fed on a diet that they read about, even though it tasted horrible to them. I think sometimes we need to turn around in the toilet and check the reality out. It is there anyways – so why not?

Number two is thinking more organically about emotions. Many people see a bad mood as something influenced by the outside world exclusively. Sleep, food, air quality, sun exposure – there are many factors. So I see my psyche as something organic. If I feel whiny, I make myself good food, go have a massage or sleep longer. Even obvious problems often get better by caring for the body first.

Number three is feeding the microbes. Every one of us has an entire organ of microbes in our gut – candy and meat doesn't feed them right. I try to eat things I like but that also are good for my microbes. A win-win situation. Cold rice, as in sushi, asparagus, sauerkraut, olives, onions and pistachios – those are a few of my favourites, but everyone has their own.

Movement

I love exercise, so perhaps it's with a touch of smugness that I jump on to my soapbox and lecture you on this very issue.

We all know that exercise has a cornucopia of benefits for our health: feeling fitter and stronger, a rush of endorphins that tend to give us a sense of wellbeing; the ability to think more clearly and to sleep better. All these factors are great contributors to our energy levels. A side benefit of exercise is that by dedicating a block of time to ourselves, we are demonstrating self-love, which is (in my not-so-humble opinion) a key to happiness.

Now, listen, I hear you if you say you're not a sporty person and you've never been into fitness. But 'exercise' doesn't have to mean running for thirty minutes three times a week on your treadmill at your local 'Fitness Is Us' gym. Try swimming. Cycling. Roller derby-ing. Join a rock climbing club. Join a tai chi club. Try Zumba or Latin dancing or spinning around a pole.

Movement is movement so do something that feels good for you. In other words, *get your goddamn arse off your satin couch and go do* something. Anything!

And if you've tried the hundreds of physical activities that are available and none suits you, just try . . . walking. Yes, with your own two feet and heartbeat. Park the car a little further away than you need. Walk to the shops. Walk to the bus stop. The very act of walking triggers a relaxation response in the body. A walk (even a ten-minute one) provides an immediate energy boost.

You can aim for the magical number of 10,000 steps a day, but you could also try just walking for the sheer enjoyment of it.[7] Like Jono Lineen says in his book *Perfect Motion*, walking brings you into contact with the environment. You feel variances in the topography in your muscles, the wind whistling through the trees, the sunlight warming your face.[8]

When I had Hakavai, I was limited in the physical activity I could do. I couldn't really leave a two-month-old baby on the beach while I went for a dive, y'know? So I started walking. I'd walk with him in my babysling, I'd walk with him in the baby backpack, and eventually he started walking beside me.

I hope Hakavai will always see his parents as active and take that as a hint that he too should get his little butt moving whenever he can, and that way he'll also experience the joy of physical activity. But you know what people assume about me? That because I'm a 'fit' person, I've always liked fitness. As a kid, sure, I loved running round and surfing and other forms of activity. But after my accident, I hated movement in any form. I felt pathetic going to a gym, getting on a treadmill and walking more slowly than the old man next to me (no offence if you were the old man, by the way).

For ages I couldn't even wear joggers because the wounds on the backs of my heels were still raw. I'd have to walk around in Crocs. I'd work out with half a kilogram of weight strapped to either wrist, since I didn't have enough fingers anymore to be able to hold the weights. That made me feel pathetic. My once tight tights, which had displayed my long, toned legs, slipped down around my ankles, so I'd have to keep them up with a belt. Sweating made my already itchy skin itchier. I was still in my black compression mask and black compression suit, and stuck out like dogs' balls. Plus, being in a gym with other people (read: the fit and attractive people that typically frequent gyms) made me feel uncomfortable, inadequate, and like I didn't belong. Here's how I dealt with all of that.

- I bought myself trendy gym outfits. No, they didn't magically make me look like a fitness model, but they did make me feel better. There's a psychological phenomenon called 'enclothed cognition', which suggests that the clothing a person wears can trigger mental changes that positively affect their performance and confidence.[9] How you look affects how confident you feel.

- I went to a gym that specialised in rehabilitation. This meant I wasn't surrounded by fit people doing things that seemed impossible for me. I was surrounded by people who had injuries, and were trying to rebuild themselves. Just like I was.
- At the start, I took someone with me as I was embarrassed about how I'd manage the machines. Sure, that someone was my dad, and sure, I did feel like a bit of a loser taking my dad to the gym when I was twenty-four, but I felt a lot more confident than if I'd rocked up solo.
- I knew exercise was part of my improvement process. I knew it was good for me (as it is for everyone). I knew I had to do it as part of my rehab. And I knew that if I wanted my old life back (or as much of it as I could reclaim), it was part of the deal. So I accepted the feelings of inadequacy and shitness, and told myself, *it will get better.*

So, if you struggle with exercise or you have a block about getting out and moving your body – hey, you know I've been there. I really do get it. Try following the steps that I took. Wear clothes that make you feel good, choose a gym where you feel safe and comfortable, take a mate and remind yourself why you're doing it. I promise you, it will make you feel better.

As Dr Libby said to me, 'It's well known that exercise can boost our endorphin levels. But you don't necessarily have to exercise with intensity to experience benefits to your mood. Many people find that gentle and restorative movement helps to reduce anxious feelings and stress, and boosts their sense of calm.'

And talking of a sense of calm ... there is something else that will undoubtedly improve your happy levels ...

Sleep

Sleep is the most important of the three foundational ways to generate energy. I remember once I was travelling solo (bliss! Bed to myself! Room service! None of my beautiful family to interrupt me!). I was training for the Kathmandu Coast to Coast, and had to fit in a ninety-minute run before I caught my seven o'clock flight. This meant a six o'clock departure from the hotel, meaning I'd have to be up at the ungodly hour of four to squeeze in the run. Just looking at those times made me feel exhausted. I was struck by an out-of-this-world crazy thought: *why don't I skip training tomorrow and just sleep until six?*

Cut to the next morning: I woke up at six to the sun filtering through the curtains. I felt great. Better than great – like every single cell in my body was soaked in a feel-good solution. For real, I felt like my body was vibrating with vitality.

And the day? Well, the whole day went my way. My fresh juice at breakfast was tantalisingly delicious. I smashed through a gazillion emails. My creativity was on fire and I punched out years' worth of content. The speech I gave in Melbourne was maybe the best experience I've had on stage. Everything I touched turned to gold!

I know it can be hard to prioritise sleep. We don't value it, and if you're struggling to fit additional activities into your day, it can be very tempting to take it out of your sleep time. Now I know in the previous chapter I suggested you wake up *earlier*, BUT this doesn't mean getting less sleep – it means going to bed earlier.

Sleep is crucial for our happiness. It's been proven, over and over again, to have the most profound benefits on our wellbeing. In fact, one study even suggested that getting one extra hour of sleep each night will do more for a person's daily happiness than getting a $60,000 raise.[10] And not getting *enough* sleep has some pretty dire consequences: hello impaired memory, weakened immune system, inability to self-regulate moods, and stacking on the kilos.[11] There's a very good reason why Amnesty International counts sleep deprivation as a form of torture.

How much sleep do you need, dear reader? Hard for me to say, having no idea who you are. My toddler has between eleven and twelve hours of sleep a night. Most of us adults need between seven and nine hours. My advice? Aim for eight hours. For several nights in a row. Pay off your sleep debt. See how you feel. Do you feel better? Happier? Like *you've* been soaked in a feel-good solution? Great. And if your body doesn't need any more sleep, something craaaazy will happen: you'll wake up of your own accord.

•

If you don't have any trouble going to sleep, staying asleep and getting enough sleep, feel free to skip this next bit.

If you *do* have trouble going to sleep, staying asleep and getting enough sleep, it might be worth trying to develop a sleep routine. I have one, and it's sleep-inducing. Before you start hating on me for being all smug-face again, I want to preface this by saying I developed it out of dire necessity, because after the fire I found it really hard to get to sleep. I was in physical pain and, to put it frankly, terrified of what had happened to me and what was going to happen to me, now and into the future. Nights were the worst. Initially in hospital I relied on a veritable pharmacopoeia to get to sleep. Effective in that I took enough drugs to tranquillise a Shetland pony, but also addictive. And when you've had sleeping pills continuously for two years, it's a really hard habit to break.

My sleep routine helped me. It might help you, or you might find the information below unrelatable and just skim through it. That's fine too.

Turia's pedantic and extremely lengthy sleep routine

Note to reader: obviously I'm not a robot. This is my sleep routine in its ideal state. If I follow this, then, yes, I do get a good night's sleep. Sometimes, though, there are other moving parts in my life (a small child! A small sick child! A partner who's away! A project I'm on deadline for!). At those times, I try to do as many of these steps as I can. And my non-negotiable top pick out of all of them would be tip number one.

1. *No screens before bed!* When we go to sleep at night, our body produces a chemical called melatonin – aka the Hormone of Darkness. Having the light from your phone shine onto your face while you're endlessly scrolling through asos.com at 11 pm will affect your melatonin production, meaning no sleepy eyes for you. When you're in bed with your partner, you'll either read, talk, have sex or shut your eyes earlier. All four are equally beneficial.

2. I get ready for bed ages before bedtime. If we're exhausted, the thought of peeling ourselves off the couch to brush our teeth/floss/put on our night creams seems too laborious . . . so we stay glued to the couch even longer.

3. I'm in bed with a book an hour before I *want* to go to bed. I think to myself: you might read for an hour, you might read for five minutes – it doesn't matter which. Just go with it.

4. I make sure I've done something physical during the day (if I don't do any exercise, it affects my sleep-ability).

5. I make sure I don't drink coffee after midday. Yes, I hear you, you drink a triple-shot latte at six every evening and still have a good night's sleep. Good for you. I'd be wired like a mechanical hare on a greyhound race track. The point is – you do you. Test and experiment and see what allows you to get quality shut-eye.

6. Breathing slowly and deeply has a relaxing effect, so sometimes I put on a guided meditation. And, I love sleep stories! Stephen Fry's 'Blue Gold' feels a shade ASMR-y but also v. excellent at putting one to sleep.*

7. If I can't fall sleep after, say, an hour, or if I'm restless during the night, or wake up and can't get back to sleep, I'll go into the

* What's ASMR? It stands for autonomous sensory meridian response. So you know how when someone whispers in your ear, you might get all tingly? That's ASMR. There's a whole ream of YouTubers who are dedicated to filming ASMR videos.

lounge room so I don't keep my family awake and do something like book-keeping or reading, which I find relaxing and unwind-y.

If I'm struggling to sleep, I try to keep myself really calm. I tell myself, 'It's okay. When your body's ready, it'll shut down.' And if I don't get a good night's sleep despite all of the steps above, I don't flip out. I say to myself, 'It's inevitable I won't have a good night every night. I know I'll be tired today, but at least I'll sleep well tonight.' I get up at my usual time and just accept that I'll probably be more tired during the day. And even if I am more tired than usual, my day isn't a complete write-off. One bad night's sleep here and there won't make you a sleep-deprived zombie. It's just when the bad nights accumulate that your body and mind suffer.

Energy-boosting quick wins

Obviously, getting into a pattern of exercise, eating well and having enough sleep are long-term changes to make. And, um, sometimes, it's not realistic to expect to achieve this holy trinity all the time.

So, I also want to give you some quick energy-boosting wins. Stuff that will make you feel good, like, right now; stuff that you can action whenever you feel like you need a boost.

1. Decluttering

This one might feel like an absolute drag and therefore to be the opposite of an energy booster. But if you typically avoid tidying and cleaning up, I promise it's an even better exercise for you – as long as it doesn't delay your bedtime, of course! Just start small. Set a time limit (like three or five minutes) and tackle one small section of your space. Put stuff away, clear the benchtops, wipe things clean.

I never used to be tidy. I just couldn't be bothered. Who cared if my bedroom floor was cluttered with clothes? Get out of my bedroom if it's a problem, you creep. But now that Hakavai is a crawling/standing/roaming kid, his stuff is also crawling, standing and roaming around with him. It doesn't matter what I do, at the end of the day his toys and stuff are everywhere. For a while there, I didn't make a habit of picking them up. But when I did, I noticed that the next day would generally go more smoothly. I'd wake up to a relatively tidy house, I wouldn't step on a book on my way to make my morning coffee, or trip over a stuffed owl.

It made me feel clearer mentally. And for me, it's about controlling the controllables. Because the truth is, shit happens, life gets in the way, and our best-laid plans go awry. So, I focus on what I can control. It doesn't matter how chaotic my day is, or what happens, I can pick up my son's toys. And that little three-minute interval makes me feel calmer. So, spend a few minutes 'picking up the toys' (whatever that means for you) every day. And, come on, don't bullshit me, you tricksy little minx, I know you're busy – but you have three minutes.

2. Change your facial expression

When you're feeling frustrated or stressed, try a simple smile. Yes, I know, it sounds silly. But our facial expressions *can* influence our emotions.[12] So a facial expression of *energy and happiness and joy* (such as a smile or a laugh) can help you to shift your mood.

3. Change your body language

Picture someone tired and drained. What do they look like? What posture do they have? Are they slumped, head down, shoulders hunched? And what about an energetic person? They're sitting up straight, right? Head up, eyes bright, shoulders relaxed. Just like us changing our facial expression, by changing our posture and our body language, we can trick our brain into feeling better too.[13] Try standing tall with your shoulders back and your head up.

4. Breathing

Breathing properly has several advantages: it calms you, it slows down your nervous system and it brings you to the present moment. Wim Hof, aka The Iceman, climbed Mount Everest wearing only a pair of shorts, and finished a marathon in the Namib Desert without drinking any water. He attributes his success in those and other extreme sporting endeavours to breathing (properly) – he reckons that breathing is key for our happiness, leading to more energy, a stronger immune system and lower stress levels.

There are heaps of different breathing exercises you can do and I've listed some recommendations in the Resources section. Square breathing is one of my favourites. Here's how you square breathe: rest your hands on your belly, breath in long and slow and deep so that you can feel your belly expanding with the air. Inhale like this for five seconds. Hold your breath for five seconds. Exhale slowly through your nose for five seconds. Hold for five seconds. Repeat.

5. Mindfulness

You'll know a bit about mindfulness if you've been paying attention for the last decade. Mindfulness is about staying in the present moment. Not thinking about the past, not thinking about the future. This is hard for most humans, since we're wired to contemplate our future. We actually think about our future three times more than we think about our past.[14]

Change, loss and death are inevitable. Hakavai has already changed so much in two years. What will he look like in another two years? In ten? And when I look at Michael, I mean *really* look at Michael, I can see change etched into him. His hair has patches of grey. His eyes have creases in them (I lecture him to wear more sunscreen).

As we have found out so potently entering this decade, *tomorrow* everything can be different, and next week things can be even more different; and what is to come the year after that and the year after that? The only certainty we have, really, is that the future will be uncertain. Hence the very present need to sometimes intentionally focus on – you got it – the present.

Some people are able to practise mindfulness without trying. Michael has beehives. Once, I was upstairs folding laundry on our bed and glanced out of the window to see him perched in a camp chair on the lawn, *literally watching the bees as they came and went from their hive.*

Obviously I thought he'd had a mental lapse, so I rushed downstairs to ask him what he was doing.

'Watching the bees, darl, and *breathing*,' he said.

'Why?'

'It's relaxing.'

'Aren't you bored?'

'No, *I'm enjoying myself.*'

I'm not great at meditating. In fact, out of all the happy-inducing activities I talk about in this book, I'm probably the shittest at being mindful. A while back, I checked out several different meditation retreats. Then I decided I didn't want to be away from my family for that long. But was this the real truth? Perhaps it was really that I didn't want to go on a meditation retreat that much! And this is the thing about being happy. Things that make me happy (geology! Reading! Hiking!) may not be your idea of happiness. But they can still be useful, and mindfulness, making ourselves stay quiet in the present moment, even for a few minutes, will give your vitality and energy levels a big nudge up.

I was introduced to Brooke Boney by a friend of a friend. She's a remarkable woman: she has a super-impressive career, she's articulate, educated, polite and diplomatic but . . . she doesn't take shit from anyone. I was interested to hear how she augments her energy levels to balance her career, happiness, and standing up for herself.

Brooke Boney, Gamilaroi woman and *Today Show* entertainment host

How has your idea of happiness changed as you've become more recognised as a public figure?

I've always been a pretty light-hearted and cheerful person. And my mum says I'm like my nephew – he walks into a room and his mission is to make everyone happy and feel good. I always thought that meant I was a bit of a pushover because I went along with things, but when my mum framed it that way I realised it was actually a great quality.

Something I admire about you is that you don't shy away from uncomfortable conversations. Why is this important to you?

I think because I've seen so many dark things reported on Aboriginal affairs and politics; and even in my own family and my own experiences, when you have things happen to you that aren't very nice or you see the world as a place that can be pretty cruel or unkind or unfair, you lean a bit harder into happiness. Because the opposite of that is despair or succumbing to it all. So for me, I lean into the light because I don't like the alternatives. But when you're guided by making other people's lives better – like other young Aboriginal people in my case, or people from the country, or disadvantaged people – you feel like you don't have a choice. You speak up when something isn't right, even if it is difficult or uncomfortable. It's a privilege to have people listening to me.

You started using the traditional Gamilaroi greeting Yaama *on Triple J, you support changing the date of Australia Day, and overall you've been an advocate for Indigenous representation on screen and in journalism. How have you managed to protect your own happiness when dealing with white privilege?*

It can be hard. It can be challenging. You need to make sure you have people around you who really care about you. I know I'm doing the right thing because people deserve to be treated equally. There's no way that in the best country in the world we should have people who can't afford to send their kids to school, whose deaths aren't investigated, who aren't treated the same under the eyes of the law, who have really poor health outcomes compared to the rest of Australia.

There's a deep sense of unfairness in that, which keeps me going. As my platform gets bigger, it's been more difficult to protect myself – I'm speaking to a bigger audience and a broader audience. For me, though, at the end of the day there's nothing wrong with asking to be treated equally – that's what makes me feel safe. It's not because I want a bigger platform or to be more famous or more rich – it's because that's what I believe.

And of course, self-care! Making sure you get enough sleep, exercise, spending time with family and friends, connecting with my community. These are the things that keep me strong when things get rough.

You practise mindfulness and meditation. What does this do for you? Does it contribute to your happiness?

I think it puts things into perspective. I've done a few different retreats in India, and meditation makes me realise that nothing matters that much, we don't have as much control over things as what we think, and for me it helps me to let go and let go of my expectations. As grim as it is, it's also very freeing! It makes me realise that my place in the world is not permanent. I'm grateful for the life that I have because I'm safe, I'm happy for the most part, I'm healthy, I've got lovely friends and a job I go to that's fun.

What makes you happy?
Talking to my mum every day, being able to have great conversations with friends, eating really lovely food, going out for a long walk. That kind of thing.

Unquestionably, regardless of whether what you're doing is pleasant (swimming for me) or unpleasant (folding clothes?), people are happiest and calmest when they stay focused on what they're doing and only that. There are also parts of the day when I'm so immersed in what I'm doing – for example, playing Lego with Hakavai and allowing myself to be soothed by following the instructions – that I lose track of time. A way of describing that feeling is that I'm 'in flow', but I guess it's a form of mindfulness, in that you're focusing so hard on what you're doing that you forget stuff that's bothering you or what you have to do next. Being in flow feels great – it makes stress disappear for the time we're concentrating, and it tends to be a sign that the activity we're doing means something to us.

And on that note, here's my illuminating interview with the Iceman himself.

Wim Hof, extreme athlete

What does happiness mean to you?
Our natural state, the way nature meant us to be.

To be on my way: my mission being to relieve suffering and to heal people, being with motivated, joyous people.

Being with my ridiculously cute child.

What kinds of activities make you happy?

Walking barefoot in the snow, hugging people.

Sharing natural wisdom, fun, music.

Spreading good news, beating ignorance with love and transparency.

How does cold water affect your happiness?

Boom, there it is. It shuts up too much thinking and brings back one's full presence. The vascular system transports your life force. Cold makes the transportation flow a lot better. The heart rate goes down. No stress, more power.

I've heard you say that to be happy, you just need to breathe and believe. Can you explain how this affects our happiness? How has your understanding of happiness changed over the years?

Breathing has an effect on our hormonal system; on our levels of dopamine and serotonin.

Over the years I see that happiness is sharing love, enlightening the ignorance that comes from too much individualism. Being happy is a natural state, sharing goes along with it.

Happiness to you all. Forever . . .

•

TL;DR

- The happier you are, the more energy you have. And having more energy makes it easier to be happy.
- To create more energy, you've got to do basic stuff well, like eating healthy-ish food, moving your body and making sure you get enough sleep.
- Having said that, there are ways to give yourself a quick boost in energy, like doing something you enjoy, changing your body language and breathing long and slow and deep.

4
Kindness

My mum is perpetually sunny. She's positively bursting with an insatiable *joie de vivre*, optimism and a genuine 'look on the bright side' attitude. When you spend time with her, she makes you feel good about yourself and your choices. Though, I'll be clear, growing up, I found her happiness to be equal parts admirable . . . and irritating, in the way all mums annoy their daughters.

When I started writing this book, I was keen to ask Mum about happiness; how she augmented hers with, it seemed, so little effort. Because I'm me, I was after a formula, where if I input X, maximised Y and decreased the value of Z, the result would be the optimal level of happiness.

Of course, she had no idea what I was talking about.

'C'mon, Mum! Just give me the basic parameters that contribute to your personal happiness levels! It's not hard.'

'Darling, the lilli pillies are ready to pick! I'm going to make jam for Hakavai! *Tama'a maitai!* Yes, happiness is good. *Oa oa no te ora!*'*

A few days later, I got an email from her:

> The lilli-pilly jam happened!
> Remember when you asked, 'Mum, how did you become who you are?', hoping for a formula? I know the answer now. Growing up, I was surrounded by kind people.

Ah, Mum. Thanks for the warm and fuzzies. And, look, she had a valid point: happy people are typically kind people. Research has shown a *correlation* between happiness and kindness. This means that happier people are more likely to perform an altruistic act like helping a stranger, or a colleague, despite their own heavy workload.[1]

But does performing kind acts actually affect your happiness? Sonja Lyubomirsky, one of the world's most prominent researchers on happiness, designed an experiment to answer this very question.[2]

It went something like this:

1. Participants were enlisted and divided into two groups (let's call them, unimaginatively, group A and group B).
2. Both groups were instructed to perform five acts of kindness per week, for six weeks. The acts of kindness that the participants doled out were varied, ranging from 'Donated

* *Tama'a maitai* is kind of the Tahitian equivalent of 'bon appétit!' *Oa oa no te ora* approximately means 'joy for the life!'. (It is very hard nailing down exact and precise meanings from my mum.)

blood' to 'Gave a homeless man twenty dollars' to 'Told my professor thank you for his hard work'.

3. Group A was instructed to perform five acts of kindness at any time during the week. Group B was to perform five acts of kindness on one day of the week.
4. And of course Sonja had a control group. She's a pro, yo.

The results? Firstly, the study showed with a resounding *yes* that performing acts of kindness does make you happier (hoorah for kindness!), both in the short and long term.[3] How? Well, in lots of ways. Being kind helps you to see others in a more positive light; it improves your self-image and sense of your own fortune; it can add meaning to your life; and on top of all that, being kind means that people are more likely to appreciate you, like you and offer gratitude for your kind deed.[4]

Lyubomirsky emphasises the need, however, not to let kind acts become part of your to-do list, because then you may resent them and find doing them tedious or repetitive, which is why it turned out that group B benefited the most.

It appears, in fact, that in a virtuous circle, being kind makes people happier and happiness makes people kinder: at the end of the experiment, group B, who had committed five acts of kindness in one day over the six weeks, had begun to think of themselves as good people, which augmented their optimism in their ability to help others.

Kindness conundrums

Something else about kindness got me thinking. In *The Little Book of Lykke*, the CEO of the Happiness Research Institute, Meik Wiking, writes:

It is not just society in general that becomes happier through altruism. We feel personally better. Try to recall a time you did something nice for a stranger, *not because you wanted to gain something from it*, just for the pure purpose of helping somebody else. How did that action make you feel?[5]

See that line I've italicised? Yeah, that's where I got myself bogged in a big conceptual kindness quagmire. I started to wonder, is being kind ever truly selfless? And if you're not being truly selfless, are you actually being kind?

So. Let's unpack this idea for all you 'people ain't kind for no reason' cynics out there.

Being kind most often engenders reciprocation. In other words, I scratch your back, you scratch mine.

Back up for a minute. So does that mean you're only kind because you sort of want something in return?

Yes. And no.

Reciprocity is widespread; all our different societies subscribe to the idea.[6] In the times of cavemen and -women, maybe you gave your share of the hunt to the medicine man of the tribe as a future 'payment' in case a member of your immediate family got sick. These days, giving back is so socially ingrained in us that mostly we do it without thinking, or analysing our motives too much. For example, Michael gives fish to his family, to my family and to our friends and neighbours. I doubt he does much internal debating about his motives for giving fish away – he does it just because he's a nice bloke. But I do know there was one guy that Michael always gave fish to. And then one day Michael asked to borrow his lawnmower and the guy said no. Do you think Michael still gives that guy fish?

So, yes, we're kind to people to keep them on our good side, because of reciprocity, but also I think the majority of us are kind to just . . . be kind. I mean, have you ever given a dollar to the person in front of you in a line when they've been short? (Yeah, me neither. JK, JK!)

When I was in hospital I noticed that my surgeon, Professor Peter Haertsch, regularly went on leave for a couple of weeks at a time. So one day I cheekily asked him where he was taking his holidays. He explained to me that he volunteered with a non-profit organisation called Interplast, providing life-changing surgery in developing countries to patients who desperately need it. Since then, I've helped to raise over a million dollars for this incredible organisation.

I don't do and never have done the work with Interplast because I'm expecting something in return. But I do reap a lot of rewards from working with them: my experiences with them have made me understand more profoundly my place in the world and the privilege of life in Australia. They have made me grateful for my own personal circumstances, and have given me a focus outside of myself. And I would say with zero hesitation that working with Interplast was instrumental to my mental recovery.

It's my belief that reciprocity is an unexpected benefit of being kind. Just as my reason for raising money for Interplast was not so I could feel happier, you're not kind to your neighbour because you want him to invite you over to his movie nights. You don't help an elderly person with their shopping with the expectation that she'll buy you lunch. Sure, if you've done someone a favour, you might be inclined to ask them for a favour of your own, but that's unlikely to be why you helped them in the first place.

Atypically, I'm not going to boss you about when it comes to how you should be kind. Be kind however you want, however kindness looks to you: helping a stranger cross the road, visiting a nursing home, picking up litter down the beach, writing your postman a thank-you note, babysitting your nephews, campaigning on behalf of Amnesty International. Just do it. Don't let your head noise get in the way of a good deed.

Have you heard the often-quoted fact that 50 per cent of our happiness is determined by our genes, 10 per cent by our life circumstances and 40 per cent by our behaviour? Sonja Lyubomirsky was one of the researchers behind the original pie chart, and she's studied happiness and wellbeing for over two decades.[7] So, I thought she'd have some interesting stuff to say.

Sonja Lyubomirsky

Some of your research indicates that practising small acts of kindness increases happiness. How could people do this?

Yes, my research shows that when people do a few more acts of kindness each week than they regularly do, they become happier. It's easy. For example, for the next month (or any period of time), do three acts of kindness (big or small, towards close or distant others) that you don't normally do. Ideally, do them all on one day – say, every Monday do three extra kind acts.

I've heard you say that short-term happiness is easier to achieve than long-term happiness. Can you explain that?

Well, most of us know how to become happier temporarily. The hard part is how to make it last – how to sustain happiness. This is difficult because we have to create new habits: for example, be more grateful or connect more with others but not just for a few weeks but forever!

Accepting kindness

Here's something else about practising kindness. You can't always be the person to offer kindness; you have to accept it for yourself, too. Yep, you need to ask for, and accept, help.

Why do we struggle with this? In the 'Goals' chapter of this book, I talk about building a support team, which comes from a step I use in my School of Champions. In other words, identifying the help you need and finding the right people to give it.

It is hands-down the most polarising step in the School of Champions course. Guaranteed, by the time my students reach this step, I'll start to get questions like, 'Can I skip this step?', 'How do you ask for help?' or 'I'm not comfortable letting my friends know what I'm doing until it's done. Can't I just do this on my own?'

I'm always being asked if I find it hard to ask for help. If I'm being honest, only sometimes. Mostly, I love to put on a high-pitched voice and coerce my mum into making me pancakes.

But the 'sometimes' when I hate asking for help? Well, I used to find it hard because I hated the reality I found myself in, and asking for help made it feel more real, and as though my dignity had been stripped away. I was no longer the fiercely independent young woman I had prided myself on becoming. I had no choice but to accept people's kindness and help.

And maybe that's been a good thing. Because I'm a pro at this now. I mean, I'll be honest, sometimes I still get frustrated at having to ask. Sometimes, particularly if I'm feeling vulnerable or crappy and if I'm struggling to get my bags in the overhead compartment on a plane, I can feel myself getting worked up. It feels embarrassing to have to show other people that my injuries do make simple tasks tricky from time to time, and on those occasions I do need help.

But for the most part I know that asking for and accepting help is just part of the deal of life. Dylan Alcott says something similar in his excellent book *Able*: 'A lot of people often try to be too independent. If asking for some help saves you time or makes things a bit easier, then don't be ashamed to ask for it. You'll enjoy life a lot better if you do.'[8]

Being a good human is not about being a superhuman. Cooking cordon bleu meals, having a six-pack and housekeeping to perfection aren't gonna make you happier. Helping others and accepting help when you need it *will*. You can't give and give and give without accepting anything in return – that would make you a martyr.

How do you know if you need help? Entrepreneur Kate Northrup summarises it beautifully in her book *Do Less*. She observes that you most likely need to ask for help, first, if you're experiencing physical stress or getting sick frequently.

For example, I got mastitis twice in the first couple of months of Hakavai's life; probably because I was still trying to maintain my pre-child levels of work and sport. I think you can absolutely crush it in multiple domains (work! Home! Kids! Roller skating!) but you can't crush it without help and support.

She also thinks you should reach out if you're constantly shitty, overwhelmed or resentful at the stuff you're spending time on; and not eating well, fitting in enough sleep or movement. Basic priorities, yo.[9]

Now that I've told you that you need to ask for, and accept, help, let me temper it all by saying: you've gotta ask the right person. For example, if you were at the supermarket and asked an elderly person to please reach up to the very top shelf to pass you down a jar of sundried tomatoes, they might baulk at the request. Whereas if you asked a youthful soul coming down the aisle, I'm sure they'd be happy to oblige.

So, asking the right person is an important consideration. And there are two other things you need to keep in mind.

1. The Value theory

Let's say you were moving to a place a couple of hours' drive away, and you asked an acquaintance at work if she could help you, *and* if you could borrow her car. No surprise, unless she was a bona fide saint, she'd probably come up with an excuse like, 'Oh, I'd love to but I have to walk my grandma's goldfish.' But if you asked your very best friend the same question, of course she'd help, right?

So here's my formula: if the time and commitment required is less or equal to the value of the relationship, yep, you help. So for example your boss might ask you if you want to be the organiser for the Christmas committee, and because you value this relationship highly, you say yes (even when you really want to say no!). So, when you're asking someone for a kindness, remember to flip things around. Consider the time and commitment required for the task, and whether the value of your relationship with that person warrants asking them.

2. Stick to your strengths

I field lots of requests to work with various charities and organisations. They're amazing causes, but I'm simply not capable of being a part of them all. Over the years of running my business, I've had to learn that if I do everything for everyone else I won't have any time for my family or friends or myself. I focus my energy on one or two things that I'm good at, and help in those areas.

So, when you get asked to do things that don't play to your strengths, say no. You can also reframe your response: 'I can't do that, but I can do *this*.' (Except when the value of relationship warrants you stepping up. For example, you'd do pretty well anything for your kid or your partner, right, but your colleague? You're not their removalist. See above.)

If I asked my mum for help with a business meeting, she'd be out of her depth and hate it. She'd be brilliant, though, at looking after Hakavai and cooking us both a fluffy omelette. If I asked my employee to look after Hakavai and cook us a fluffy omelette, and then massage my hair with coconut oil, she'd probably quit.

Moral? Pick the most appropriate person to help you. And in return, offer the help you're best suited to provide.

Saying . . . 'No (thanks)'

So, if you've figured out that you're not the right person for the job, *how* do you say no? As humans, we want to say yes to the things people ask of us. We want to be socially obliging, to be part of a team. We say yes because it's easier than saying no. It feels kind to say yes. But, here's the thing: what if you ask yourself, kind for who?

All it takes is a few easy yeses and suddenly you're taking on an extra project at work, making a six-layer birthday cake for your second cousin's wedding and going on a yacht cruise party the night before a major project is due (but, ahem, that does sound fun. Send me an invite 😂).

All these commitments pull your focus away from the things you actually want to spend your time and energy on. That's not being kind to yourself. Saying no can be the ultimate act of kindness. To yourself, *and* to others. Saying no isn't selfish, it's self-care, and we need to practise it more.

Here are my tips for saying no more easily:

- Don't dally. If you know you can't commit to something, be straight. Don't confuse things by saying 'I'll check', 'Maybe I could make it work' or 'I'll think about it'. Those responses only delay your eventual no, and make things harder in the long run for the person asking. Be brief, respond promptly and don't delay the inevitable.
- If you have a reason, sure, share it. ('I can't come to your cousin's softball game *because* my thesis is due on Monday.'). Research shows that giving a reason provides context and makes people more likely to be fine with your no.[10]
- Having said that, don't lie. I know, it's tempting to soften a no with a white lie, but it can get you into sticky situations. You could try something like, 'I won't be able to make it. I've been working really hard and I promised myself I wouldn't take on another commitment until I've rested and restored my energy.'

- For social events, think about whether or not the event would genuinely suffer without you. Let's say the obligation is your best friend's wedding, and you're the maid of honour or best man, then, yeah, that obligation will suffer without you there and really you should go. But the baby shower of a colleague you worked with four years ago? Nope, it's probably not gonna suffer without you. Now, I know you're hilarious and charming and every social obligation would benefit from your attendance. (Am I right?!). But remember, each commitment you say yes to means you're saying no to something else.
- Consider the 'Two Days' rule. Sometimes we say yes to things ('Yeah, of course I can come with you to that three-hour movie you really want to see') because we think they're *ages* away. I am guilty of this, over and over again, but what helps me is thinking about whether or not I'd say yes if the event was in two days' time.
- If it's appropriate (and if you want to), offer an alternative. If there's a time in the future you could commit to, or someone or something else to offer instead – offer it!
- I know that saying no feels uncomfortable. But saying yes to commitments that will overcrowd, overwhelm and overcommit you – that's more uncomfortable. We've all said yes to things we wish we said no to. And what happens? We end up being shitty and resentful.

Long story short: sometimes being kind is exhausting. Saying no is the ultimate act of kindness to yourself.

There's one last thing to remember when we're talking about accepting acts of kindness. When you ask people for their help, they're going to help in *their way*. If Michael's with Hakavai, I have to accept that he could feed Hakavai a milkshake for lunch and let him bring the worms and dirt from the garden into our bedroom. That's stuff I wouldn't let Hakavai do (if anyone is getting a milkshake when my boy and I hang out, it's me).

To enjoy kindness, it's a good idea to decide you're not going to give up your happiness over little things that you can't control. So drop the expectation that everyone will do things the way you would, and choose to be appreciative for the people and the moments that you have.

•

TL;DR

- Performing acts of kindness and being an overall good human make you happier.
- Don't overthink it. Helping a stranger cross the road, picking up litter, babysitting, campaigning on behalf of a charity - all of these (and many more!) are acts of kindness.
- Learn how to accept kindness from others. You can absolutely crush it in multiple domains, but you can't crush it without help and support.
- While you're shaking this kindness thing like glitter, sprinkle a little bit on yourself. It's okay and sometimes necessary to say no!

[illegible]

[illegible] their [illegible] they become [illegible] to help the [illegible] with [illegible]. Indeed, I think it's clear that he could feed his [illegible] and a mile [illegible]

[illegible]

[illegible]

[illegible]

[illegible]

5
Self-talk

Gosh. Self-talk is everything, isn't it? I really could have written a whole book about it.

What is self-talk, you ask? Once again you've posed an excellent question.

Self-talk is that little inner voice we all have. It's the conversations you have with yourself, and the words you use to describe yourself. You know when you walk past a window and think, 'Wow, it looks like a rat set up camp in my hair overnight'? That's self-talk (not very nice self-talk, at that rate, either. I'm sure the rat was only a passing visitor. Nothing a hairdryer can't fix).

I believe self-talk is critical for our success in life, our relationships with others and, most importantly, how good we feel about ourselves. We all know people who, ostensibly, *should* be really happy, but they're not. Why? Well, maybe they give themselves too many rules in order to be happy. They need to keep their house immaculate, keep themselves immaculate, never lose their cool with their kids, be a perfect blend of fun and sexy for their spouse, and win 'Employee of the Month', um, every month.

On top of that, what do you reckon the voice inside their head is telling them? Do you think it's saying, 'Wow! Go you! Your house is spotless! You're a beautiful parent and friend! Your hair looks great parted like that!' Or is that voice constantly harassing them?

An inner critic – we all have one. Mine used to be really mean to me, too. Looking back on my high school years, I remember how, like many young women, I was overly concerned by my weight and my body image. My inner critic would pipe up real loud if I had a second serving of cake. I'd berate myself endlessly. As an adult, I question how a fourteen-year-old girl can be so mean to herself. (Not to mention that being mean to yourself is probably the most ineffective way to enact a change. The only thing it does is make you feel like the bits of dog shit that you can't get out of the tiny crevices on the bottom of your shoe.)

Changing your self-talk helps you feel better about yourself and your choices. Which in turn helps you to be happier. So, how do we change our self-talk? Let's focus on some areas of interest. First up, language.

Language

I believe that the words we use influence our emotions, so I'm pretty particular about the ones I use in my day-to-day life. Those haven't always been received well. In fact, people have told me (the nerve of some people, honestly) to change the language I use because it's too informal/childish/surfie/immature etc. Like, far out, man, I can't help the amount of time I spend in the green room, y'know?

I choose to use these types of words ('sick', 'fully sick', 'awesomely sick', for example) cos they make me feel fun, light, not-take-self-too-serious-y and overall *happier*. I'm not saying you need to drastically overhaul how you speak because you, my love, are special and unique and there is no one (and never has been anyone) like you in the world, so why should you try to speak like anyone else?

What I'm advocating is that we all broaden our vocabulary (I'll think of a better slogan for my placards, I promise) because the more words we have to describe an experience, the richer those experiences can become.

Think about this: when someone asks you how you're going, and you reply, 'Flat out, life is so busy and full on,' well, that's the only way you can see it – busy, messy, too fast, stressful. But if you say, 'I'm so excited, there's so much happening at the moment!' there are different connotations. Can you see how the two descriptions change the way you feel?

If someone asked you how your weekend was and instead of just saying, 'Oh yeah, it was all right,' you said, '*Marvellous!*' or '*Extraordinary!*' and maybe even SHOUTED IT (or maybe not, your call), would that change how you felt about the weekend, and even how you felt now?

Note: I'm not asking you to bullshit your way through life. To be a super-positive Pollyanna all the time would be, firstly, very fucking annoying to everyone around you, and secondly, mean that you were a bit of an ostrich with your head in sand. You can't deny that bad stuff happens. So when I reference self-talk, I'm not asking you to lie to yourself. Like, if you just broke up with your boyfriend and your cat died, when someone asked you how your weekend was, you'd probably be lying if you replied '*Spectacular!*'

(Unless of course your boyfriend was a loser and you hated the cat you inherited from your Aunt Maude. No judgements from me, promise.)

However, I *am* asking you to turn off your autopilot and use new words to describe your experiences. Because the more words we have at our disposal, the more colourful and alive our experiences feel. The language we use shapes the way we perceive and understand the world.[1] The Japanese have a word to describe sunlight filtering through the trees (*komorebi*), hence they look out for this occurrence. The French have *flâner* – leisurely strolling the streets with no destination in mind, simply for the sake of soaking up the beauty of a place. Serbs have *merak* – the feeling of bliss and one-ness with the universe that comes from the simplest of pleasures.

Does this mean that if you're not familiar with the German word *fernweh*, you can't experience a longing for far-off places, especially those you haven't yet visited? No, of course it doesn't. But by having a word at the ready, we may be more capable of recognising and relishing a feeling as opposed to if we have only a vague description of it. Dr Tim Lomas, an expert on positive psychology, has created a positive cross-cultural lexicography which, in his own words, is an 'evolving index of "untranslatable" words relating to wellbeing from across the world's languages'.[2]

According to Lomas, 'Life is just this great diffused river of sensations and stimuli. It's hard to pin things down, but if I have a label for it, it's slightly easier to grab hold of a passing feeling.'[3]

So, in my pretty little head, it's simple – if you want to feel a certain way, use the words associated with that feeling.

Here's a test for you. Grab a quill and a stack of papyrus sheets and write down all the negative emotions you felt last week. Go on. Here are some examples:

> I was embarrassed when my boss yelled at me.
> I was annoyed and frustrated when I had a fight with my partner over whose turn it was to take the bins out.
> I was angry when the next door neighbours reversed into my fence, damaging my prize-winning gardenias.

Done?

Now write a list of all the ways you felt good last week. Again, some examples:

> I felt sexy when my partner playfully slapped me on the bum in the morning.
> I felt so proud when I watched my prize-winning azaleas blossoming (you green thumb, you).
> I felt like a total frother when I caught a really sick wave in front of all my mates.

After completing this assignment like the gold-star student you are, count up the number of negative words you had at your disposal compared to positive ones.

Were there more negative words on your lists? If there were, it doesn't necessarily mean you're a downer. Our brains are very clever and have helped humankind to stay alive for the past half a million years, but one thing they don't do as well as they could is to pay good attention to positive emotions. In fact, our brain is top-notch at noticing the *bad* things in our lives. That makes sense from an evolutionary perspective.

Cavepeople who didn't notice a lion would get eaten. Cavepeople who weren't worried about their food stores starved. Cavepeople who weren't slightly pessimistic about the chance of snow might leave behind their furs and freeze to death. In the past, being optimistic and positive would have led to us dying and not being able to pass on our genes.

These days, though, this negative bias doesn't help us to stay alive. Remembering the dressing-down that Brian from Accounts gave you doesn't increase your life expectancy. Mentally listing all the ways your morning has gone wrong doesn't make your day easier. And thinking of all the ways your appearance is flawed frankly does bugger all except make you feel like shit.

And yet studies have shown that no matter your age or culture, we have far more words in our vocabulary that express negative emotions than positive ones.[4] Again, we developed this way for a reason: for example, is that bad feeling I'm getting because of the sabre-tooth tiger approaching me? Or is it because I feel guilty about betraying a friend? Feeling good usually means we're okay, we're safe and our lives aren't in danger – and therefore feel-good emotions need less distinction.

Robert Schrauf, a professor of applied linguistics at Penn State University, undertook a comprehensive search of scientific literature to try to uncover the most common words people use across the world to denote emotions. He found that 'cross-culturally, there are maybe five to seven basic emotions that show up in every language, that seem to have the same meaning'.[5] They are: 'joy, fear, anger, sadness, disgust, shame and guilt'. How many positive words are in that list? Yes, you read it right – *one*!

But I feel as though this is a bit like saying the only colours in the world are the primary colours. Just because we can all agree on five to seven basic emotions, it doesn't mean those are the only emotions we can experience. I pride myself on 'feeling' the broad spectrum of emotions that we are able to experience. I want to be painting with the whole goddamn palette, not restricting myself to a couple of primary colours.

So, what's the takeaway?

Well, start noticing the different ways you feel positive emotions, and develop a vocabulary to describe them.

If you're thinking 'Turia, it's that easy, is it? Just use happier words and I'll feel happier?' – um, yes. That's exactly what I'm saying. Chapter over, yeah?

JK, JK! I know that you (like me) approach self-help books with a healthy dose of cynicism and a dash of scepticism and a sprinkle of pessimism so I'll elaborate further. Read on!

Self-descriptors

I'm pretty careful with the words I use to describe myself. For example, I'd never call myself a burns victim, or disfigured. I'm not lying to myself. The descriptors 'burns victim' and 'disfigured' have vastly different connotations to others I could use – 'burns survivor' and 'different'. Using other words to describe myself makes me feel better about myself and therefore happier.

Have an honest think about the words you use to describe yourself. Which words have negative connotations? Could you replace them with more positive ones? It's a small and simple switch but it packs a big punch.

Self-talk faux pas

Change 'have to' to 'get to'

Life with my son is delightful, magical, incredible – and relentless. Kids sleep (sometimes), but until they do there's no off button.

When I first had Hakavai, I was always telling myself that I *had* to do stuff. I had to prepare his food. I had to take him for a walk. I had to clean his room. I had to play with him. I had to do this and I had to do that.

Consistently telling myself that I 'had' to do stuff for my son made it feel as though I was telling myself that spending time with him was a chore. So I started saying I 'get' to do stuff with my son. I get to feed Hakavai. I get to wash his clothes. I get to be around and watch him grow up.

This simple shift in my language instantly changed my attitude: It shifted the focus from one of obligation to one of gratitude.

Using '. . . yet'

In Year 5, when I was about ten years old, I was doing remedial maths. I found it so difficult. Every night I'd sit down with my homework and look at the numbers in front of me and feel overwhelmed.

One night I was sitting in the kitchen while Mum cooked lentil stew, my homework spread out across the table in front of me. I remember it so distinctly: the stew bubbling quietly in the pot, Mum chatting away loudly, the rain coming down outside. And the overwhelming feeling that *I just couldn't do it.* I burst into tears and said to Mum, 'I'm so stupid, I don't get this, I can't do it.'

And my mum, my beautiful mum, said, 'No, Turia. You can't do it *yet*.'

Simply by adding that little word 'yet', I was reminded that just because I couldn't do something at the time, it didn't mean I wouldn't be able to find a way to make it happen in the future. And that gave me hope. Whatever you're working towards, even if you can't see results right now and even if you might not be where you want to be, it doesn't mean that you're not making progress.

Use 'yet'.

You will get there.

I don't have time

I cover this in my 'Goals' chapter, too. But, hey, I'm happy to talk about it a lil more here, first!

Just like saying we 'have to go to work', telling ourselves we 'don't have the time' is disempowering. All it does is refocus our brain (and its delightful negative bias) on what we *don't* have. And I don't know about you, but I'm not exactly fond of remembering that I don't have an in-house chef, forty-six hours in one day, and (awkwardly) ten fingers – which made the physical typing of this book . . . ahhh, rather slow, I might add. (Cue tiny violin solo for each of my fallen finger friends.)

It feels shitty to dwell on the stuff we don't have. You know this already from the first chapter of this book. Saying you 'don't have time' can make you feel like you don't have a choice at all.

There are twenty-four hours in a day. That fact is something we all share. But we all have different priorities that shape how we use that time. If you're not doing something with your time, it's likely because that task is not currently high on that list of priorities. That's okay. If it needs to be placed higher, you can make that decision and do the work to figure out how to make it happen. In the meantime, instead of saying, 'I don't have the time to exercise/declutter the linen cupboard/work on my interior design business,' you could say, 'It's not a priority for me right now.' It reminds you that *you've got options.*

Inner critics

You might recognise your inner critic from such classics as *I'm a Stupid Failure, I'm Fat and Ugly, No One Will Ever Like Me* and *I'm Going To Fail School/Be a Disaster in This Job.*

Sound familiar?

Sometimes the inner critic in my head can be mean, especially if I'm tired, recovering from an operation, feeling vulnerable or just having a bad day.

So if I'm feeling crappy, and I'm out with Michael, sometimes my inner critic will whisper insidiously, 'You know people are wondering how you snagged Michael, right?'

If I'm recovering from an operation and therefore feeling vulnerable, and I'm struggling to carry my groceries, my inner critic will screech at me, 'You're pathetic! You can't even carry a bag of milk and bread!'

Or, if I'm running and I'm in a shit mood, my inner critic will sneer, 'Wow, motherhood has definitely slowed you down hasn't it?'

My inner critic is a sassy bitch if I let her out for too long. So I've got some management techniques that I've honed over the past decade to keep her on a tight leash. I reckon they might help you keep your inner critic walking within the lines of decency too!

(And, a quick note on inner-critic catching: typically, your inner critic will sound just like you. This means she – or he! – can be hard to catch. Your inner critic runs rampant whenever you feel uncertain, scared, angry, embarrassed, negative or sad. So, the next time you feel down, and you hear something negative about yourself like 'You always stuff things up, what did you expect?' BAM! That, my friend, is your inner critic.)

1. Be your own bestie

You've probably heard it before – we're our own worst enemy. Think about how nasty and mean and toxic the stuff we say to ourselves is. Would you ever talk like that to someone you loved?

If your partner had a rough day at the office, would you say, 'Yeah, you're a failure.' Would you sit down with your daughter after she lost a running race and say, 'Why did you even bother – you're crap at running.'

So next time you catch that negative mental tape switching on, think about how you would talk to someone you love. Instead of saying, 'You always fuck things up,' I want you to say something along the lines of 'It's okay, mate, everyone makes mistakes. You're human! And this feeling won't last.'

2. Change your inner critic's voice

The best and sneakiest trick of the inner critic is that it has your voice. It sounds just like you!

So I like to take away its impact by giving it a different voice – one that's easier to spot, and one that makes me laugh.

Every time you notice your inner critic throwing you an insult, catch it, and then repeat it out loud using a sultry and seductive voice. It's harder to believe 'You alwaaaaayyys fuck things up' when you hear it coming from Zsa Zsa Gabor.

3. Harass your inner critic

Let me kick this one off with a story. When I was heavily pregnant with Hakavai, I went to an aqua aerobics class with my mum. A stranger in the class wearing a purple bathing suit and a floral ruffled swimming cap waded over to me and said – I quote verbatim – 'It's good to see you being active!'

Immediately I felt this irrational kind of hormone-fuelled anger bubble up inside me. My inner critic was running rampant, running giant, looping circles in my head.

Everyone thinks you're an invalid. They think a gentle aqua aerobics class is all you can do. Ha! You did Ironman and people still think you're weak! Why did you even bother! See? No matter how you try, people will always think you're not capable. (You look ridiculous in your rainbow one-piece, by the way. It's showing off your knobbly knees.)

After the class, I urgently re-told the story to Michael (poor bloke).

Me: 'This lady was such a bitch to me at the pool! Like, she was sooooo rude!'

Michael: 'Wow, what happened, darl?'

Me: 'She came right up to me and said, "It's good to see you being active!"'

Michael: [silence]

Me: 'It was so mean! She didn't say it like I said it. She said it in, like, a really mean way.'

[Even after it came out of my mouth, I still didn't realise how ridiculous I sounded.]

Michael: 'Mmmm. Um, darl, I'm not sure if she meant it meanly? Like, I'm not even sure if that's a mean thing to say?'

Me: [blowing up] 'You weren't there! She was pretty much telling me that I can't do ANYTHING.'

Michael: [annoyingly calm as usual] 'Darl, can you be *sure* that's what she meant?'

He was right. I didn't know what she had meant.

And what had I done? *I had assigned my own meaning to her words.*

We all have our story, don't we? We're all so focused on our own insecurities and concerns that we think that's what others are focused on, too. Our inner critic makes sure we feel that way. But what *do* we know for sure? We know that our inner critic is a liar! So, interrogate it!

After that conversation with Michael, I thought of all the possible other meanings the woman might have intended. I pulled up the Notes app on my phone and jotted down the following:

- She thought it was nice to see me keeping active while heavily pregnant.
- She just thought it was good to see me.
- She was trying to make conversation.
- She thought it was nice to see me with my mum and that we have a great relationship.

Looking at all of those different possibilities made me realise that Michael was right – we can't ever assume we know what other people are thinking. And we certainly can't rely on our inner critic for a reliable assessment of the situation.

My friend tells me that whenever someone tells her she's looking 'well', her inner critic immediately goes into overdrive.

Does that mean they think I look fat and don't know what else to say to me? Or that I was looking fatter last time they saw me, and they're pleased to see I'm looking less piggy and disgusting than I was then?

See? Our inner critics are crazy. Stop listening to yours.

Here's a challenge for you:

- I want you to think about something that's been said to you in the past that made you feel angry, annoyed, upset – anything that triggered an emotional reaction from you. It might be a glance someone gave you on the street, someone who pushed in front of you in a line, or a word said in passing.
- Now write down all the possible meanings the perpetrator might have had for that look or their words or action. For example, if someone pushed in front of you, yeah, maybe they were a rude person. Maybe they didn't see you. Maybe they have bad vision. Maybe they just lost their job and weren't really with it. Make sure you actually write everything down – we want to get this stuff out of your head and on to paper.
- Then, review your list. See how there can be many interpretations of one experience?

Remember, when you assume you know what someone thinks about you, you're only limiting yourself and your perspective of the world.

4. Sometimes you've just got to acknowledge your inner critic and let it be

I'll give you an example. A few months ago, I was up early, driving to Sydney for a TV appearance. It was four on a Wednesday morning. Five days after I'd had surgery. And to be honest I didn't really feel up to it. But I'd agreed to do it long before the surgery had been scheduled, and I hadn't wanted to be rude and cancel.

So there I was in the car, all bandaged up, driving through the early morning. It was cold and rainy. I was sore and not nearly as caffeinated as I would have liked. I kept thinking about Hakavai and Michael snoozing happily, all snug and warm in bed. I was feeling sorry for myself. Big time. So, to cheer myself up, I turned to my bag and rummaged for my little lunchbox. And, shit. I'd left it at home. I had a vision of my snacks (a blueberry muffin bar, banana, and some almond butter) sitting, forlorn, on the kitchen bench.

Fuckkkkkkkkk.

Three long, hungry hours later, I arrived in Sydney. I hobbled up the stairs to the studio and through the doors, catching the side of my bandaged foot in the glass as I walked through. Ouch. I was now most definitely in a Bad Mood. I walked into the waiting area, and found the lounges overtaken by a big group of cool girls, in cool outfits, clutching warm coffees and chatting brightly among themselves. They all seemed to know each other.

'Hello!' I said, in the cheeriest voice I could muster. They glanced up, said nothing, and kept on chatting. No one seemed to know why I was there, and they didn't even offer me a seat. I felt mortified. Like I was the wrong person, in the wrong place and definitely in the wrong outfit.

So, because I am a grown up, I left the room, went straight to the toilets, locked myself in a cubicle, and cried. It felt like my first day at high school all over again: despite my protests, my dad had dropped me off right at the school gate and as I hopped out of our 1987 rust-coloured minivan wearing an *ankle-length* plaid skirt, I realised I had made a huge mistake. Before me was a sea of mini-skirt-clad girls who had definitely not followed the skirt-length restrictions laid out in the school guidelines. Wrong person, wrong place, wrong outfit.

But I was no longer a thirteen-year-old girl with a nerdy penchant for guidelines and systems and rulebooks! I was a thirty-year-old woman with a nerdy penchant for guidelines and systems and rulebooks! I splashed some water on my face, chucked on some lippy, looked in the mirror and said to myself, '*Pull yourself together, Turia!* You're a successful woman who's kicking goals all over the place, with a damn sexy man and arguably the cutest baby in the whole universe. You're going to go out there and let your magnificent bubbly personality shine through!'

And did that work?

A bit. It helped. It wasn't the best day. But I got on with it. I did my interview. I hobbled back to the car and that night I got into bed with Michael and Hakavai and I went to sleep.

We can never quite escape the situations that embarrass us, or make us feel small. They're part of life. But luckily we get to experience some wonderful things too. If you're having a bad day, or your inner critic is making you feel properly shit, that's okay! You can always hem your skirt and start again tomorrow.

Make sure your bank is stacked high with gold bullion bars

Preferably imprinted with the words, 'Be kind to yourself'. We all have a self-esteem bank account. Being kind to yourself, being able to look at yourself in the mirror and give yourself a compliment, accepting compliments graciously – all of these things put a deposit of self-esteem cash in your vault.

The same goes for positive interactions with people – each one makes you feel good about yourself, and leaves a net deposit in your account. However, someone saying to you, 'Do you really need that second piece of cake?' Looking at yourself in the mirror and saying, 'Gosh, who is that old bag staring back to me?' These are withdrawals from your vault.

It's okay to have withdrawals, as long as you deposit enough to create a cushion. Research shows that because of the negative bias in our brain, we need to have three positive experiences to outweigh every negative experience.[6]

Gahhhhh. What a depressing thought. May as well give up now.

NOT! Haha. No, what we've been building up to in this chapter is noticing more of these positive moments and appreciating them, and now we'll be describing them in a way that will amplify these moments even more.

I'd like to close with some words from superb human being, author and research professor Brené Brown. Brené Brown advocates 'wholehearted living'. She describes this as 'engaging in our lives from a place of worthiness'. Our inner critic does a very effective job of reminding us of our imperfections (or *glaring* imperfections, as the inner critic might describe them). To counteract that, try to remember these words of Brown when you go to bed at night: 'Yes, I am imperfect and vulnerable and sometimes afraid, but that doesn't change the truth that I am also brave and worthy of love and belonging.'[7]

•

TL;DR

- Self-talk is v. important for our happiness.
- The language we use to describe our experiences is also v. important. If you want to feel a certain way, use the words associated with that feeling.
- Our brain has a negative bias so we naturally pay more attention to the bad stuff.
- We've all got an inner critic. They can be mean. Rethink the words you use to describe yourself. How do they make you feel?
- If you change 'have to' to 'get to', it'll help you to appreciate your life more.
- If you can't do something, try saying 'I can't do this *yet*.' It'll remind you that your current situation is not your final destination.
- Saying that you don't have enough time is pretty disempowering. Try saying, 'It's not a priority.'
- One of my favourite strategies for my inner critic is to talk to myself in the same way I'd talk to my best friend or my son.
- Ensure that you've got enough deposits in your self-esteem bank account to cushion any withdrawals.

6
Self-love

A few years ago I found myself in New York for Christmas. I'd never experienced a white Christmas so when it started snowing, I was frothing like a rabid animal. I wanted to head out to explore and take it all in. So Michael, my colleague Grace and I made our way down to the subway. Michael and Grace clicked through the turnstiles with their subway passes, which worked pretty well since they, unlike me, had remembered to bring them.

I called out to Michael, made the universal 'no subway pass' signal, and headed back to the vendor at the top of the stairs, a $20 note in hand (because I'd also forgotten my EFTPOS card).

Here's something you should know about me. Because of the injuries to my hands, I find handling coins awkward. Like, I can do it: if something costs $4.50 and I've handed over a crisp $5 note to get 50c back, I can handle that. But if I've given someone a $10 note for something that costs $2.15, when I put my hands out to get the change, the serving person (sometimes) gets awkward, so I get awkward, so . . . I don't like getting change back. Now, if it was really important to me to get better at this skill, I could work at it, but we're almost living in a cashless society, so I just manage as best I can when I have to handle small change.

This server is a jerk. I can hear him yelling at people in front of me for being in the wrong place, for having the wrong money, and probably mainly because he hates his job.

I'm getting nervous, cos I *know* this interaction will involve small pieces of metal that I will fumble with. And, sure enough, when I slide the $20 underneath the Perspex divider he yells at me for not having change, and because he's a dick he gives me the lowest-denomination coins possible; literally, he starts pouring nickels and dimes underneath the Perspex.

I grab the ticket and walk away, leaving the pile of coins behind me. He starts screaming at me. 'COME GET YOUR GODDAMN CHANGE! COME BACK HERE NOW! YOUR CHANGE IS CLOGGING UP MY DESK! COME AND GET IT!'

I know I should use my skinny legs to run away, but I walk back to him. 'Um, I'm so sorry but I'm unable to get my hand underneath the Perspex, so you can keep the change.' (I was being servile and humble and polite: just so we're clear, it was very out of character.)

'YOU THINK I CARE? GET IT OFF MY GODDAMN DESK! I DON'T WANT YOUR GODDAMN CHANGE! I'M SICK OF YOU PEOPLE TREATING ME LIKE THIS.'

He continues to berate me and badger me. I burst into tears because people are staring. I wish I had the ability to permeate the concrete floor I'm standing on. Do I feel just a smidge self-conscious? No. I feel a fuck-load self-conscious. I am being yelled at by a strange man, *because of an injury that wasn't even my fault and I never asked for*, in front of loads of people.

Now, I know we all feel self-conscious at times. I know that even supermodels feel self-conscious. And that's okay because you can love yourself and still feel embarrassed and ashamed and self-conscious from time to time. 'Self-love' doesn't require you to *never* be self-conscious or self-critical or self-analytical or self-whatever.

So, what is self-love? Self-love is treating yourself how you'd treat your best friend, your partner, your kids. Self-love is recognising that you're not perfect, but you're perfectly you. Self-love is being okay with your foibles and flaws. Self-love is being compassionate to yourself. Self-love is accepting yourself for who you are *but also recognising that you are a work in progress and you are allowed to evolve and still love yourself for who you are.*

As for the elephant in the corner: what about how we look? Does this impact our self-love-ability? Well, yes and no.

Yes, because of course how we look impacts how we feel. For example, if I were to give a speech in Ugg boots, sleep in my eyes, wild-woman hair and unbrushed teeth, I sure as shit wouldn't be as confident as if my hair and makeup was on point, I'd been to the gym that morning and I had on some cool threads.

But, no, because you don't need to be a certain height, have a certain weight, *look a certain way*, in order to love yourself.

Here's how I came to terms with my new self after my accident, and regained my self-love. Although my journey is obviously unique, I think in it there are lessons everyone can benefit from.

Baby steps

It's less than a month since I've been burnt and I'm trapped in the intensive care unit with a tracheostomy, covered head to toe in bandages, tubes going up each and every orifice to empty contents and replace fluids.

I'm also pleasantly high. Not like later on, when I'm moved upstairs to the burns unit and my pain medication is reduced.

So, I'm high as a kite and a nurse comes into the room. She busies herself at her wheelie-table. Big bottles of fluid are snipped open. Crinkly packages are ripped open. Latex gloves are snapped over painted fingernails. She proceeds brusquely in my direction, an efficient blur, and methodically starts shearing through my bandages with her shiny scissors. I hear the scissors go 'snip, snip, snip' and feel the thick bandages fall away from my damaged skin. A rank smell hits me. I shift my head ever so slightly so that I can see the nurse. Her lips are pulled back in revulsion, her head is leaning in the opposite direction to my body.

And then she lifts my leg so that I can see it in all its glory. I'm whipped out of my high and into reality. My beautiful long tanned and toned legs, my pride and joy, my reason for wearing denim cut-offs at each and every opportunity, are not what I'm looking at right now. My leg, the one the nurse is clutching, is a pallid grey with big blood clots all down it. My toes are black, the top of my feet look like desiccated cracks in mud. The stench – of my own two legs – becomes too much. I squeeze my eyes shut.

I am revolted. And I am revolted by me.

So how did I get from self-hatred and loathing to self-love and happiness?

Big question. With a really simple answer.

I started small.

I had to. In that immediate year after the fire, my self-love level was literally at zero.

I'd found myself in a hospital bed with my physical abilities completely stripped away, a pair of gross limbs for legs, clunky hands that I couldn't use, and having been made redundant from my job. I was socially isolated (my friends were all off working or travelling the world), I was forced to wear a compression mask that made me stick out like a sore thumb, my boyfriend became my carer and I was completely dependent on him and my mum to do the most basic of tasks.

I had zero confidence and zero pride in my appearance. I would wear Michael's t-shirts and trackpants with Crocs (stylish, I know) and he would have to brush my hair on the rare occasion that I let him. Instead of us spending weekends rock climbing in gorges, we were spending weeks at rehab centres and I was constantly in and out of operating theatres.

I hated how I looked, I hated how *unable* I felt, and I hated the pithy platitudes people would dole out to me on a daily basis: hearing 'beauty is only skin deep' from the chick at the servo only reinforced my feelings of woe and inadequacy and not-beautiful-ness. I continued to squeeze my eyes shut when my bandages were changed, as if I were somehow wiping out what had happened to me.

The enormity of 'getting my life back' was too vast for me to comprehend, so I focused only on getting through the day. And if the day seemed too overwhelming, I'd just get through the hour.

Baby steps, baby. The early baby steps were related to self-image. The first one? Getting my mum to paint my toenails while we were in hospital. And then? Wearing 'cool' gym clothes over the top of my compression suit. Having a shower every day. Wearing deodorant.

Then I moved on to taking some steps to regain my independence and confidence. I walked around the block by myself. I bought a tricycle and did laps around the cul-de-sac where Michael lived. I forced myself to go into Woolworths to buy milk.

These steps might seem very fucking trivial. Just like a brick by itself doesn't mean shit. But it's the bricks on the bricks on the bricks that build you a mansion.

It doesn't matter where you land on the spectrum, whether you're loving yourself sick, or you hate yourself. It's always about the baby steps. Doing the small things every day that make us feel good about ourselves.

In his book *Tiny Habits*, B. J. Fogg has a behaviour formula: 'Make it easy, make it fit your life, and make it rewarding.' He reminds us that 'people change best by feeling good, not by feeling bad.' He suggests a simple exercise we can all do to remind ourselves of this:

> **Step 1:** Write this phrase on a small piece of paper: 'I change best by feeling good, not by feeling bad.'
> **Step 2:** Tape the paper to your bathroom mirror or anywhere you will frequently see it.
> **Step 3:** Read the phrase often.
> **Step 4:** Notice how this insight works in your life (and for the people around you).[1]

And to feel good about yourself, whatever vehicle you take to get there (getting a mani-pedi, going for a surf, cooking a delicious omelette for breakfast, reading a book) is worth it.

Because there's so much shit in our world that makes us feel bad about ourselves already.

For me, well, I discovered that working on rebuilding my physical body made me feel good about myself. As did working towards a goal. My early goals were modest (see above). Then I moved on to more lofty ones. Raising money for Interplast. Going back to uni. Telling my story on *60 Minutes*. Starting my business.

But essentially what got me through those first years was forgetting about where I wanted to go and just doing the work every day, small step by small step.

Lean into the work

Like with everything, and everything you've learnt in this book so far, you don't get something for nothing. If you want to build your self-love stocks, you need to accept that there'll be some work involved.

For me, the 'work' was doing those baby steps. The 'work' was forcing myself to not run away when the postman came to the front door. The 'work' was walking around my block without my mask on. The work was forcing myself to look in the mirror. The work was doing makeup courses, trialling different outfits to see which were most flattering, seeing what I was (and wasn't) comfortable with. The work was surrounding myself with people who made me feel good about being me. The work was going to a psychologist every week. The work was getting comfortable with being vulnerable. I didn't just shed my compression suit like a snake one day and then, hey presto, was down the beach surfing. The work was slowly moving from long-sleeve shirts and pants to three-quarter-length clothes, and then shorts and skirts and tees and singlets.

It was getting comfortable, slowly, with the new me. I did the small steps every single day.

So, doing the work doesn't involve a quantum leap over an immense chasm. It's the many baby steps. Don't think you have the confidence to eat dinner at a restaurant solo at night? First of all: is this important to you? If so, go smaller. What about lunch? What about breakfast? What about getting a coffee? Don't feel confident in shorts? That's fine. Want to be able to wear shorts? That's a different story. Again, start small. Wear seven-eighth-length cargo pants. See how you feel. Go shorter. Wear three-quarter pants. See how you feel. Go shorter.

As I've said before, I'm all about the power of the mind; I think that anyone can do anything if they do the work, if they develop their mental fortitude. And that goes for developing your ability to love and accept yourself. I'll talk more about the idea of *practising* the work below.

And with self-love and your appearance, it's not about being consumed by your appearance or becoming a total narcissist, but spending ten minutes putting on moisturiser, lip gloss and mascara: you're investing in *you*, and that reinforces to you that you are worth investing time in (and that you're worthy of love, friendship and an all-round happy life). Don't fall into the trap of thinking you need to be able to wear a G-string to the beach to be 'confident in your own skin'. What you wear, how you look, is your prerogative.

Be kind to yourself

A crucial step to having an insatiable approval and love for yourself is to practise self-compassion. Remember how in 'Self-talk' I asked you to speak to yourself like you would your bestie? That's self-compassion in action, yo. At its core, it's simply being kind to yourself.

It's understanding that you're not a robot, that life experiences, however varied they might be, can be painful, and it's okay to be in pain; it's okay to be upset; and feeling those feelings doesn't mean you're weak, it just means you're human. And humans, by definition, are flawed, imperfect, fallible and fuck up on a regular basis.

So it's also okay if you do on occasion upset other people, or make mistakes. Those actions don't mean you're an awful person.

When I was at preschool, a little girl was showing me her marbles and other toys that her grandma gave her. *I stole them off her while she was asleep and put them in my bag.* At the end of the day, I remember watching her crying because she couldn't find her toys and I was not the slightest bit compelled to give them back to her. Sometimes when I'm making Michael a toasted sandwich, I'll make his smaller than mine and I'll put the crap bits of tomato on it.

Sometimes I'm just a bit selfish.

And that's okay. The more you practise being 'you' and owning yourself, the sooner you'll learn to love yourself, even though there are things about yourself that you think are bad.

Back yourself

Here's the cold hard truth: if you don't back yourself, how can you expect anyone else to believe in you? If you're walking around with a large neon sign, or even a small one, which flashes from time to time, saying 'I'M A FAILURE', why would anyone put their confidence in you?

I know that seems harsh. And I know if you haven't had any practice at 'backing yourself' it might seem like a far-fetched concept, maybe even insurmountable for you to have a crack. But backing yourself is, in its essence, *just another skill*. Like tennis, mahjong or public speaking. If you have the desire and drive to do anything, you *can* get better at it. The more you practise it, the better you get at it. The more you evaluate and critique your performance, the better you get at it.

Again, my advice would be to start small. If you're too nervous to give a presentation, ask your boss if you can lead your team huddle. If the idea of abseiling is terrifying, start by going to a trampoline centre.

The concept of 'backing yourself' can be hard, especially if you live in Australia, where tall poppy syndrome runs rife. What's tall poppy syndrome? My youngest brother, Toriki, used to like to pretend he was a ninja. He'd jump around the garden, air punching and rolling around on the grass like the hyperactive little boy that he was. One day I watched, gob-smacked, as he beheaded every single one of the agapanthus in our garden with Dad's steel graphic-design ruler.

That's an extreme example of tall poppy syndrome. Literally, if any flower is too tall (or too successful/smart/beautiful/fit or whatever) there's a temptation to strike it down.

Also, women, in the past, though hopefully less so now, have been reluctant to back themselves, to talk about their achievements, for fear of seeming arrogant, or boastful, or (gasp) up themselves.

We can conform to society's expectations ('Maybe I shouldn't put my hand up for that presentation because Kevin and Cindy will bag me out') or we can defy them. Because at the end of the day, if you don't have tickets on yourself, you'll miss out on the show. YOUR SHOW!

I'm sometimes accused of being arrogant, brash, full of myself or 'on myself'. After three decades on the planet, I'm starting to come to terms with that. I know I'm not an arrogant human being; I'm a confident, kind, generous, courageous individual, who can talk to a roomful of people or chat comfortably with strangers. It's important to be clear to yourself about who you want to be, who you can be, and to aim for that when you back yourself, and not to be put off your stride by people who might perceive you in an unflattering light because they're perhaps a bit envious of your apparent confidence.

You, my love (just like me), are a force, with immeasurable power to create the life that you want for yourself. The essence of all of this is to start *somewhere.* Anywhere will do. Start, keep taking the baby steps, and above all: back yourself.

But, let me be clear: sometimes it is useful to quietly listen to critical feedback. Backing yourself does not mean closing your ears to people who want to help you. It does not mean hogging the conversation. It does not mean you never admit to mistakes you make. Everyone makes mistakes, goes the cliché, and someone who likes themselves can admit when they have.

Backing yourself does not mean that the world revolves around you. It does not mean that you're better than others. It does not mean you're always right. It does not mean you're an all-round wanker and braggart.

The contrary.

You can be gracious, you can be humble, you can be generous. You can admit when you're wrong, you can concede defeat, you can own up to your insecurities.

One does not exclude the other.

Own yourself

Here's the thing: there's always going to be something about yourself that you don't love that much. Did I like wearing a black compression mask that made me stick out like dogs' balls? No.

Do I like having operations and having to see people when I have inflamed red skin and black eyes? No. Do I like the fact that I can get really worked up about the most trivial things? No, of course not.

But if you can't own yourself, if you can't own your challenges, if you can't own what makes you different and unique, *no one else will be able to do it for you.* And if you're (mostly) proud of who you are, and you don't care, no one else will either.

As a kid I had really bad eczema. I used to have to slather myself in moisturiser and wear little white cotton gloves to school. Like Michael Jackson in his later years. Of course, if you're a kid and you're wearing white cotton gloves *to school*, you feel self-conscious. And my dad would say to me, 'If you own it and walk into the classroom with your head held high, no one will say anything to you. All the other kids have got their own issues to worry about.'

My dad was right. He wasn't being disparaging, it's just how all of us are wired: to think about ourselves. You want proof? Say you go out to a party on the weekend and come Monday the group chat is firing and someone sends through photos from the party. Who's the first person you look at in that group photo? It's YOU! I'm not saying you're an egomaniac, I'm saying that every single person on the planet is a little bit self-absorbed.

So, own yourself. Own what makes you different. Either give zero fucks or pretend to give zero fucks. And at the end of the day, remind yourself that most people are too busy with their own lives to think about yours.

It's me

Your past doesn't define your future. I'm never going to be the Turia of the past. So I may as well reinvent myself into a new version. No matter what's happened to you in the past: I'm giving you permission to be whoever you want to be, as long as you can nurture that version of yourself, and accept her or him or they for who they are.

I've given myself permission to be loud and proud and confident, but it's also okay if I feel like crying and watching Netflix. I've given myself permission to wear whatever I want, but it's okay if some days I'm more comfortable wearing long pants and a long-sleeved shirt. And I've given myself permission to love myself, the person who I know the best in the world. The person I've been in the longest relationship with. But it's definitely okay to sometimes feel that this self-love stuff is like pushing shit uphill.

Feeling insecure is part of being human. Start with forgiving yourself for your perceived flaws, accepting yourself, being okay with yourself (most of the time), liking yourself (most of the time). The road to self-love starts with YOU and um, confusingly, also ends with YOU.

Stop comparing

We humans are excellent at constantly comparing ourselves to others. The problem is, sometimes we compare ourselves against standards that aren't relevant. Some clever researchers did a study on this.[2] It went something like this:

I ask you, reader, to eat potato chips.

I ask a random person to eat the potato chips while there's a tub of rancid sardines on the table.

I ask one more random person to eat the potato chips while there's a Hershey's Cookies'n'Creme bar on the table.

Who do you reckon enjoyed the chips the most?

The person who ate the chips with the sardines on the table enjoyed them twice as much as the person who ate them while there was a yummy chocolate bar staring at them.

Extrapolating from this info, it seems we can be perfectly satisfied with our lives, with nice things we're doing, and to be honest, quite content all round . . . *until* we start comparing our lives to other people's.

According to the research, being exposed to people who are richer/smarter/more successful/more powerful/sexier than you can cause your self-image to plunge.[3]

I mean, you've probably experienced this, yeah? Think of how you'd feel down Bondi surrounded by all those lifeguards and fit people busting out a million chin-ups with the sun sparkling off their bronzed and toned abs. Or talking to a group of Nobel Prize-winning scientists.

Comparing ourselves to others is very normal; it's also a game we can't win. There will always be someone who's better looking, smarter, funnier, richer, nicer than you. Period. We've all got things we're great at, which means a) we're probably more interested in those things; and b) we spend more time on those things; and c) we don't invest energy or time into things that other people are really good at.

In other words: we can do anything, but we can't do everything. Our attention, energy, money and time are finite resources. If we spend them on becoming the world champion of chess, that might mean we can't simultaneously be the world champion of surfing. So comparing ourselves to someone else doesn't make a whole heap of sense because we've got no idea what they've decided to spend their finite resources on.

No seriously, stop

The kicker with our tendency to compare ourselves to others is . . . we've invented a whole new way for us to feel bad about ourselves!

Give me an S, give me an O, give me a C . . .

Okay, okay, I'll just tell you. *Social media!*

Now, I personally love it. Social media is crucial for my business; in fact, for my livelihood. And it allows me to connect with long-lost friends and my second cousin Annika.

But . . . social media can also instigate a festering pool of self-loathing and hate and constant comparison. Sure, you might think getting a degree in architecture from UNSW is pretty good, until you see your friend living the high life in France, with an apartment right next to the Eiffel Tower.

The pool of talent, which once was six other contemporaries in your village, has now expanded to be EVERY SINGLE PERSON IN THE WORLD. It's okay to feel inspired or to look up to someone to check out what they're doing with their lives. But it's not okay to feel less-than or worthless by comparing yourself to someone else.

And you know what they say (or, more specifically, what Theodore Roosevelt said): 'Comparison is the thief of joy.'

Don't let that shit get in there, stealing your joy!

So, what can you do to combat comparison in all its forms?

Practise gratitude. Practising gratitude for your own life will reinforce to you all of the great things that you've got going on.

Remind yourself that what you see on social media is a highlights reel, not real life. Most influencers have a highly curated feed, use lots of filters and know their best angles. And if you find yourself on Instagram, looking at beautiful models on vaycay in the Bahamas, and feeling like shit, may I suggest you change your feed up?

Self-love, self-compassion, self-worth, self-esteem and . . . .. a selfie stick

Help! What's the difference between the 'self-whatevers'? All of the above are important concepts when it comes to understanding the knotty idea of self-love.

Well, we've covered self-love and self-compassion. To unpack how we should differentiate between self-esteem and self-worth, I asked the fabulous Zoë Foster Blake for her thoughts.

This is how she thinks we should define self-esteem and self-worth:[4]

Self-esteem

- is how you feel about yourself based on what you do and what is in your control, as well as your actions
- is being proud of who you are and what you do, in a positive way, not fuelled by insecurities, or with arrogance
- is how you measure and compare yourself against what you think is the ideal human; working out your value on a (personally meaningful but arbitrary) universal scale you have created
- is learning from experience, getting better at challenges and opportunities
- is whether you trust yourself to get the job done, in your abilities
- ends in the word 'esteem' not the word 'worth'.

Self-worth

- is how you perceive yourself and your worth (i.e. your opinion of you)
- is what you believe your value to be

- is what you believe you offer the world
- is knowing that no matter what happens, good or bad, you are you, and you are proud of that
- is knowing you are greater than your accomplishments and success, your failures and losses
- is being okay with your shortcomings
- is treating yourself lovingly, and with acceptance and kindness.

In short, '*self-esteem* asks: are you proud of who you are, and the life you've chosen to live, and the actions you take each day? *Self-worth* asks: do you feel you deserve to be here and be happy?'[5]

Here's my breakdown of this. Self-worth is inside. It's like sitting in a log cabin, warmed by a cosy fire, with a mug of hot cocoa in your lap. Irrespective of the storms that rage outside your window, or the amount of snow that falls, your interior doesn't change.

But self-esteem is outside. It's taking pride in the appearance of the cabin, sweeping snow and sleet off the porch, pruning the fruit trees, catching some fish.

Despite my very clever analogies, I still had some more questions for ZFB. Such as, how does she see so much from a place of positivity? And why is her skin always so dewy and lovely?

So I organised to meet up with her on a cold and blustery morning in Melbourne. She was a glowing and vibrant vision, with luminescent skin. Almost cherubic, but without being a fat little baby angel. She ordered a coffee (piccolo), I ordered a coffee (double-shot latte) and we began talking. Zoë's answers were articulate but not super-efficient. In a good way: when she was talking I found her so engaging that I sometimes forgot the question I'd asked her (also, it was kind of hard not to be distracted by her big blue eyes) and forgot to look at my notepad with my prepared questions, so at the end of an informative answer in which Zoë managed to touch on happiness, parenthood, her cult skincare brand and, profoundly, the meaning of life, I found myself just ogling at her from across the table.

Here's our interview.

Zoë Foster Blake

You've mentioned that you prefer to provide solutions on social media to challenging times, rather than sharing those challenges in the moment. Why is that important to you?

It can be a huge help and intensely validating for others going through the same thing when people share their challenges on social media. And it also helps the sharer, because they receive support, and understand they are not alone. This is one of the diamond benefits of social media.

While I sometimes impulsively go to share my trying times on social media, usually I stop and think, 'Why?' Why am I sharing this at a time when the real focus should be healing it, and working through it? And so I prefer to share the outcome, and how I got through it, or the help I sought, and share it as a whole story, with a useful conclusion for others at the end. To me, that feels like a meaningful use of the platform. It also boils down to what you put out, you get back, so I'm careful about putting negative stuff out there when I am hot with anguish or upset, as it generally tends to bring more my way.

Tell me more about how your mum influenced you from a young age to manifest positivity. How did she explain that to you?

When I was five or six, I kept breaking my thermos at school. So Mum sat me down and said, 'If you believe that you will smash your thermos, you will. Because what you think about, you bring about. Your words become your world. Good or bad.' It stuck with me forever. It's my most powerful perspective realignment tool and attitude shifter.

From my perspective, your products, books, Instagram captions – everything you craft – seem to be created to bring a sense of joy and wonder to the world. Is that your intention?

Yes, unashamedly. There is enough heavy stuff going on. If I have a chance to give someone a giggle, or learn something new without realising it, or save them some time with a useful recommendation, I will choose to do that. I am acutely aware of the privilege and the fortunate circumstances that allow me to live and create in this vein, and live in gratitude for my life, health and family. I am very lucky to live a life that fills my tank with joy and creativity, and gives me outlets to share it.

How do you do that, when you're going through a hard or challenging time?

I will opt out of social media and go inward till I'm through. (As an introvert, going dark and hermit-y is my preferred state anyway.) I rely on nature, my husband and kids, my mum, my loving-and-no-bullshit friends, and comedy to lift me back up again. I definitely create better things when I am feeling good, so feeling good is fundamental not only to my wellbeing and the mood of the house, but also my productivity.

How have you trained yourself to spread that kind of joy? Because that's hard for some people to do.
It is a learnt skill, I suppose. But from my very early days as a journo, in 2002, I felt lucky, and grateful and genuinely enjoyed my work, and this came through in my writing, I think. Would it be fair to say that if you choose a place and space where you enjoy your chosen work, and feel competent and confident about what you do, (whatever that may be) and who you are, you are more likely to have an output that is positive?

What tips do you have for people who want to start feeling happier?
That's a toughie. As I get older it has started to feel patronising to tell people how to buck up and smile. There are all kinds of really valid reasons people feel unhappy, and I know I can give off the vibe of being uncaring, or too problem-solvey when I jump in and advise people how to feel better. (Yes, I wrote a book on break-ups that *literally* does this for a whole book.) Anyway, I will just say that having the courage to try to feel happier, that's the best starting point. Making the decision to *want* to be happy, that can do so much.

•

TL;DR

- 'Self-love' doesn't require you to *never* be self-critical or self-analytical. You can love yourself and still be embarrassed and self-conscious. Self-love is treating yourself how you'd treat your best friend, partner or kids.
- Whatever makes you feel good about yourself – getting a mani-pedi, going for a surf, cooking, reading a book – is worth it and must be prioritised.
- Own yourself. Because if you can't own your challenges, if you can't own what makes you different and unique, *no one else will be able to do it for you*.
- Comparing yourself to others on social media or IRL can make it harder to own yourself. There's no one in the world who's better at being you than you! The key to short-circuiting comparison is practising gratitude for your own life.

7
Love

I want you to do something for me. Close your eyes and think of the last time you were happy. And don't get caught up in this instruction! Just think of the last time you felt good. Were you out walking? Having dinner? Watching a movie?

Got it?

So here's my next question.

Were you with someone? With your family? On a group phone call? Walking with your Shetland pony?

Meik Wiking reckons that the best predictor of happiness is our social connections.[1] It follows, then, that the more satisfied you are with your relationships, the happier you'll be.

I wrote this chapter, and then wanted to rewrite it. (That's a lie. I blatantly DID NOT WANT TO DO ANY MORE WRITING. But my editor is a real task master, y'see.)

Because in the months after the manuscript was delivered, coronavirus happened, social-distancing laws were enforced and things like 'catching up with your girlfriends for a glass of wine' were no longer an option.

Did it change how I viewed my relationships?

Well, you know how when you go camping and then you come home, you're excessively grateful to have the 'basics' like running water, a cold fridge and an electronic lazy Susan?

The global pandemic affected me in the same way as camping does.

You follow?

Let me elaborate.

See, I always tell myself I'm an introvert. I think to myself, 'I'd love to move to Alaska, get away from people, have a nice little log cabin, be canning crowberries and smoking salmon and be completely self-sufficient.' Not sure why Alaska, since I hate the cold, but this is my go-to dream whenever my everyday life and people in it get annoying.

Like, if I'm dropping off my son at preschool, and the driver in front of me is going excessively slowly, I'll feel myself start to get irritated. Or, if I'm in a queue for a coffee and the person in front of me has a super elaborate order, I'll do an internal eye-roll. Sometimes, all of these interactions with people make me annoyed, and I tell myself that I'm an introvert.

So many people all around the world were massively impacted by the pandemic. I had friends whose relatives died as a result, I had friends who lost their jobs overnight. But where we lived? Our local economy was definitely rocked, but all in all, it was relatively low-key.

Still. By week two of the lockdown, I really started to fucking miss people. I missed patting people on the back. Laughing with someone and touching their arm. Kissing my friends on the cheek. And although the amount of bonding my family did was extremely meaningful and special and a time I'll never forget, I also just wanted to catch up with my girlfriends for a glass of wine.

Not being able to see people emphasised how much I needed them. It made me realise how valuable my relationships are. I had zero FOMO, but I experienced a lot of SOMO.*

To me, the pandemic has crystallised how important our social connections are. How most of us very truly need people in our lives in order for us to be happier.

The thing about relationships, though? They can be hard. Y'see, cos it's not just *you*, dear reader, but you *plus* someone else (friend, spouse, kid, Shetland pony, etc.).

This is further complicated by the variety of relationships we have: you might have a relationship with your spouse of five decades, with your mother-in-law, with your postman (maybe). And all relationships have different statuses, different dynamics, different needs.

Maybe your family is on the precipice of perfect and you play Scrabble and Scattergories every night together, but you've got zero in the way of a sex life. Or maybe you've got fantastic friends who've always got your back, but your family causes you no end of problems. Maybe your friends *are* your family. Maybe you have intimacy issues. Commitment issues. Or maybe you find every single person on the planet annoying, except your neighbour.

It doesn't matter what types of relationships you have. Underpinning every single one, from your barista to your mother-in-law, is trust.

So, let's get into it, shall we?

---

* Sadness of missing out. It's an acronym I literally just made up.

Trust and community

I live in a pretty cool place. It's a small coastal town, and there's a high degree of trust among its inhabitants. After all, it's easier to trust people when you know their first and last name, what they do for work, how old their kids are, that they like snowboarding and that their favourite beer is a Carlton.

Take a sample morning for me in my home town. Hakavai and I head to the post office to collect my mail from the little 'hole in the wall'. Hakavai presses the red button next to the hole in the wall (his highlight of the morning) and Ann (post office lady, whose dog attends work with her) pulls up the concertina window. We make small talk as she gets my parcels. I hand her Hakavai (he loves Ann's dog) and carry the parcels to the car. I come back, collect Hakavai, say thank you to Ann, and jump back in the car. I drive up the hill to my favourite coffee shop, and order a coffee for me and a babycino for Hakavai. I drive to the beach and meet up with a friend. Hakavai totters down while I wrangle towels, coffee, babycino, car keys and sunscreen. A woman picks up Hakavai and starts walking with him to the beach. Luckily she's not a stranger, it's Cathy, who I see in the surf all the time. As I start to wind my way down the stairs Rod stops me and asks me to thank Michael for the fresh kingfish that he dropped up at his place. He tried Michael's recommendation for how to best cook it and all of his kids loved it and he didn't have to pretend it was chicken.

As a teenager who wanted to go out at night and party without her parents knowing, I found my home town suffocating. Now, as an adult with a family of my own, I find it envelops me, like that feeling on a rainy day when you're snuggled up with a doona and a mug of hot chocolate.

Because underpinning my life here is a sense of trust. Trust in my community and trust in the people I interact with.

Trust is at the centre of our society. Think about it: on my trip-to-the-post-office morning, I assumed a lot of stuff. I assumed that a gunman wasn't waiting at the front door to shoot us. I assumed that a truck wasn't going to veer into my car on the drive to the post office. I assumed Ann wasn't going to feed Hakavai to her dog. I assumed that the café's payment system was not going to scam me. I assumed the coffee wasn't laced with arsenic. I assumed Cathy wasn't going to run off with my son.

(Gosh, I can be morbid.)

Placing trust in each other and in the world has helped us to be who we are today. On the whole, most of us are good. Of course, there are the token worm-ridden apples in the barrel. But they are few and far between, and they aren't going to seriously threaten our species' survival.[2] If we trust each other, we feel safe and have less to worry about, and we see others as potential co-operators, not as competition for resources. When you think about it, as a reproduction strategy it's imperative for us to trust each other and form social bonds.

Bottom line? Without trust, it's very hard to feel happy.

Meik Wiking,

CEO of the Happiness Research Institute

What makes you happy?

I think I am very ordinary in this sense – bringing together good people over some good food is good for my mood: I am about to go on a summer holiday with my girlfriend to a small island where I have a summer cabin. But I think happiness is connected to a lot of things – a sense of purpose, freedom and resources to do what you want, connection with loved ones, a job you enjoy and so on.

How has your understanding of happiness changed over the years?

Since I have been working with happiness, I have grown to understand how similar a perception of the good life people have across the world. We might be Danish, American or Chinese, but we are first and foremost people.

Your research shows that the happiest countries have a strong sense of community and that you can't develop a sense of community, without trust. What practical steps would you recommend someone take in order to improve their sense of trust in others, and in their community?

I do think trust and a sense of community goes hand in hand. People who feel they have someone to rely on in times of need will also be people who feel they can trust their neighbours. I would advise taking small steps to get to know your local community a little better. Chat with your neighbours or just start saying hello. Get to know the name of your butcher or fishmonger. Set up a mini-library with the take-a-book-leave-a-book principle, or create a street directory like Shani did in *The Little Book of Lykke* – she was the lady who took a street and turned it into a community.

I feel like a bit of a fraud telling you to just trust people: especially when I'm not familiar with your personal circumstances. Like, if you just moved to the middle of a new city and you don't know anyone, it's going to take time to build up that community and that trust in people in the stores and cafés, your neighbours, your local doctors.

When our trust in our place in the world has been violated, it gets even harder. According to Daniel Goleman, a psychologist and author of the bestselling book *Emotional Intelligence*, violent acts – perpetuated by a fellow human – are far more pernicious, when it comes to trust, than natural catastrophes (like, say, getting trapped by a bushfire). Why? Because being attacked by a fellow human being 'shatters assumptions about the trustworthiness of people and the safety of the interpersonal world, an assumption natural catastrophes leave untouched. Within an instant, the social world becomes a dangerous place, one in which people are potential threats to your safety'.[3]

Losing trust in others also amplifies your own pre-existing insecurities. After I was burnt, I lost friends. Like, a lot of friends. It was really upsetting. It was upsetting when people didn't acknowledge what'd happened to me, it was upsetting when people didn't visit or reach out, it was upsetting when I stopped getting invited to people's birthdays and then I'd see the photos on Facebook.

Now, 'Rational Me' tries to logically understand this behaviour. There are a lot of reasons why this might have happened. For example, I was young when I was injured, people my age were pretty wrapped up in their social and work lives, I received my injuries in the west of Australia so it was hard(er) for mates to see and visit me, when I moved back home none of my mates were living there . . .

Yes, but that's no excuse! I would have been there for them! It hurt my feelings!

Pipe down, Irrational Me. It's not your turn to write.

Irrational Me, especially on days when I'm feeling fragile, or in a bad mood, or have woken up on the wrong side of the bed, in certain situations, will think bad thoughts like: *Well, all my supposed mates have let me down before. Why should a different group of friends be any different?* Or *I wonder if she's buying my coffee because she's my friend, or maybe she wants something from me?*

Thinking 'bad' thoughts is okay. It makes us human. It doesn't make you a terrible human to be at times uncharitable, ungenerous or unkind. And when we're feeling blue, it's natural for our insecurities to be amplified . . . but this doesn't mean we should take out our behaviour on our loved ones, on those who we trust and like and have our best interests at heart.

After all, handling personal relationships can be hard work. It's inevitable that sometimes we get angry, feel slighted, snubbed, misunderstood, even by people we trust deeply. Of course, we don't want to be the metaphorical doormat, and, yes, we want to (and need to!) stand up for ourselves when dealing with our friends and family, *but* we don't want to alienate them by over-reacting in the heat of the moment.

What am I saying? Often, to maintain that sense of mutual trust between you and your social circle, if someone is getting to you, it's best to step away, think about what happened, try to put yourself in the other person's hiking boots, give it some time and space and *then* think about whether or not a response is warranted.

I'm sure you can think of plenty examples from your own life, dear reader. The time you bit your tongue when a friend or relative commented on how you need to start brushing your hair. (*I normally do but as it's Sunday and as I've been gardening I haven't got to it yet, have I!?* you screamed in your head.) Or the time you lost it when your mum casually asked when you last did laundry. (*I have a life! I have to work! I have children! I have other priorities!* you screamed at her.)

In my experience, our trust and wellbeing levels are likely to be higher if we're gentle rather than angry with people close to us who we feel have behaved badly. And with ourselves when we have those irrational thoughts.

•

One exercise I like to do when thinking about who to trust (and conversely, who not to trust) is to think about the contexts in which I trust. I'll give you an example. A few hours south of me is a beautiful little seaside town called Eden.

Between around 1840 and 1930, orcas in Eden's Twofold Bay worked in cooperation with humans to help them to hunt larger whales.[4] In fact, there are reports that people of the Yuin nation* had been collaborating with the orcas for thousands of years.[5]

The orcas would wait at a corner of Eden's cliffs. There, they would hear the other whales coming towards them from a couple of hundred kilometres away. Acting like cattle dogs, the orcas would start herding the incoming whales into the shallows of Twofold Bay, then one of the orcas would swim into the bay and alert the whalers to the presence of the larger whales by flopping his tail continuously on the surface of the water.

---

* The Australian Aboriginal people from the south coast of New South Wales.

Into the longboats the whalers would jump, and they'd follow the orcas out to the whales. When they were near enough, the humans would kill one of the whales by harpooning it. They'd anchor the dead whale there, the orcas would take their share (the lips and the tongue) and the whalers would come back out the next day and drag the rest of the carcass to shore.

This relationship was mutually beneficial. Orcas don't typically hunt bigger species. Sure, they go after calves, but not the big momma. But by enlisting the humans, the whales in Eden were able to trust that the humans would leave them a good meal. And the humans? Well, they were alerted by their orca partners to any passing whales, and they trusted that the orcas wouldn't eat the entire whale carcass.

So what happened to the fabled orcas of Eden? One day an orca beached itself, and a vagrant on the shore stabbed it repeatedly until it died. And that was the beginning of the end of the relationship between the orcas and the men of Eden. (If you think this tale is too much of a stretch, go to Eden and check out the Killer Whale Museum. There are hundreds of articles and eyewitness reports to support these claims.)

Like I've said, the foundation for any relationship is trust. And once that trust has gone – your partner has cheated on you, a friend has stood you up one too many times, or um, a human has killed one of your pod – it is pretty darn hard to restore it.

Trust in others is very much contextual. Do you have a friend who's awesome, lovely to spend time with, but habitually late? This doesn't necessarily mean that you can't trust them, just that the evidence shows that typically they run late. Maybe your partner is a great sounding board for you, but you also *know* that they'll forget to fill up the car with petrol.

You can trust your barista to make your double almond cap, but you'd probably be reluctant to let them manage your shares. You might trust your brother to mend your car, but not to cat-sit.

Being able to trust people in *all* contexts is a very high standard to hold them to: most people are flawed and imperfect, just like you. But the people you're closest to, like your partner and best friend? You definitely should be able to count on them. And conversely, you should be this person for them, too.

Friends

So, trust is fundamental to any relationship. Which includes relationships with friends.

Here's a quick few disheartening facts about having (or not having) friends. Did you know feeling lonely and isolated increases your chances of DEATH? No idea why I capitalised that. I guess for emphasis. Anyway. This finding was pulled out of lots of different studies,[6] but the one that's most well-known is referred to as the Harvard study.[7] Harvard University conducted a longitudinal study of around seven hundred male sophomores, over a period of eighty years, in the hope that it would yield some clues on happiness, health and living an all-round good life. It's not a perfect study (consisting of the pale, male and now stale group) but still, the insights gleaned from it were pretty impressive.

The study's findings supported the idea that our relationships contribute to our happiness vastly. And how happy we are in our relationships impacts our health vastly. Our relationships trump money or fame or myriad other factors in adding to our happy tanks.

The Harvard study found that people with warm, well-functioning relationships lived longer and were happier. People who were lonely died earlier. In fact, Robert Waldinger, the fourth director of this study, stated that 'loneliness kills and it was as powerful [a predictor of death] as smoking or alcoholism'.[8]

Note that *feeling lonely* is by no means an objective measure. You can be lonely in a crowded room, you can be lonely at a mate's barbecue, you can be lonely in a marriage. And not being lonely is about the quality of the connections and relationships, not the quantity.

When I was in Year 5, I was bullied by my classmates. There was a group of five girls who I tried to be friends with. Except, of course, they weren't my friends, because they bullied me (haha, how one can jest twenty years after the fact). One day one of the girls came to class and announced in an exaggerated voice how *awesome* her birthday party was going to be. She proceeded to hand out her party invitations to each member of the class. Her pudgy little hands were encrusted with thick gold bracelets. She gave out the gold-embossed party invites with a voice dripping in a cloying honey: 'Yes, Tom, *you* are invited. And here's an invite for you, Dani. Ahh, and Steve. Here's yours.'

Everyone in the class got an invite. Except me.

The girls conducted a 'hate survey' to see what percentage of the class despised me and were overjoyed to report that 97 per cent of the class agreed with them. (I took heart in the fact that 3 per cent were ambivalent.) They created hate certificates for people who hated me. We had class diaries which we were supposed to write in every day and, as the ultimate nerd, of course I did my homework to the extreme and wrote in mine every day. My classmates stole my diary and sniggered their way through the contents, reading them aloud to the class.

And, yes, I'll repeat, I was trying to be friends with these people!

What did I learn from this experience?

Number one, some people are just arseholes. Number two, bad relationships are bad for you. It's preferable for our happiness and our health to exit a bad relationship as the cost of maintaining a bad relationship is far more detrimental than not having a relationship at all.[9]

What about good relationships? Well, we only need go back to Meik Wiking's finding that I told you about at the beginning of the chapter, and the Harvard University study. Yes, good relationships are extremely beneficial to you.

So, I've taken the initiative and written some guidelines to strengthen and forge your social connections.

Note: some of this stuff might seem as though it's right out of *Teaching a Psychopath How to Make Friends*. Look, it's always good to revisit the basics, no matter how much of a socialite you consider yourself to be.

Emotional contagion

People can catch your emotions (emotional contagion, yo). So if you're a downer, this will obviously influence and affect people around you. If you're a positive, happy person, this too will influence others. It might not be fair, but it's true: people like spending time with those who make them feel good. Never forget what legendary writer Maya Angelou said on this subject: 'I've learnt that people will forget what you said, people will forget what you did, but people will never forget how you made them feel.'

That's not to say, though, that if you see a friend when you're feeling down, you should lie and be super-positive. Of course you want to, and should, confide your sadness and problems to your friends. But the pendulum can only swing so far. Remember the episode of *Sex and the City* where Carrie is complaining about Big to her mates, and they tell her that she should see a therapist? Well . . . can I suggest very kindly and gently that if *every* time you see a friend you complain about how awful your life is, it might be time for you to seek professional help too.

Smile

In fact, just smile more. Again, emotional contagion comes into play here. It makes you more approachable and it makes you seem friendlier.

Practise

Let's say you wanted to become a piano virtuoso. Most people would understand that to get to that level of piano-playing proficiency, it would involve a massive (potentially life-long) input of time, energy and commitment. But social skills? A lot of people assume you're born with or without them.

And yes, some people do naturally have better social skills than others. But just like getting better at tennis, you can improve yours (and hopefully make some more quality friends along the way). That might mean dragging your ass off the couch to a friend of a friend's housewarming and making small talk with people you don't know. It might mean buying Dale Carnegie's book *How to Win Friends and Influence People* and rampantly highlighting chunks. It might mean joining a virtual tap-dancing class or starting a bird-watching club.

Or, it might not.

It might not be a priority for you to improve your social skills. Heck, you may have impeccable social skills and you might simply not like going to parties. You might find being in a room with strangers and remembering everyone's name and speaking to that guy about his new dating app that makes him a modern Hitch totally and utterly exhausting.

That's okay. It's your prerogative. But if you want more friends, or you want to establish more trust in your community, you'll need to put yourself out there and practise.

Self-talk

If you're not great at making friends, but you feel you need more social connections, it's not helpful to say to yourself 'I'm shit at making friends' or 'It's too hard, I'm better off on my own.'

Remember how we talked about our brains filtering the plethora of information they receive every second? Well, saying 'I'm shit at making friends' tells your brain to find evidence to support this, and your statement then becomes a self-fulfilling prophecy – whether you're the belle of the ball or you live in Antarctica and haven't seen another human IRL for two years.

Try saying something different to yourself, like 'I'm actively looking for new friends' or 'I'm really proud of the work I'm doing to be more social.' I know, I know, it might seem corny and trite. But try it, and see how you go.

Lower the bar

Ellen Hendriksen, in her book *How to Be Yourself*, talks about how hard it is to make friends as an adult (word, Ellen, word). She writes: 'A meta-analysis of 177,000 participants in the prestigious journal *Psychological Bulletin* found that social circles expand until early adulthood and then shrink from there'.[10] In other words, making new friends, and keeping old ones, is hard as an adult.

My advice? If you feel you need to make more friends, start by lowering the bar. They don't need to be funny, adventurous, popular (wait, sounds like I'm describing myself) and agree with all of your political views. Just ask yourself this question: is this person nice to me? Is this person kind? If it's a yes, then open your friendship gate (not wide, but enough to let this person in). Can you trust them? It's too early to tell. But the only way you'll be able to ascertain whether or not they're going to be a potential friend is to give them a go.

Aim for quality

Just a note on the previous point. We all have limited time available to us and thus limited time to dedicate to the social networks available to us. So if you'd like more friends, and/or you feel genuinely like you didn't have anyone to count on in a time of need, the step above is a good one. But friendships require time. Emotional energy. Caring about someone deeply can be exhausting. And you might feel that you already have enough relationships to nurture and enjoy. So, don't stress if you don't have ten close friends on speed dial who you check in with on an hourly basis. But if you hang out with someone whose behaviour makes you feel uneasy, discontented, uncomfortable or used, you should probably question what you're getting from that friendship and your motives for continuing it.

Have you heard that quote, 'You're the average of the five people you spend time with'? Now I know there's no scientific validation to support this (except for, say, Dunbar's number*), but the people we spend time with of course have an influence on our psyche.[11] If you hang out with kind, funny and generous people, this will impact your behaviour and mood. We can't always control who we spend most of our time with. But I also know that when you hang out with people who make you feel good, life is infinitely better.

Disclose just a bit

You need to share and be vulnerable with your friends, but not to overshare or be too vulnerable, as this can come across as manipulative and off-putting. Let me give you an example. After three months of you catching up with Jane for a coffee after yoga, she mentions her brother is seeing a psychologist for his anxiety. If you open up to disclose that you, or someone close to you, has been through a similar thing, you're sharing something personal and no doubt important about yourself, which makes it clear you see Jane as a friend who can be trusted. That kind of disclosure can advance friendships. Being vulnerable goes hand in hand with trust. But remember, it's always your prerogative as to how much or little you share. And of course, disclosure isn't a one-way street. If you want to be a good friend, it's your responsibility to show interest in your friends' lives, to ask them questions, to listen carefully to the answers.

---

* Dunbar reckons that the highest number of people with whom we can have a genuinely social relationship is 150, with our innermost circle consisting of three to five people.

Be specific

If you genuinely want to spend time with your new friend (you friend, you!) be specific. Rather than, 'Wanna do something sometime?' try, 'Want to go to yoga tonight? I can pick you up.' Being vague results in vague results.

Make time

You can't spend years turning down invites to your friends' barbecues and fundraisers and then expect everyone to drop their lives and come running when you have a big ice-skating competition. When I was writing this chapter, I reflected that although, through the past few years, it was easy to make time for my family or for my work, often my friendships got the leftovers, the sad, squishy stale piece of cake, sitting there after everyone had had their fill. I realised I had to make time for my friends, but I didn't have to make time in the way I saw other people do.

The answer to 'How can I be a better friend?' is actually quite simple: show up, but show up in your strength zone. For example, I don't love talking on the phone. I prefer to write a thoughtful text or email at night and schedule it to send the next morning. I'm great at giving people thoughtful gifts, but not necessarily on their birthdays. If something involves organisation on the computer or booking tickets, I'm pretty competent at that. But helping people set up for their birthday? Not good. Helping people move? I'm terrible. So 'be there' for people when they need you, but it's okay to 'be there' how you be there best.

Gossip

Look, we all love a bit of gossip. Hey, we're only human! We're wired to be intrigued by gossip. And in the past it served a vital function: as we shifted from small hunter-gatherer societies to larger communities, we needed a way to communicate social norms and keep bad behaviour in check.

But now? Well, we live in the twenty-first century. We have plenty of ways to communicate social norms and plenty of ways to keep bad behaviour in check (like, um, our mobile phones, which can film us doing anything at any time). And even though when you gossip you may feel like it increases intimacy, the opposite is true. The energy behind gossiping leaves people with a sour taste in their mouth. Avoid it to build trust into your relationships.

Families

On a cold blustery day wayyyyy back in 1997, Mum was asked to perform a Tahitian song at my brother's preschool. My brother Heimanu couldn't wait to see Mum's performance – after all, it had been all she'd talked about for weeks.

In Mum's mind, she was going to impress the children with her *pehepehe*,* her incantations, her percussive skills. She had all the gear: tribal necklaces, a *hei*,† traditional Tahitian dress, and a set of bongo drums from Vinnies (as unfortunately she was unable to source a pig-skin-covered drum).

Another mum had been in the day before, and the children had adored her blue-spangled-guitar rendition of 'Twinkle, Twinkle, Little Star'. But Heimanu knew Mum's performance would be way, way better.

The children gathered round the preschool teacher, as she proceeded in the standard sing-song voice: 'Now, today,

* A song

† Tahitian flower crown

children, we are going to have a *very* special performance by Heimanu's mum. Today, she is going to delight us all with a traditional Tahitian song. Let's give Celestine Vaite our usual Green Street School welcome!'

There was a smattering of applause. Mum stood in the centre of the room. Internally she was calling on her ancestors: for strength, and guidance.

She let out a high-pitched cry: 'Ahhhhhhhyieeeeeeee!'

The children were taken aback.

'*A haere tātou!!*'*

She was singing with *mana*.† She started beating on the drums, to a faster and faster pace. Before she reached the end of the first verse, Thomas looked at Jack and they started giggling. The giggling spread like a virus through the room.

Was Heimanu embarrassed? Probably, but Mum's mum. She is who she is. She's loud, proud and unapologetically herself. My dad's the same, except louder and prouder and an extremely unapologetic person in general. I know that I'm lucky. I get along (mostly) with both of my parents, with all three brothers and even my third cousin, who's a fruitarian.

All of us – including you! – deserve to be loved unconditionally. But maybe you didn't get that from your parents or siblings. Maybe you don't have a good relationship with them. Maybe you can't stand them. Personal relationships are hard, *family* relationships are even harder. I'm not a specialist in family dynamics, so if you don't have a good relationship with your family and you wish you did, I'd recommend seeing a

---

* Let's go!

† Energy and power, often spiritual.

therapist or seeking support from one of the services listed in the Resources section.

Check your mood

Have you ever noticed you have to be in the 'right mood' for certain people? Family is no exception to this. So, for example, my entire family is intense. (Except me, of course! I'm not intense at all!) If I'm feeling energetic and playful, I love spending time with my mum. *She's awesome.* But if I'm tired or if I'm feeling a tad cynical, I can find her upbeat nature tiring. You might like spending time with a certain friend if you're feeling pensive and reflective, and you might like spending time with a certain family member when you're feeling pumped. That's normal, and it's a good idea to work with it, which leads me to . . .

One-on-one time

If you find spending one-on-one time with a family member draining or depleting, you could aim to always have a buffer around (and let's be honest, hanging out one on one with someone can be intense). A buffer is an additional person (at least) who defuses the situation, pulls the focus away from you, and changes the energy in the air.

Accept them as they are

As a kid, I was rather neat and conscientious. For example, after every surf I'd turn my wetsuit the right way around, hang it in the laundry and make sure all the sand was perfectly rinsed away. I'd place my board neatly in the board rack Dad made, the leg rope wrapped tightly around the tail.

My brother Genji was the opposite. His wetsuit would

be strewn haphazardly over the back fence, his surfboard dumped in the middle of the pathway up from the rocky beach below.

I guess that's why after one particular surf his stuff got stolen but mine didn't. His two wetsuits and his three boards (he was sponsored so he got cool gear) gone. Vanished into thin air. Dad was ropeable. Later that day my uncles came over and Dad furiously told them what had happened. My Uncle Insect reckoned that crims always return to the scene of the crime. And with that remark, a plan was formulated. My uncles would stay the night, each taking turns with Dad to keep an eye out for the thief. Mum disapproved of the plan. She didn't say anything, but she muttered under her breath and swept around everyone's feet with a kind of determined energy. In Tahiti people borrow stuff from each other all the time. It's rude to lock your door when you go out. What if one of your cousins needs to borrow money, thongs or have a shower, and they can't get in?

As the shadows in the backyard grew longer and nightfall approached, the criminals got bigger and scarier in my mind. It was a bikie gang. On the warpath. They probably had tattoos. Knuckle dusters. Guns. And a couple of big scary German shepherds with spiked dog collars. In bed I tossed and turned. I must've fallen asleep at some stage because the sound of the door crashing open and footsteps running across the front yard jolted me awake some time after midnight. Terrified, I leapt to my feet and quickly pulled back the curtains. Under the pale white glow of the streetlight I saw it all unfold before me. My uncle, wearing nothing but his undies, was wrestling someone to the ground.

It's him! The thief!

A second later, Dad and my other uncle run into the picture, carrying a roll of chicken wire between them. Together, they begin to bundle up this man, like a lumpy spring roll. The vigilantes stand back and look down at their bounty, rolled up on the driveway before them. There's a long silence and then they all start talking and gesticulating at once. I can't discern any actual words but it's clear they disagree on what to do next. The next thing I know, Dad's back in the house dialling the local police station. 'Hi there. I've performed a citizen's arrest. I've caught a thief and secured him outside my home, ready for collection and processing,' he barks down the line.

A few minutes later a cop car pulls up, and two portly policeman climb out. Flabbergasted, they stare at the scene before them, the surfboard thief yelling wildly for help, struggling in his wire cocoon. They rush to his side, kneel down and begin to unroll him, one of the cops lecturing Dad all the while. 'Look, mate, you just can't go around rolling people up in the dead of the night!'

Finally free, the surfboard thief leaps to his feet and runs to the cop car, jumping in the back seat and locking the door behind him.

All of this is to say: you can pick your friends, but you can't pick your family. Whether you like it or not, you're stuck with them.

What works

A gentle reminder about your family. Don't expect that you'll get everything you need from them. Michael is awesome at showing his fishing gear to Hakavai, but inept at scheduling social media posts (JK! As if I'd trust him to do that). Maybe your mum is particularly good at taking pleasure in your successes, but not well equipped to help you through hard times. Maybe your partner is practical and kind, but unspontaneous and quiet. No family member can be everything to you, no matter how close you are to them.

Romantic love

I guess you could say Michael and I have had an intense relationship. (Who am I kidding? I'm the intense ingredient in the relationship.) We went from girlfriend and boyfriend to patient and carer, back to boyfriend and girlfriend and then on to become parents. We've had massive changes in our careers, and, not that I'd ever go so far as to say that we've experienced fame, but we're both recognisable and we've had to navigate a pretty intense media spotlight from time to time.*

Consequently, people always seem really interested in our relationship. Not in a 'put your keys in a bowl and join us in the red room' kind of way (but, you know, different courses for different horses), more in a 'how did you guys do it?' kind of way.

The thing is, the stuff we've been through sounds unique, and of course it is unique to us, but underlying it is the same web of issues and complexities that most couples encounter.

In this section, I'll attempt to offer a few thoughts on how to navigate those complexities and build a positive attitude towards finding and growing romantic love. I want to preface all of this by saying that I come at this conversation as a straight woman. That's been my perspective in life. Feel free to change my references to specific genders and my advice as it

* I'm being modest. It's obviously me that's famous, not him.

applies to you, and know that I'm limited by my experiences. As with anything, take what works for you and throw the rest out. I'll only be mildly offended, I promise.

And, if you don't have that fabled 'someone' and feel like punching me on the nose: please don't. There'll be advice that would apply to platonic relationships (though some advice, true, you'd definitely only want to apply to your lover).

So, light a candle and slip into something sexy. Not the leopard print, though. I'm wearing that.

What's good about a partner?

Look, we all have certain itches that need scratching. But aside from that, romantic relationships play a pretty big part in our overall happiness. From a physical standpoint alone, their impact is significant. Falling in love literally changes the inner chemistry of our bodies. It raises our oxytocin and progesterone levels – biological responses linked with lifelong bonds, trust and intimacy. Even hugging someone for a minimum of six seconds promotes the flow of oxytocin and serotonin (both mood-boosting feel-goody biochemicals that enhance and promote bonding).

A good relationship can be magical. It's enriching to build a life with someone. *But* that's not to say an intimate relationship is necessary to your happiness. In fact, the very opposite can be true. Relationships are hard work. They inevitably mean constant compromise. Couples who dislike each other are more likely to suffer from infectious illnesses (colds, flu, and so on) than other people. You argue about money and the in-laws and everything in between. And then get sick from the stress of all the fighting and disharmony.

That's not what we want.

So, here are my tips for creating the good, magic, oxytocin-rich kinds of relationships.

Have your own thing going on

Whether you're in a relationship, or happily lying like a starfish on your king-size bed, there is nothing (*nothing!*) more attractive than someone who has their own thing going on. Whether it's hiking up mountains, or reverently making their coffee *just so*, or a podcast about coffee and hiking that they host with their cat – you get the picture – they have a *life* going on.

Think about if you walked past two restaurants on a Friday night. One of them has no patrons in it. The wait staff are pressing menus into your hand and giving you pleading eyes as they gesture for you to 'please come in'. The other restaurant? It's full of people, laughing merrily while they clink their oversized glasses of wine.

Which restaurant would you go into?

I'm not saying you need to become a cool new vegan restaurant, or even that familiar local Italian place with the crunchy pillows of garlic bread. You're your own unique restaurant. Fill it with the stuff you love, the people you like to hang out with, the art you like to look at and the drinks specials that people remember.

You are a wonderful, funny, clever person. You are! You don't need to push your menu into the hands of strangers. Turn the lights on, pump your fave tunes and let others peer through your windows in delight.*

* Not a euphemism – unless you'd like it to be.

Have your own thing going on, part two

If you do have a wonderful partner, as wonderful as they are, pleaseeeee don't forget . . . *you!* Yes, glorious you! The you that adores soft-sand jogging, playing Bananagrams and volunteering at the homeless shelter. Don't ditch your life because (or for) your wonderful partner. You need a life outside of your partner. You need your own hobbies, you need your own social circles. It's okay to cross over, but carve out your own space in your life.

No guarantees

Nothing is guaranteed in life, especially not love. First of all, you need to be willing to put yourself out there. We talked about this a little bit earlier in the chapter. Say yes to that coffee date. Offer to pick up Jane for rock climbing. Accept your colleague's invitation to their dinner party.

If you come straight home from work, put on your PJs and fire up Netflix, please do not have the brazenness to say 'There are no good men/women out there.' Cos you, my friend, aren't 'out there'. You're inside, watching Netflix. And if you want a relationship, you're going to have to run the risk of rejection, and you're going to have to be vulnerable. Yes, your date may not like you. Yes, you might have a great thing going on for two years or three decades and still have your heart broken.

Life is an absolute wizard at putting your expectations through the ringer. To reiterate, there are no guarantees in love or in life (I know, just when you were feeling positive).

Lower the bar

We all want a dreamboat who's extremely fit, a great listener, gives you career advice, has deep and meaningful conversations with you, always organises cool adventures for the weekend, is sensible with money, is clean and tidy and a great cook, is particularly handy around the house, makes heaps of cash, picks his towels up off the floor, is funny, never in a bad mood, makes good decisions and is thoughtful and kind *all at once*.

Yes, these perfect dreamboats do exist, but only if you're in a Mills & Boon novel. So what does that mean for the rest of us? Well, we need to stop expecting our partners to be everything for us. Relationship guru Esther Perel said it best: 'We turn to one person to provide what an entire village once did.'[12]

Drop your expectations.

Not that low!

But low enough that the person you're with can be a regular flawed human (just like you).

Everyone is different

Case in point: I've been in the US with Michael for three weeks and he is driving me insane. I want to go out and explore, he's happy to go the gym for a workout and read the paper. I want to go out to a nice restaurant and have a gin and tonic and look at the sunset, he wears his old clothes, yawns all the way through drinks and continually checks his phone because 'the fish are on at home'. I want to go to the Rose Bowl Game in Pasadena, California. Michael doesn't want to go, but does the obligatory 'I'll go with you if you want me to, darl.'

No, I don't want to feel like I'm coercing someone into attending what's sure to be a super-fun and super-energetic *American college gridiron game!*

But luckily we're in the US for my work, so I have Grace with me, who's as enthused as I am.

Me: 'OMG, so you know they have something called "tail-gating"? What *is* that?'

Grace: 'Yeah, it's crazy! They, like, take food and fully cook it up right there and then in the back of their ute!'

Me: 'Wow! They cook food in the back of their *car*? Ohhhhhh – that's why it's called tailgating!'

Grace: 'Yeah, and everyone visits each other and drinks and it's like a street party but with rows of utes instead of houses!'

For some reason, Michael's decided he *now wants to come with us*, but tbh his (lack of) energy is a bit of a downer. He's also wearing an ushanka hat (those sheepskin hats with the big ear fluffs on them) and a big black coat that looks like it's made from the inside of Ugg boots.

In short, he looks like a serial killer.

We arrive at the Rose Bowl, make our way over to the entry point and line up. It's a long line, and we're in it for more than forty minutes. Grace and I excitedly point out things of interest to each other.

'Wow! It's fully obvious what team they're going for! Like, they're all so kitted!'

'Man, these Americans come prepared! That family over there has brought an actual dining table!'

Michael is sitting on the ground, stretching his hamstrings.

We talk to the other line participants. Everyone is so keen for the game, and giving Grace and me advice about who to go for. The excitement and buzz and froth factor in the air are palpable – everyone looks high (on life) . . . except for one person, who's standing with us, in an ushanka hat and an Ugg-boot black coat.

And then we are only *two people away* before it's our turn with security . . . and then one person away . . . and finally we're at security! Mere steps away from the action! And *then* the security guard promptly tells us we have to go buy a clear plastic bag for our stuff.

Fuckkkkkkk.

Still, our enthusiasm can't be stopped. 'No worries, mate!' Grace says. 'Where can we get a bag from?'

Mr Security Man points into the distance and we head off in the opposite direction to the one the line is heading. I can see Michael's Ugg-boot black coat parting the crowd, exactly the way you'd imagine a serial killer would.

Even so, I'm brilliant at being optimistic and bubbly, and Grace is still in high spirits. We join the transparent zip-up-bag line, purchase an overpriced bag and make our way back to the security line to queue for the second time.

Once more, we are *two people away* and I can feel my excitement starting to make me all giddy and silly. We get to Mr Security Man and Grace hands over her ticket and I hand over my ticket and we look at Michael expectantly. *He doesn't have his ticket.*

Grace and I are flabbergasted. 'Check your pockets!' I urge.

'Don't worry! We'll go see the box office!' Grace suggests.

'Nah, don't worry, girls. I'll just walk home.' The hotel is eight kilometres away. He pecks me on the cheek and is gone, his ushanka hat bobbing through the crowd until we can't see it or its wearer anymore.

Grace and I look at each other, shrug, and line up for beer and nachos.

Should I have been pissed that Michael put a dampener on the day? Nah. Why? Michael was simply being Michael. He's been consistently 'Michael' ever since I've known him.

And just because he doesn't love everything I do, in exactly the same way as me, that doesn't devalue his role in my life or what he brings to the table. It doesn't mean I need to force him to change.

The point? If you're unhappy with how someone is at their core – the way they *are consistently* – don't be the one who thinks you can change them. You either love this person and are willing to invest in them and build a life with them, or they aren't the right person for you.

Communicate

When I was writing this chapter, I started reading John Gottman's book about making marriages work.[13] And of course I started to miss Michael deeply (he was in the Mentawai Islands on a surfing trip). So on the spur of the moment I sent him what I thought was a risqué text: 'You look sexy and tanned atm 😉.'

As an afterthought and an after-text, I sent him a love-hearted emoji 😍.

And then . . . three days passed without me hearing anything from him.

On day three of radio silence, I was sure that Michael had run off with some sort of beautiful, leggy creature and that we were going to break up. (He didn't, and we haven't.)

I've said it before but I'll say it again: relationships are hard. You may not have the same way of showing love for your partner as they do for you (side note: I personally found Gary Chapman's book *The Five Love Languages* incredibly illuminating on this point).[14] You may be more of a brusque and upfront person; they might be more of a subtle and nuanced person. You might be the type of person to tell the waiter the steak was overdone if they ask and . . . your partner might be the type who says, 'It was great, thank you.'

Remember: the person you're in a relationship with may very well communicate differently from you. And that's okay.

On day four of radio silence, I received a love email from Michael that I found incredibly tear-inducing and happy-making.

Oh, all right, you voyeuristic pest. Here it is.

> I'm sitting on a ferry crossing the ocean from the Mentawai Islands to Padang. The weather is humid, the ocean rolling and the ferry . . . well, it's a typical Indonesian ferry. Indonesians fill the seats; some sleep, others smoke, and a few tourists . . . we just give each other weird looks every time the ferry rolls dramatically. Lying covered with sarongs and with an intravenous drip in her arm is a sick local Indonesian lady. I thought she was dead when they loaded her onto the boat. It hurts me to see someone so vulnerable having to travel in dire straits to the hospital.
>
> I think immensely about our beautiful family every day. I love the photos you sent of Haki being cheeky. He is beautiful, a little charger who has been blessed with his mother's feature button nose, olive skin, thick black Turia hair. Although, I know his stubbornness will see us in many stalemates as he develops into a teenager.
>
> I feel such high levels of euphoria knowing we have created another human together. I daydream sometimes and wonder how Haki will absorb the world we immerse him with. You have been the dream mother. Hakavai loves your energy, the cuddles you give him, the books you read to him and the way you tickle him making him squeal with laughter. I'm happy I asked if we

were going to kiss at the bbq all those years ago, the smartest words I've ever exhaled.

Although our time together hasn't been as smooth sailing as the *Moana Tane Tahiti*, I'm happy we have been mature and strong enough to have lived and shared life the best we possibly could have under the circumstances. I know the anniversary of the fire is coming up and I'll be away. I have forgotten how long it's been as it's kind of irrelevant to our lives now. I honestly thought I would never get over what happened that day, but I have, there are no ill feelings anymore. I've emotionally and spiritually moved through that phase of our life together. I'm proud of the woman you were when you were sick and I'm proud of the mother you are today with Hakavai.

You deserve all the success you have achieved within life, the media, business and motherhood. You made the choice to live and thrive again and I'll never know where you found that strength but you did. I'll always remember your first steps and they will continue now as we build our family together. A family that lives and breathes life, appreciates the sand through our toes, ocean on our skin, sun to warm us when we are cold.

I love you, love Hakavai, and can't wait to meet our second baby boy. One day we will all drift away as a family and live upon the ocean. It will allow our kids to see the true beauty of life, with the fresh air in their little lungs, and the hunter-gatherer to form within them. I will be truly at peace watching this unfold.

Love you, beautiful woman, see you all soon. But for now I'm off on a boat, to drift somewhere in the ocean, daydream about my beautiful family, my second child, maybe even choose his name . . .

Michael

•

TL;DR

- People with warm, well-functioning relationships lived longer and happier.
- Relationships are built on trust.
- Families are hard. We usually don't get to pick! Try to accept yours as they are. If you find spending time with them draining, try to minimise it or make sure you have a person (or two) as an energy buffer.
- Regarding your relationship/s with your significant other/s, don't forget about you! Glorious you!
- If you want a successful relationship, it's important to accept your partner for who they are.

8
Money

We'd been down at the river camping for a week. Long enough for us kids to go feral. Blackened feet, dirty nails, unbrushed teeth, hair as thick and matted as a possum's tail. Now it was time to go home. We clambered into Dad's 1987 rust-coloured minivan, jostling to get into our preallocated seats. Genji got to sit all the way up the back. Heimanu next, he was on the side. Toriki closest to the gunmetal-grey sliding door with the racer stripe (he was prone to being car sick). Cos it was just us kids, and Mum wasn't there, I got the coveted front seat.

'Should I do a skiddy, kids?' Dad asked, motor throttling, car revving.

'Yeah!' we all shouted (me clapping my hands with glee).

Vroooom! Dust flung out around us, filtering sunlight like a translucent teabag. I could identify the gear changes by the sound of the car. The windscreen wiper was on, moving the dust and grime back and forth.

'You all hungry?'

We nodded.

'KFC?'

More emphatic nods all round, our eyes bugging out of our heads like one of Margaret Keane's paintings. No one spoke. If you spoke, it was easy to distract Dad and send him off on a totally unrelated tangent, which might make him miss the left-hand turn to fast-food heaven.

We pulled up, and piled out. Me first, hauling out Toriki, then came Heimanu and then Genji from the back. Excitedly we jibber-jabbered to each other.

'I'm gonna get a Zinger Burger!'

'I'm getting one large chips, with two tubs of gravy!'

'I'm getting popcorn chicken!'

We joined the queue, the air con making us stamp our feet and put our hands under our armpits. I stared at the billboards above my head: plump pieces of chicken hanging off the edge of a soft white bread bun, chicken drumsticks steaming as they were dunked into warm puddles of mashed potato and gravy, decadent pots of vanilla-frosted cheesecake.

'Hi there, what can I get for you today?'

Dad asked us all to order. (When you're speaking to someone, you must look them in the eye, be as articulate as you can, and definitely do not mumble.) We don't need to be asked twice. One by one, we clearly enunciate our orders.

Dad hands over his card.

Beeeeeeppp.

'I'm sorry, sir, your card's been declined.'

'Right.' Dad looks at us, one by one. We wait with bated breath. There's a queue behind us.

'Right, c'mon, kids. Back to the car.'

Let me be clear, I had an idyllic childhood. I grew up in a house on a cliff overlooking one of the best surf breaks in town. As soon as the sun peeked above the horizon, I'd sit up in bed and check the surf, and if there was none, I'd go for a run. Days were spent exploring the chutes and side paths of the cliffs, scrabbling over rocks and clumps of dirt and flora, only stopping when we heard Mum sing out at dinnertime. But, like most families, we had financial difficulties. You know that song by Simply Red, 'Money's Too Tight to Mention'? That was the soundtrack to my childhood.

We weren't poor. There was enough for school uniforms, school books, school excursions and surfing paraphernalia. When I wanted tutoring in Years 11 and 12, my family found the money to make that happen. But we certainly weren't well off. There were no big family holidays. Our house was messy and chaotic. There were four kids. We had shit cars. We didn't have a dishwasher and everything always seemed to be broken.

What point am I trying to make?

My childhood was awesome, despite our lack of cash.

We all know that money doesn't 'buy happiness' (and if you don't, um, maybe get out more?). But, let me unpack this statement a little. It's fairly common for Westerners to contrast their lives (and their happiness) with people in developing countries: *Oh, we just got back from *insert developing country* and the people were so poor, they had nothing, but they seemed* so happy*!*

Yes, and it's true, people in developing countries who have sound family structures, access to some education, a house of whatever kind, but little money, *are* leading lives that we would probably see as content. Although . . . you should know by now, dear reader, that *seeming* content and *being* content are two different things. Because there are vast numbers of people living in developing countries who would not be content because of the troubles they face, and many of those are made harder by, or are due to, a lack of money.

So, when I hear people say 'money doesn't buy you happiness', I have to resist the urge to shake them like a Polaroid picture. Because it does make life much easier, which kind of means it buys some happiness . . .

If you're reading this book, you're probably living in a developed country. And in the 2020s, that means you probably live in a house or apartment, drive a car, have electricity and running water. You can get to the supermarket, where there's a veritable buffet of food before you, the quantity and range of which have never been seen before in the whole of human history. You've got access to medical care, dental care, you're educated: you might not have an MBA from Stanford but you've more than likely graduated from high school. And you have access to most of the world's information instantly and free of cost, thanks to the internet (in fact, a Masai warrior on a cellphone in the middle of Kenya has better mobile communication than President Reagan did in the late 1980s. And if they're on a smartphone and hooked up to Google, they've got more instant access to knowledge and information than President Clinton did in the late nineties).[1]

We have more disposable income than ever. Our purchasing power has increased. Our standard of living has gone up. In Australia, we have incomes that are three times higher than they were in 1950.[2]

When asked what they'd choose if they could have anything in the world right now, many people respond 'more money' (at least according to the blogs and forums I scrolled through one caffeine-fuelled night). Because, let's be clear, not having money sucks. It's awful feeling under financial stress, worrying about how you're going to manage your liabilities, getting harassed by debt collectors, not being able to meet your mortgage repayments. Married couples with higher levels of debt have more marital conflicts.[3] Throw kids into the mix and it's obvious why money figures prominently in reasons why couples get divorced (the ultimate irony being that divorce is usually financially crippling).[4] I mean, they don't get divorced *because* a big fat wad of cash started sleeping in their bed, but because of the stress a lack of money creates.

•

Money is complicated, and so, mostly, is our relationship to our money. Two different people with different genes, a different upbringing, different environmental factors and different experiences will likely also have very different ideas on money and what to do with it. Michael and I were both raised in the same coastal town, had relatively similar upbringings, and we still have vastly different opinions. Our arguments about money go something like this:

Michael: 'Save more!' [Michael's underlying beliefs about money include 'You work hard, pay off your mortgage as quickly as possible: don't owe money to the banks, or to anybody.']

Me: 'What are we saving for?? Let's live!!' [My underlying beliefs about money include 'I love money. You can go on holidays with it.']

Like I said, it's complicated. Some people are financial ostriches, ignoring bills and debt collectors and so on and so forth. Other people take great care of their income and try to do their best with it.

You and your significant other may see eye to eye on what you do with your money, or maybe you don't. I have married friends who record who-spends-what-where on a spreadsheet. You might have a friend who you know is a bit of a tight-arse, and never pays the bill when you go out to lunch. You might have mates who put everything on their credit cards. You might have a friend who's addicted to online shopping (or you might have several). You might have a friend who was super-stingy with money while you were at uni, and then managed to buy a Sydney property while *still* at uni.

It's not for me to tell you how to spend your money. But I do have some pointers on how you could spend your money to be happier, and studies have shown that this is something we can all take time to consider and enact.

What's the difference between having money and being wealthy?

Well, look, love, I'm no expert, but I know the illusion of having money is fairly easy to convey.

If I asked you to describe a stereotypical multi-millionaire, what description would you give me?

Maybe they'd live in a snazzy waterfront mansion. They'd drive an Aston Martin. They'd work in the city, at an important job, like . . . I dunno, something to do with corporate finance. They'd wear beautifully tailored suits, they'd have weekly manicures, they'd lunch at posh restaurants and they'd wash their hands with Dom Perignon.

Now this person could indeed be very wealthy.

Or they could be up to their eyeballs in debt. Maybe

they're just renting their place. Maybe they're leasing the Aston. Maybe they put their lunches and suits on their credit card.

Most of us define wealth by how much people spend – on designer clothes, expensive makeup, flashy cars, bling rings).[5] Not by how much money they have in the bank account. Not by the size of their super fund. Not by the assets that they own.

•

You might have read about, or seen ripping through your Facebook feed over the past five years, a well-known study on money and happiness. '$75,000 BUYS YOU HAPPINESS!' was the link I clicked. A psychologist at Princeton University, Daniel Kahneman, and Princeton economist Angus Deaton undertook the study in 2008-ish.[6] It had a huge data set of participants, close to half a million (the more data you have, the better your averages will be). The study measured two different elements of happiness. One was emotional wellbeing: the *frequency* and *intensity* of experiences of joy, stress, sadness, anger and affection. In other words, our daily emotions. The other was the thoughts people have about their life in general.

Here's a lil diagram I made to show the difference:

Emotional well-being	**Life evaluation**
'This guy on the bus talking loudly on his phone is pissing me off.'	'I'd have to say I'm overall pretty happy. I mean, my boss is a dick, but I love my family and I feel lucky to have such a supportive bowls team.'

TIME →

Short term (i.e. being temporarily annoyed)	Longer term (looking at your life as a whole)

It turns out that these two measurements of happiness are affected by different factors. Greater levels of income and education positively affect life evaluation, but our emotional wellbeing is largely determined by health, care-giving, loneliness and (randomly) smoking. An article about the study reported: 'Researchers found that life satisfaction rose steadily the more people were paid. Happiness rose with income too, but plateaued when people reached an annual salary of $75,000.'[7] (A caveat: this study was published in 2010, and the number quoted was in USD. So if we do a straight extrapolation it's probably closer to $150,000 in AUD in 2020.)

But also, let's not get too hung up on the numbers. Scott Pape, aka 'the Barefoot Investor', is Australia's most trusted independent finance expert, and reckons that $70,000 per year in Australia is enough to meet your essential needs. Once you earn beyond this point, you hit what is called 'the economics of enough'. Every dollar thereafter provides a diminishing rate of return on your happiness.

It's not for me to say how much money you, dear reader, need to make you happy. Just know that after a certain point, having more money don't do jack to improve your emotional wellbeing.

But we still need that 'certain point'. And to rub salt into the proverbial wound, the study showed that 'low income exacerbates the emotional pain associated with such misfortunes as divorce, ill health, and being alone'.[8] And this makes sense to most of us. Being broke is shit. Being broke and freshly divorced is extra shit. Being broke and freshly divorced and getting sick is shit with a flashing neon FUCK sign hanging overhead.

Whereas if you're rich and you get divorced, you can always get away to a meditation retreat in Bali to 'reflect'. And if you get a cancer diagnosis on top of that, at least you'll have the funds to stop working if you need to, and to pay for the top health care available. It would still be fucked, but money would ease the stress a tad.

All this money talk was making my head hurt. Do I diminish inflation at a compounding rate to increase my happiness at an exponential rate? Do I offset the measure of happiness by my annual salary adjusted for inflation?

And then I decided to stop pretending to be a financial expert and just ask one. Here's part of my interview with the inimitable Barefoot Investor.

Scott Pape

What amount of money makes us happy?

Once you earn over around $70,000 you hit what is called 'the economics of enough'. You have enough money to put a roof over your head, food on the table and clothes on your back . . . Once you have your basics covered, look to other things (outside of wealth) to provide happiness.

Do you think you can be happy without having a handle on your money?

Bob Cummins from Deakin University conducted one of the largest wellbeing surveys in Australian history (that's been going for over fifteen years). What he found from this research was what he calls the 'Triangle of Happiness'. It shows that people need to have a sense of purpose (beyond yearning for a large amount of money) and a sense of contributing to other people and their community.

The second finding was that humans need to have strong and loving relationships. The final pillar is financial security, and what we take from that circles back to the 'economics of enough': once you're earning around $70,000 per year and you're not in debt; if you can look yourself in the eye and say 'I've got this.' Even if you have credit card debt, you don't have to wait until you're out of credit card debit, or Nimble debt, or AfterPay debt to feel free. Once you have a plan in place, it is then a matter of time. You just need to adopt a plan to get you moving closer towards getting out of debt. A financial plan provides contentment; it's not about becoming a millionaire.

If you've got enough money, you're probably going to live longer, have the opportunity for more leisure time with friends and family, be healthier, eat better-quality food, have a more meaningful job, have better medical care. If you have lots of money, you have the vast array of choice of the Planet Earth laid out before you. You can virtually do anything you want. And with that freedom, one would imagine you'd be happier.

At its cold little heart, money gives you choice. It gives you options.

So, money can buy you happiness in that sense. It can and does improve your quality of life, and, yes, will likely make you happier. Initially.

Let's say I gave you the life of billionaire. You would be heady and excited about the thought of what you could do with all that money, and perhaps you'd spend it on lavish holidays and silk clothes and giving some to your family and friends, and then . . .

Remember hedonic adaptation? (No? Go back to the first chapter!)

You'd get used to it. And when we get used to something, it no longer makes us any happier. So, after a while, the lavish vacations and the silk blouses of your new billionaire status would start to feel run-of-the-mill.

'Ah yes, getting used to the life of a billionaire would be *terrible*, Turia. Please don't make me do it.'

I hear you, dear reader, I hear you. And luckily for you, I also have some good news about the connection between money and happiness. Yes, money can make you consistently happier . . . if you spend it on the right things.[9] YAY! You *can* be a billionaire and keep getting happier!

So, what are the 'right' things – what should we spend our money on if we want to be happier? Luckily for you, some clever researchers investigated this exact issue.[10] Read on, dear reader, read on.

1. Skydiving good, new handbag bad?

We should buy more experiences and fewer material goods. So skydiving gets a tick. What about forking out for a new handbag – is that a black mark? Well, let's not lump people together here. Because if you absolutely *love* handbags, then the feel of that leather strap, the weight of your long-coveted bag hanging from your hand *is* an experience. Individual choice, yo! (But remember old Hedgy – your handbag purchase might not mean *eternal* happiness 😉.) Know what an experience is for you, and save your money for it.

2. Buy time, but not a Rolex

Time is a precious resource. It's finite, and we have no idea how much of it we'll get on this planet.

The concepts of time and money promote different mindsets.[11] When we think about money, we usually think about it in a cold, rational manner, whereas thinking about how we spend our time helps us to focus on our social relationships and our happiness in general.[12]

Are we happy with how we spend our time right now? Well, some researchers broke down a number of daily tasks and ranked them in order of how much happiness each gave. Unsurprisingly, sexy time with someone else was number one. Commuting was people's least favourite part of the day, with work a close second, which, when you think about it, is not cool. We spend over a third of our lives at work, so if you hate your job it's probably not a great exchange for the salary you get.[13] (More on this in the 'Purpose' chapter.) Childcare and housework came next.[14] (If you don't have kids, please feel free now to shout out loud HAHA, SUCKED IN PROCREATORS! If you do have kids, may I kindly remind you that packing your toddler's bag for school and making them a breakfast they don't eat is not the same as watching them marvel at the autumn leaves or making them giggle with your Thomas the Tank Engine impersonation.)

With this in mind, if you have the advantage of not worrying about putting a roof over your head every night, one way that extra money could buy you happiness is by buying you more time. If chores like housework don't do it for you, and you have a little excess money, why don't you consider paying someone to do them? Like, of course I can clean my own home, but I wouldn't clean it as well as a professional cleaner and it would take half of my Saturday, and I'd rather spend my Saturday bushwalking with my family.

I order my groceries online. Yes, I could get them cheaper by wrangling Hakavai into Aldi, finding everything I need with him wriggling in the trolley, and then driving around the corner to Woolworths to get the rest of the stuff they didn't have at Aldi. I choose to pay the premium, though, to avoid losing two hours of my day to that very average experience.

Now, if you're a student living on mi goreng, you're probably not going to spend more than you need to buying your groceries online for the sheer convenience. But if you can afford it, and your happiness is a priority, then using your money to buy time is money well spent.[15]

3. Lattes are better than a Lexus

Hedonic adaptation means we get used to good things (a new handbag!) and bad things (ever gone into a room that reeked of fart and found that after a couple of minutes, the fart smell has diminished?). Because our money is limited, we're better off spending it frequently on little things, like lattes, as opposed to infrequently on big things . . . like a brand new Lexus.[16]

Why? According to the research, the more easily you can explain an event (I bought a new car!) the more quickly you adapt to it.[17] And when you buy a new Lexus, every time you jump into it, it's the same car. Whereas if you go down the pub and there's a new craft beer to sample, that experience ticks all the boxes of variety, novelty and surprise.

4. Save for some brown pants

When I was fifteen, I had three part-time jobs. On a Friday arvo I'd ride my bike to our local video store and do the night shift there. Saturdays, I'd ride my bike to the fish and chip shop and do my shift there. Then I'd ride my bike to the video store, get changed in the cleaning closet into my uniform and do the Saturday-night shift. On Sundays I did the dishes at our local pizza joint.

What did I do with my earnings? Well, I was on minimum wage to start with. But I had my eye on a pair of brown cords from a local surf shop. I put them on layby. Every time I went to work I imagined being able to wear them to a party. Around town! Skating! (I didn't skate, but I had a colourful imagination.) I anticipated how different I would be once I was wearing the brown cords. I would be cool! I would be the *it* girl! I would have to fend off multiple romantic advances! (I stayed pretty much the same after I bought the cords, but owning and wearing them still gave me lots of pleasure).

Fast forward five years to Turia at university. One day, I got sent a piece of magenta plastic. My name was embossed on it, along with a sixteen-digit code. Running my fingers over the minuscule lettering, I fantasised about what this piece of plastic would allow me to do. I could finally buy a leather jacket! I could go on a surfing trip to Bali! I could go down to the snow and buy a new snowboard, snowboard boots, bindings, helmet, goggles and everything else the sales assistant pressed on me in the store. I could go out to nice dinners! I could drop $500 at David Jones! I cou—

And then I ran out of money. I reached my credit limit in under a year.

Going into debt made me very unhappy. Miserable, in fact.

The takeaway of these two anecdotes should be clear. Delaying consumption (saving for a pair of brown pants) makes you happier than buying stuff straightaway you can't really afford (the whole floor of a ski shop). Debt is the anti-happiness.[18]

5. Make like a saint

I'd read that spending money on others makes us happier. But there's nothing like finding out for yourself.[19] While I was writing this chapter, my brother told me his headphones had broken. As a musician, not having a pair of headphones is a big deal for him. And because he's a musician, of course the new pair he wanted was exorbitantly priced. The Louboutins of the ears, if you will.

The same day he told me about his expensive hearing problem, I was eyeing off a nice little geological hammer on one of my favourite online stores (individual choice, remember!). I sent my bro a text asking if he still needed new headphones. He replied to say he'd already got some but I was generous for offering.

'Man,' I thought, 'these scientists are on to something!' I did get a huge boost by feeling as though I'd made a generous offer (and without having to spend any of my own money, so it truly was a win-win). What a time to be alive!

In my example above, I was beatific and generous . . . but at the same time, not really, since I didn't have to follow through. Would the boost I received been even *more* powerful if my brother had needed the headphones and I'd bought them and sent them off to him?

Thank goodness for clever researchers, because they investigated this very issue for me.[20] They gave participants a $5 or $20 bill, having asked them that morning to rank their happiness, and then instructed them to spend it on themselves or give it away. When they contacted the participants the same evening, those who'd given away their cash were feeling happier than those who'd spent it on themselves.

•

So here's what I think about all that money talk. I think money does make you happier if you have enough not to wake up at night worried about how you'll pay the rent or the next bill that comes in; and if you're spending any spare money you have on things that, well, make you happier. Like, if you feel guilty after handing over cash to the dentist who just glued diamonds onto your teeth, that's obviously not a way for you to feel happier. Spending the money that you work bloody hard for *should* be exciting, and joyful. If you love flowers and flower-arranging, and you have the opportunity to go to a flower-arranging course in your neighbourhood, and you froth on it and it gives you so many new ideas about how to intersperse sunflowers with banksias – well then, I would say that's excellent expenditure on your behalf.

Again: you do you.

I *love* buying a double-shot soy latte every morning, but you might detest the feel of a warm beverage in your hand and the kick in your step delivered by a hit of caffeine.

You might think New Zealand is the best country on Earth to visit, or you might decide that caravanning around some remote part of your state is an absolute necessity for you.

Maybe you want to own your own home so you can spend DIY-filled weekends making it perfectly yours. Or maybe putting 40 per cent of your wage straight into your mortgage is not a way you want to use up your money. Maybe you'd prefer to rent and save all of the mending bother for the landlord, your nights free to sample spaghetti at every Italian restaurant in town.

Know who you are, what brings you joy and spend your money, judiciously, to enact it.

Don't know what you love? Try this

Print out your bank statement, and circle the transactions you feel good about.

Use those circles as a guide.

And if there's nothing circled? Well, you, my friend, need to get out more.

A flan is not a financial plan

A flan is delicious, but it's not an action plan for your financial future.

If you don't have a fitness plan, how can you expect to be fitter? If you don't have a business plan, how can you expect to be, um, more business-y? If you want to get better with your finances, you need a plan.

There are plenty of books out there that give financial advice on all things money, from budgeting to planning. This one you're reading right now isn't one of them! I personally love the straight-talking style of Scott Pape, aka the Barefoot Investor. You might find someone else's advice and voice resonates with you. Don't waste your life stressing about money or feeling guilty about it. Get a plan, or find a reputable advisor, and then enact it.*

Forget the Joneses

When I was a poor uni student, we revelled in our not-wealthy circumstances. Hearing stuff like this was not uncommon: 'I can't afford a pillow so I've just blown up the bladder from the cask of wine we drank last night.'

Out of the confines of student life, it is, however, easy to fall into the trap of unfavourably comparing your life circumstances to others (see pages 120–22 for more info on overcoming this trap), and how much money we have, as displayed by how much money we spend, provides a super-simple way for us to compare ourselves to others. In fact, research shows that we are biologically and intrinsically wired to defer to symbols of wealth.[21]

Don't feel bad if you want to be the rich alpha human; blame your wiring. But keep in mind that what 'buys' your happiness will be different to what buys happiness for that bloke Steve in Accounting. Try to avoid the trap of comparing yourself to others. Focus on what makes *you* happy.

---

* There's lots of sharks out there (as in shoddy financial advisors). *The Barefoot Investor* has a brilliant guide on how to pick a reputable advisor. And see the Resources section.

How much was your engagement ring (asking for a friend)?

Way back in 2011, after I was burnt, Michael received pretty hectic news from my surgeons. 'She might not live.'

They asked him if he wanted to see me, but they warned him I looked different (my head was the size of a pumpkin, plus they'd shaved it). He thought, 'If Turia's going to die, I want to remember her how she was, with long dark hair and her big smile.'

And then he had a second thought: 'If she survives, I'll marry her.'

I survived and unbeknown to me, using his inheritance from his grandma Michael bought a ring from a charming shop in Kununurra; the diamond in it was even from the mine where I'd worked as an engineer.

Fast forward four years, Michael's proposing to me in the Maldives and I'm saying yes and we're going midnight snorkelling with manta rays.

I've always loved diamonds – they're literally the hardest shit on earth. Despite my affinity for them, I thought it was weird that stuff that was almost exactly the same as graphite was worth so much money: the average amount spent on an engagement ring in Australia is close to $7000.[22]

So, where's my ring now?

When I went to the south of France, it was on a necklace, accompanied by a very bourgeois pearl that we'd bought in Broome. Fancy, but still with that Aussie twist, y'know?

On the way to the airport in a taxi, I was swinging my pearl-and-engagement-ring necklace back and forth in front of Hakavai and laughing at his grunts and squeals of delight.

It was only when I started to walk through our departure gates that I realised I had *left it in the fucking taxi.*

So I did what anyone would do in this situation. I hid from Michael that I'd lost the ring and made up vague excuses for months for why it was no longer around my neck. ('It doesn't suit what I'm wearing,' 'I'm getting it cleaned,' 'I've read I need to dry out my diamond so it's in the sun drying.')

Inevitably he worked it out, and inevitably he was annoyed. I guess because he'd bought it with his inheritance from his grandma and decided he'd propose if I lived, and all of that stuff?!

I lose shit all the time. If I'd wanted to make 100 per cent sure I had my diamond ring forever, I could have never worn it and kept it in a safe my whole life. But instead it had a great (albeit short) life. It was with me through the best times of the past five years – it came to Tahiti, the Maldives, watched me finish at Ironman Kona, walked the Kokoda Track and, best of all, was there to give Hakavai a metallic welcome to the world.

At the end of the day, it's not about the ring or whatever precious commodities you have squirrelled away. Life is short. Go and enjoy it. And remember that diamonds and other 'valuable' stuff only have the meaning that we give them. And by that logic, money only has the meaning that we give it, too. Yes, we need it. And yes, it can make us happier. But not as happy as we might assume.

Scott Pape again

What kind of attitudes around money do you see make people the happiest?

Generosity and gratefulness. One of the things that we find consistently is that poorer countries in a global setting are some of the happiest countries, as they're not trying to keep up with the Joneses and generosity is a really big thing for them. What I've seen among very wealthy people is their overwhelming fear around losing [their wealth]. It's important to have an understanding that money alone does not provide happiness. People on an average wage in Australia are still living in one of the wealthiest countries on the planet. Australians have access to a world-class education, a world-class health system, a HECS system where students don't have to face large upfront debt for tuition fees. We are so lucky to be living in Australia.

What makes you happy and/or how has your understanding of happiness changed over the years?

What makes me happy is spending time with my family on our farm. That has changed over time. I used to be one of the most heavily booked public speakers in Australia – I was working extremely hard. When my son turned one, I decided that real happiness is spending time with my family and kids. Over the last couple of years, I can count on one hand the number of speaking events I've done – they've all been for not-for-profits and events for communities.

For me, real happiness is being able to dictate my time and to spend that time with my loved ones.

Are there any habits or practices that you undertake daily that contribute to your general sense of happiness?
I love living on the farm because it's a reminder of life and its seasons. We're around animals that we care for and love and this connects us to nature. Being able to play with my kids and go for walks with them in nature each day is a wonderful way to give back to each other. I also have an Apple watch and a remote team that work from home. I try to compete with my team on our exercise goals because I know that one of the ways to beat the blues is to get moving. My family and I also give money to things we're passionate about and often do so anonymously. One of the other things I'm really proud of and passionate about is that we sit down as a family for dinner every night (with the TV off). There may be spaghetti being thrown but we are all at the table and all talking about our day – it's a ritual in our house every single night and is very important to us.

•

TL;DR

- Remember, there's a difference between having money and 'having money'. It's easy to paint an illusion of wealth with credit cards and bad debt.
- Money can definitely make you happy if you have enough to pay for life's fundamental needs (food, shelter, transport), and if you're spending it on the right things.
- What are the 'right things'? For example, new experiences, buying your time back and using your money to help others.

9
Purpose

You want to know what I hate?

Penguins.

And also . . . purpose.

There's so much pressure surrounding the idea of your 'purpose', right?

As kids, we're always being asked what we want to do when we grow up. As teens, we're asked what our passions are. All through our lives we hear platitudes such as 'Do what you love and you'll never work a day in your life' and 'Decide what you want, then make it happen.'

I mean, honestly, do any of us know exactly what we want in our lives?

Like, I'm an extremely decisive person. When I go to a café, I don't bandy about perusing the menu for twenty minutes wondering if I should get the whipped salmon mousse omelette or the fairy-floss pancakes. I take an inordinate amount of pride in my quick and effective menu decision-making.

But if you asked me what my purpose in *life* was, I'd find it hard not to feel crushed by the existential weight of that question.

So, if you, dear reader, want to know 'what you should be doing with your life', read on.

Let's start with work

Given we spend so much of our precious time on our jobs, it's easy to mix up your work and your purpose – and confuse them.

And it can be hard to find a career path that feels 'right', right? You know, one we have a natural aptitude and affinity for, makes some sort of difference to the world AND gives our lives meaning. I mean, we're not asking for much!

Dr Terri Janke is a brilliant lawyer, runs her own law firm, and has a doctorate in Indigenous cultural and intellectual property rights. So, yeah, you could say she's pretty accomplished! I've known Terri since forever (she's my aunt!) and what I have always loved about her is her style: she's calm, humble and extremely gracious. I admire her passion and focus and pride in her identity, and for me she epitomises that perfect balance – she has a career for which she has a natural aptitude and affinity, plus it's meaningful and makes a difference to the world.

Dr Terri Janke, Wuthathi/Meriam lawyer, leading international authority on Indigenous cultural and intellectual property.

I'm interested in how your work, purpose, identity and happiness all intersect with one another. Why do you find your work fulfilling, what drives you to do it, and does it make you happier? (Sorry, that's three questions in one!)

I find work extremely fulfilling. As a lawyer I knew I wanted to work in Indigenous social justice issues. My first path was to think I'd work in the courts, but I was often mistaken for a defendant. I didn't enjoy that side of the law; I wanted something more positive. I love the arts, I love writing and reading, I love performances, I love learning about culture. I have always found my work fulfilling. I've wanted to focus on copyright and Indigenous arts and knowledge since the start of my career. It fulfils me because I am able to help Indigenous people, and I can help with engagement between Indigenous and non-Indigenous people, and we raise awareness through our work. My identity is closely aligned to my work and I have a purpose to make a better future for Indigenous people, but also for all Australians. I am driven because I can see the difference that engaging on an equal-value platform, negotiating deals and having intellectual property valued equally can bring so much change for Indigenous people.

I love it when I see the results of our work – in a project, a piece of public art, or shifts in how a company engages. We act for all people in business, and I love being a part of the growing Indigenous business sector. It drives me to make Indigenous sustainable, but also I am driven to see Indigenous ways of knowing as part of the Australian business landscape. That motivates me so much: I am rewarded by seeing the difference – over twenty years it's been great. I have younger lawyers working with me now, Indigenous and non-Indigenous. We work for large non-Indigenous companies and small non-Indigenous businesses who share our values.

Obviously being the boss means I can control and manage my vision and set the values for the company. I like to listen to clients, and to my staff, and I always want to grow.

What makes me happy is being able to meet a challenge and deal with it in my way. I like to treat other people with respect, I listen, I want to always improve. I am happier when I am helping people, getting good feedback and engaging with all levels of community. I like that we get great feedback and I am happy that over time my work has been recognised, not just by awards but by people in the community, Indigenous people. I loved winning the NAIDOC Award in 2011. That was great to be recognised by the Indigenous community!

You look after yourself extremely well physically – you don't drink alcohol, you're a vegan, you exercise every day. Why is it important for you to do this, and do you think it helps your wellbeing and happiness?

It goes in waves, my eating and exercising; no doubt I feel better when I do well in those. But I think giving up alcohol was one of the best decisions I have ever made. Being healthy really helps my wellbeing, happiness, mental ability, but as I said, there are waves. I think I also slip up with not finding the work–life balance.

What makes you happy?

My family – my husband, Andrew, and my two children, Tamina and Jaiki. I feel very connected with them, and I love it when we are all together. Being in a close relationship with my husband has been the secret to my success. We are different but we are committed to understanding each other and supporting each other. We have always been focused on being able to nurture our children so they can be strong and independent, sharing great experiences, learning new things, dealing with problems, and having deeper conversations about the world, social, cultural and political discussions.

My mum – calling her always makes me happy. She sacrificed so much for us kids, encouraged me when I was down and unconfident and I love talking to her: she naturally makes me feel happy.

I like being part of the Indigenous community and the connections with the land, the sea and other people. I like hearing stories about my culture, the stories of survival, and I want to advance Indigenous rights. Being Indigenous gives me a strong identity – Wuthathi and Meriam - and I am centred by this.

I like being in natural spaces – on the beach or in a forest.

I like being able to have choices, to be able to think and focus and set goals, and to think deeply about their impact to me, others and the world. I want the world to be a better place; I want to leave a legacy and a good message for future generations. I like to think that I bring positivity and hope and that through what I do I might inspire others. I especially like it when I get emails and cards and letters from young Indigenous girls who are thinking of studying law and tell me 'Thanks for being an inspiration.' I never had role models when I was a kid. I would never have had the guts to write a letter to someone. I think the next generation is going to be much better than me.

I like it when I reach my goals. Some of them are small and short term but others are long term, and I get happiness from meeting the long-term goals. Seeing the shifts over time.

How has your understanding of happiness changed over the years?

I always had altruistic goals, but I did also have short-term happiness goals and perhaps material ones. There is no doubt that I am happier with money than having no money: it gives you more choices and options. But you actually do have choice and options even without money. I always waited for someone else to notice me or give me things, but I learnt how to set goals and work on myself. I learnt that happiness comes from me. I think there is a deeper spiritual path and way of the world, and that has given me happiness when I connect with it. That said, many times I lose that connection and I am lost in materialism, envy, taking things personally. I don't think you have to always be happy – there are other emotions that you need to feel life. I know happiness, or that connection, is something you always have to work on.

When I think of a proud Aboriginal woman, you always come to my mind. Have you always been proud of your culture and your identity?
This is very nice of you – thanks. I didn't see this question before I wrote my response to what makes me happy, but I would say my heritage, culture and identity play a strong part in my life and outlook. When I was a kid, I was subjected to racism every day at school, and the world seemed aggressive. I didn't know how to deal with that; I never knew how to respond. There was always the confusion of how history was taught, and the invisibility of Aboriginal people continued to justify taking up the land.

It's a very challenging time for young Indigenous people, and as a young kid and adolescent I remember thinking 'I wish I didn't have to deal with this.' There were so many complexities and times I had to speak up to racism: I have always been proud to be an Aboriginal woman, but as a kid I wished I was like everybody else – I wanted to fit in, I really did not want the racist attention! I am happy my kids don't seem to have the same confusion.

I know that for me personally, celebrating my Tahitian heritage helps me to feel more connected and adds to my happiness. Has your connection to your culture and heritage done the same for you?
Yes, it has. I feel the connection to my heritage very, very deeply – it's a connection that runs deep, is timeless, and spiritual. It's a harder journey given the history of our country and that our ancestors were either killed,

died young, were made not to practise culture or speak language, but every time I learn more, every time we reclaim language, every time an Indigenous person revitalises cultural practice, I am stronger.

I remember when I saw the masks of Mer of the old people, at the Encounters exhibition at the National Museum of Australia. They were taken from Torres Strait 150 years or more and kept in the British Museum vaults. This was their first time back in Australia and we got to see them. I cried because I felt a sense of awe, a sense of connection, a sense of loss, but also because I was overcome by the beauty of them. How I felt, seeing them with my kids, could not be described in words.

•

It's my humble opinion that one of the reasons it's hard to find the *perfect* career path is because we have so many bloody options. In the 'olden days', maybe you could've been a blacksmith, or maybe your uncle was a baker so that was also an option.

These days, you can be anything! Do anything! Which, yes, is a very exciting prospect, but is also rather overwhelming. According to Barry Schwartz, in his highly regarded book *The Paradox of Choice*, having too many choices produces 'psychological distress, especially when combined with regret, concern about status, adaptation, social comparison, and perhaps most important, the desire to have the best of everything'.[1] Saying yes to the spaghetti bolognese means we're saying no to the seafood risotto, the margherita pizza, the calamari salad.

And the more options there are, the easier it is to regret the option that you went for.[2]

Applying this rationale to our careers means that because we can do anything, it's easier to be dissatisfied with what we end up doing.

Now, if you're in a job that matches your natural skill set and creates meaning and you love it and you have extraordinary colleagues who you sit around a campfire with every weekend, singing Disney tunes, go you!

For the rest of us, I have some advice . . .

What flavour shit sandwich do you most enjoy eating?

Because all jobs have some element of, you know, shit – hard work, grind, *stuff you don't want to do*. Knowing what kind of shit you're not up for is a huge help in figuring out if you have the right job – in the future and in the job you have right now. For example, if you like the idea of being a vet nurse and working with animals, but can't handle the thought of dealing with needles or blood . . . maybe that's not the right job. Likewise, if you dream of being an actor but can't handle the idea of being rejected . . . that's maybe not the best shit sandwich for you.

It's okay if your job isn't 'perfect'

In my previous life as a mining engineer, I often struggled with the dilemma *am I doing the right job?* Don't get me wrong, there was lots of stuff I adored about my job – such as settling in front of my dual monitor to work on an Excel spreadsheet, or doing new rehabilitation slope designs in MineScape (kind of like AutoCAD for mines). There was, however, a lot of stuff I didn't love about my job, such as the long hours, working with people who I didn't have much in common with, and being bossed about on a daily basis. But, despite my frustrations with parts of my job as an engineer, I still had a sense of purpose and contentment during that time – I was challenged intellectually and I spent my time outside of work doing the stuff I really loved (camping, adventuring, running and being an all-round legend).

Now let's look at my mate Susan. Every morning Susan pops her two kids in the car, and drives five minutes down the road to the award-winning daycare they're enrolled at. After handing them over to the smiling brunette in the playroom, she hops back in the car and drives another five minutes to her office, parks in the free undercover area, and walks into her light-filled building. The sun streams through the windows, the rays soaked up by the potted fiddle-leaf figs that dot across the gleaming wooden floors.

After making herself an almond milk cappuccino in the impeccably appointed work kitchen, she walks purposefully into her first meeting of the day – a catch-up with her team filled with enthusiasm and energy. They all fist-bump each other, before walking away to start their mornings on a high. Her work is meaningful – she raises money and provides resources to families in need. Her team is efficient, generous and smart, and she has an annual take-home salary of $120,000. Her managers understand that she has carer duties and allow her to be flexible with her working hours so she can take lunch to her elderly mum's place a few days each week, as well as be around to see the kids after daycare.

Where does Susan work and how do I get a job there? I hear you ask.

I'd ask her but . . . SUSAN DOESN'T EXIST.

I mean, maybe she does, but I don't know her. For the purposes of this book, I invented her.

See, Susan's job ticks all the boxes that the World Happiness Report suggests contribute to contentment: a short commute, a decent wage and flexibility to balance work and non-work commitments.[3]

Yep, there are certain things we need to feel content in our jobs. But even if your job doesn't tick many of these boxes – my mining job didn't – it's quite possible that it's still a satisfying role and gives you the sense of purpose you need to live a fulfilled life.

Finding meaning in your job

Let's boil this down simply: we find meaning when we see a connection between what we value and what we spend our time doing.

And there's an argument that everyone, no matter how tedious they might think their work is, can find this sense of meaning in what they do. David Ulrich, a professor of business at the University of Michigan, and psychologist Wendy Ulrich, mused on the question of 'The Why of Work' in *Forbes* magazine.[4] David related a fable about three bricklayers all working on the same wall:

> Someone asked the bricklayers, 'What you are doing?' The first said, 'I am laying bricks'; the second bricklayer replied, 'I am building a wall'; and the third answered, 'I am building a great cathedral for God.' The third had a vision of how the daily tasks of laying bricks fit into a broader, more meaningful purpose. Likewise, employees who envision the outcomes of their daily routines find more meaning from doing them.[5]

Wendy went on to say, 'I learnt long ago with therapy clients that their misery often had less to do with their circumstances and more to do with what they told themselves those circumstances meant about them ... changing the story, seeing a different perspective, or getting creative can turn a problem into an opportunity.'[6]

I'll wrap all of this up by saying that if, no matter how you try to frame your job, your workplace makes you genuinely unhappy, you probably should think about changing jobs. Easier said than done, I know. But that's something you can work on. Work occupies *so* much of our time. And if you enjoy most of what you do, the shit sandwiches are palatable and you can derive some form of meaning from it – you'll be able to apply more of yourself to it.

Mark Manson, author of mega-bestseller *The Subtle Art of Not Giving a F*ck*

I think when people talk about purpose, what they really mean is simply feeling that they are using their time well. If you spend your time doing something important or fun then you feel as though it has meaning or significance for your life. If you spend your time doing something frivolous or dumb then you feel as though you're wasting your life. So, the question of purpose is really just a question of finding something valuable or meaningful in the world and committing to it. The mistake most people make is they get it backwards: they look for purpose first, so then they can make the commitment to it after. But you make the commitment first, then feel a sense of purpose later.

> What people perceive as purpose or happiness or success or whatever, it *is* the work. It is the feeling of sacrifice or struggle that generates the sense of meaning and satisfaction. Trying to be happy or have purpose without sacrificing anything is like baking a cake with no batter . . . you're just left with some shitty frosting.

Other ways to feel purpose

Yes, having a sense of purpose contributes to our happiness. I mean, all the smart people say so. In fact, according to Sonja Lyubomirsky, the concept of 'happiness' refers to the experience of joy, contentment or positive wellbeing, combined with a sense that one's life is good, meaningful and worthwhile.[7]

So how do we create this feeling of 'meaning' and 'worthwhile-ness'? I know for me (and for a lot of people) a large part of it does come from my work. But there are many ways to derive a sense of purpose and meaning from our lives beyond how we make a buck.

Making progress

When you make progress on tasks, either big ones (see the 'Goals' chapter) or small ones (this weekend I'm going to replant our veggie garden) you're pretty much guaranteed to feel some kick of purpose or meaning. The act of making progress, of immersing yourself in something, of working towards something, of focusing wholeheartedly on something, gives you structure in your days and yes, gives you purpose.

My Ironman journey ticked all these boxes. When I woke in the mornings, I didn't think, 'What is my purpose in life now?' Instead I'd think, 'I've got to do that ten-kilometre run today as part of my training. Need to get it done this morning because we're going up to Sydney this afternoon for my cousin's birthday.'

Ironman gave me a focal point to my days, and in doing so created meaning and purpose in my life.

Caring for others

Most caring roles (partner, kids, parents, chickens – you name it) bestow the carer with a glow – or at least a faint shimmer – of purpose. Sure, it can suck to be woken up by Hakavai for the fourteenth time in the night, but it sure as hell signifies I have a role to play in his life.

Caring for something, or someone, beyond yourself, gives you a greater perspective of the role you play in the bigger picture of life. Now, I'm not suggesting you start popping out a bunch of kids in order to find meaning in your life! But I am suggesting you find ways to connect with, and care for, other living things – be it a herb garden, a dog, a friend or family member.

That brings me to . . . connection.

You know this from my chapter on love (unless you have skipped ahead, assuming all the juicy lessons were at the end of the book – in which case you're wrong: I'm running out of insights to share! Go back to the beginning when I was full of zest and joie de vivre!) but growing a community and participating in it are integral to your happiness, and to your sense of purpose.

So, join that book club you were invited to. Bake those cookies from the recipe your neighbour gave you and share some over the fence. Sign up to a running group. Being connected to others, and investing in a shared experience will help you feel part of something bigger.

Take the pressure off

So, what's my purpose? Well, I'm not sure if I have just one. I love what I do for work and, yep, I'm happy with the shit sandwiches I get served. I love my family, looking after my business and my team, keeping myself healthy and active, figuring out where my next challenge will come from, working towards that challenge. To me, all those things give my life meaning.

So, for you dear reader, if the lofty idea of 'purpose' is something you've struggled with, here's what I want you to do. Stop asking yourself 'What is my purpose? What should I be doing with my life?' Instead, I want you to focus on answering questions like: 'What am I interested in? What should I try first? What do I want to know more about? What question do I want to find an answer to? What do I love thinking about?'

Most successful people don't start out with an all-encompassing vision for their life. They pull at an area of interest, chase an idea that excites them, or look at answering a question they don't know the answer to. Forget purpose. Follow your interests. Be curious. And I bet where you end up will be pretty damn meaningful.

Marie Forleo, entrepreneur and author of the number-one *New York Times* bestseller *Everything Is Figureoutable*

What makes you happy?

Connection. Growth. Contribution. Creativity. Collaboration. Music. Dance. Food. Laughter. Nature. Hard work. Great coffee. Playing with my dog. Rollercoasters. Zombie movies. Cheese. Travel.

How has your understanding of happiness changed over the years?
I've learnt that happiness is an inside job. It's a choice that we get to make moment to moment.

Marie, you talk a lot about finding your purpose (and I know this is one of the main things you help people all around the world with). I would assume that if you've got a strong life purpose, it would make you happier. Do you have any thoughts on how happiness and purpose work together?
I actually think the concept of 'finding your purpose' can keep people navel-gazing and lost. I'd rather people start taking action and find a way to be of service to others. To get moving. I usually talk about sharing your gifts and contribution. We all want to feel useful in life, as though we're somehow making a difference to others. When you have your attention off yourself, and you're fully immersed in helping others, you tend to feel a sense of fulfillment, connection and meaning – feelings that many people would associate with happiness.

I believe that life is all about progress – figuring things out, overcoming challenges and working towards the life that you want for yourself. Do you agree that making progress helps happiness?
We human beings thrive off progress. It's essential for happiness. I believe it's also critical to our mental, emotional, and spiritual health.

Having said that, a lot of people believe that happiness is about being content with what you have. How do you reconcile those two beliefs?
Paradoxes exist everywhere. For example, 'Water, water everywhere and not a drop to drink.' That's certainly true if you're stranded on a raft in the middle of the ocean. Similarly, you can be grateful and appreciative of what you have right now, and you can be excited to grow and create different experiences in the future. Happiness and progress are not mutually exclusive.

What do you wish more people knew about happiness?
That it's something you must choose, cultivate, and practise. Daily.

•

TL; DR

- We have so many options and so much choice that it can make us completely dissatisfied.
- All jobs have some kind of shit in the sandwich they serve up. So it's helpful to know what you are (and aren't) up for when choosing what you do for work.
- It's okay if your work life isn't perfect – there are lots of ways to feel like you have purpose and meaning, such as making progress and caring for someone (or something) else.
- Stop asking yourself 'What is my purpose?' Instead, focus on answering questions like 'What am I interested in?' and 'What do I want to know more about'?

10
Hard Times

It's counterintuitive but I believe with every minuscule cell in my body that going through some challenges and hard times is crucial to our happiness.

Hard times can reaffirm your sense of identity. They can give you a deeper understanding of who the fuck you really are. In fact, they can force you to step up, to become *more* of who you are. They can make you realise that, YES, you are infinitely stronger than you've given yourself credit for.

Hard times can even benefit your relationships. Adversity acts as a relationship filter, separating fair-weather relationships from ones that will endure, and further strengthening those.

Experiencing and coming through hard times also flips your priorities. For me, going through what I have means that I always make time for my loyal friends and family, for my health. Well, almost always. I think we all sometimes get bogged down in the minutiae of life; of needing to send that email *right now* and make sure the house is *immaculate* and that presentation is *perfect*. I think that's okay, and is very much human nature, but it's good for us every now and then to have a perspective shift to remind us of what actually matters in life.

When you go through hard times you gain the ability to see a perfectly normal day for what it is – a perfectly normal day and how fucking good is it to be alive and to feel the sun's warmth on your face and to hear the kookaburras singing and to feel the warmth radiating out of your heart.

Nope, I'm not high, but I'm intoxicated by the idea of this glorious life that you, dear reader, and I get to live. Am I like this every day? Of course not, you goose! But the hard times I've faced have made me realise how strong I am, and how I can guide my future by my actions. A part of me is embarrassed to be so unashamedly *positive*, and the darker part of me doubts the veracity of this sentence, but another part of me thinks . . . well, aren't I?

Humans are remarkably resilient. As we grow up, we make and lose friends, we pass and fail tests, we move house or country, we get a job, we might lose the job or get a promotion, and through these ebbs and flows we get used to our new normal. When we're faced with a challenge – be that divorce or going through cancer or living through a global pandemic or having to foreclose on your family home – we eventually adjust. Have faith that we are adaptable, and that we have the ability to adjust to the new normal. It's hedonic adaptation in reverse. So, just like I gave you strategies so you don't become terribly accustomed to the good stuff, in this chapter I'm going to give you tools to help you with the hard times.

Now, a serious note. I haven't personally experienced every type of trauma, and the trauma I *have* experienced in no way makes me an expert, and it doesn't make me immune to additional trauma either. The trauma you may or may not have experienced is unique to you, and your exact personal circumstances.

So. If you have been through a traumatic experience, however big or small, I would encourage you to see a professional. Yes, if you have a fantastic support network, that's awesome. But friends and family aren't trained in, or always the best at knowing what to say, how to frame things, and approaches, strategies and tools that are going to be beneficial to your long-term mental health. Think about it. You'd get your car fixed by a mechanic, your teeth cleaned by a dentist, your face beautified by a beautician. Your heart and head deserve nothing less than a professional to help you.

The first time I saw a psychologist I was in hospital. It was too soon: I was still coming to terms with what had happened to me. I didn't see another psychologist for another six months, and they weren't right for me – I didn't feel I could talk openly to them. I saw someone else a month later. Meetings with her were pivotal; she was instrumental to my recovery.

There are also some incredibly helpful organisations out there that can help you to work through hard times: see the Resources section for some of these.

An unordinary interview with Leigh Sales (don't you love it when people butcher your book title for their own amusement, Leigh?)

In your book Any Ordinary Day *you describe the hard times that you have dealt with personally. Would you say you're happier now, because of what those hard times have taught you?*

> I really believe that you can't seek out happiness, that it's not something you can find. It's a by-product of what you do, how you treat others and your relationships with people. Happiness is quite fleeting, I find. It's a momentary emotion. I think contentment is a more permanent state of being and I think that comes from being comfortable in how you are living your life . . . I definitely wouldn't say I'm happier now, I would say that overall, I'm less happy. I'm less happy because I'm more conscious of how quickly life can change for the worse and I carry some pain from the memory of things that have happened to me. Also, I'm a single mother of two young children and so my everyday life is just harder than it used to be in sheer logistics! But I do think that hard times have made me a much better, more empathetic person. And I would say I get more moments of happiness from simple everyday things, like the sound of magpies or the look of the ocean. I'm way better at being 'present' because I know not to take it for granted. I'm way better at thinking, *Okay, I only have to get through today, I can do that*, and setting aside worries about tomorrow.

Sharing

We've all been through hard stuff. Life is *not* a competition for who's had the 'hardest' stuff, and we don't get little medals for going through the hard stuff and coming out the other side with our selves generally intact. Whatever 'hard' was to you, know that very probably it's been faced before. I'm in no way trying to diminish your experience, but research has shown that sharing your experiences with others who've been through something similar helps.

Sheryl Sandberg, Facebook's Chief Operating Officer, became a widow and a single parent when her husband died unexpectedly. In her book *Option B*, she says that 'getting to know people who also lost a parent or a spouse provided much-needed comfort'.[1] I know that in my experience, getting to know some of the others who were trapped by the fire, and talking to them about what we had been through, was so helpful. When I complained about being itchy to Mum and Michael, they were sympathetic but would annoyingly say, 'Well, scratching is only going to make it worse.' Whereas if I complained to Kate, who also got burnt that day, she'd say, 'Tell me about it, it's the worst. I like to use a fork to really get in there.' A shared experience with someone means that they get you, because *they've been you.*

And if you've just started on your adversity path and time is moving at a painstakingly slow pace, I want you to say to yourself, 'I'm still here and that's a win.' Or if you're very much in the thick of it, I want you say to yourself, 'I have the inner resources to deal with any situation that comes my way.'

And if you feel like you 'should' be 'over it' and you're not – well, my friend, that is perfectly okay too.

You know what I don't do when I feel like crying about what I've been through? I don't say to myself, 'You're a stupid girl for crying.' I don't say, 'Gurl, get over it already, it happened almost a decade ago.' I don't say, 'Yeah, go ahead, keep crying those ugly tears.' (Remember what we learnt in the 'Self-talk' chapter!)

I talk to myself like I would talk to Michael or my son or my mum: 'I know, mate. What you've been through *was* really fucking hard and upsetting, and you're allowed to cry.' And because I've allowed myself to sit in that feeling of frustration and anger and disappointment and hurt, those feelings dissipate quicker than if I had denied them.

Now, you might feel this is very much against the grain of the premise of this entire book (happiness!), but feeling like shit is okay, and normal, and actually very necessary. So don't judge yourself for feeling a negative emotion – that's what our biological wiring tells us to do. And, look, when you think about it, it's actually rather thoughtful of our minds to try to anticipate problems and avoid pitfalls.

Our emotions tell us something. They're useful. Tap into them. Don't deny them. If you're angry, allow yourself to be angry. Be curious about the feeling. All of our emotions, including the 'negative' ones, are valid.

The truth is, 'pulling yourself together' takes energy. And if you feel like shit, it feels completely inauthentic to put on a fake smile. I'll concede, sometimes we can't let how we feel dictate our behaviour. Sometimes you have a massive fight with your partner, and then need to go to your kid's Easter Parade with all the other mums. Sometimes you'll find out about your dad's cancer diagnosis just before you're about to go into a meeting. In those moments, yes, you do just need to keep your shit together until you're in a safe space.

But if you do have the luxury of not needing to 'pull yourself together', why not just allow yourself to feel disappointed or hurt or angry or frustrated or however you're feeling? Accept it and acknowledge it. Say to yourself: yeah, I feel shit, and that's okay.

Kate Sanderson, my friend and fellow survivor

Fate thrust Kate and me together: we were both trapped by the fire during that ultramarathon in 2011. We tackled our recoveries very differently – Kate quietly gets the job done, whereas I wanted validation at every single step – but we are both in a place now where we think we are happier than we were before the fire.

Kate works in the Coroner's Court (meaning she sees death on a daily basis), volunteers with the Country Fire Authority (meaning she regularly spends her free time with FIRE, the very thing that nearly killed us) and spends any leftover time she has with her animals, or competing in an extreme endurance event.

T: Kate, are you as happy now as you were before the fire, or happier, or not as happy?

K: I'm going to say happier. Before, I was on a path of career, property investing, achieving my financial goals. I was running from A to B, always trying to catch up. The fire has put a lot of my life into perspective, made me slow down, and I've reprioritised spending time with family and friends, and hiking and doing things that I enjoy. Almost losing my life also me realise that things like trying to get as far as you can in your career aren't important.

T: what about living with your injuries? Does that affect your happiness? Like with me, for example, if I can't open a jar, sometimes if I'm feeling vulnerable it's a painful reminder of my inadequacies. Can you relate to that?

K: What do you mean you can't open a jar? Who reminds you you're inadequate? [Kate is nothing if not exceptionally literal. One of the many things I love about her.]

T: Okay, so I want Vegemite toast, and I need to open a new jar of Vegemite.* I try to use my jar opening tool,† and I still can't open the jar. If I'm feeling normal, I'll say 'Oh well, I'll ask Michael when he's back from his surf.' If I'm feeling shit or vulnerable, I'll get really upset.

Does this stuff ever happen to you?

K: Yeah. I'm in the CFA, so when we get a page, we have to turn out within four minutes.‡ If my foot brace is off I can't respond to a call within that timeframe. I get upset about that.§

T: because your injury has affected your ability to participate in something you want to participate in?

K: Yep. And it's the same if it's a 45-degree day, and you have to wear all the gear, and a few times I've had to say no because it's just too hot. That makes me feel like I'm being judged because I'm saying no to a lot of stuff.

T: Yeah, obviously people wouldn't be judging you – they'd understand. But I can for sure see how that would make you feel.

---

* Vegemite was probably not the best example, seeing how a jar of Vegemite lasts forever.

† See turiapitt.com/happy-resources for more information about the tool I have.

‡ 'Turn out' means getting dressed in the uniform and getting into the fire truck.

§ Kate had half of her foot amputated due to her injuries.

K: I can understand if people do judge, because I haven't explained my injuries to them and how I have to wear a brace and stuff, so they're probably not aware of it.

T: And would you want to explain it?

K: There are instances when there isn't a full truck of volunteers and I feel bad as I just couldn't get there in time. So, yeah, I will have that conversation and explain it. Also, going hiking in the heat, I don't do that anymore. So they're probably the only things I still get upset about.

T: Kate, I know I rely on Michael to do things for me (like opening jars) that I can't do for myself. Is living alone for you to your benefit – in that you just figure out a way of doing things – or to your detriment?

K: I guess it depends on how you look at it. Like, if someone is there and willing to help you, then why not? Living by myself, it's made me more self-sufficient. But in a way it makes it harder for me to ask for help.

T: Yeah, I think it's awesome to be independent and self-sufficient, but it's also a good skill to be able to say, 'Hey, I need help with this.'

K: I had to do that when I got out of hospital. And it was funny because as soon as I started saying 'Yeah, I need help,' everyone around me was like, *Thank god!* They were so happy to help. They helped at the drop of a hat. I hadn't experienced that before because I hadn't asked for help before. So I don't find it hard now. I will ask for help if I need it.

T: When you look at the experience we've been through, do you spend much time thinking about it and ruminating on it? Are you grateful for it, or are you like, 'Yeah, it happened, let's get on with things?'

K: Definitely the latter. It's like, yeah, that thing happened to me eight years ago.

T: So do you think you're the same person?

K: Yes. Just more appreciative of my friends and family. Appreciative of being able-bodied, and appreciative of being back doing the things I want to do. Yeah, I can't run, but I can hike and I can get on my mountain bike.

T: See, if I think about me, I'd say I was happier than before the fire, because it's given me more appreciation and perspective of life and of the little things.

K: Yeah. I just think, *These are the cards I've been dealt, just deal with it.* And I guess maybe it's a bit of a mindset thing.

T: For sure. So what kind of things have you done to help you get to where you are now mentally? For example, I practise gratitude in the morning. [Kate gives a dismissive grunt.]

K: I don't know. Like I said, I'm pretty much the same person, but I have found volunteering has helped me, it's grounded me. I volunteer at a homeless breakfast, I visit the Burns Unit. It's just a reality check, and reminds me there are people who are so much less fortunate than me. It stops me from automatically judging people.

T: So through giving back, you're always getting a fresh perspective on your life. Do you spend much time on social media?

K: No. I'm sporadic. I have Facebook, I might check it every day for three days and then not check it for two weeks. I try to distance myself from it.

T: Why?

K: I don't want it to rule my life. Like I don't want my phone to rule my life. So if I catch up with a friend for a coffee, I put my phone away.

T: See, I think doing things like that has helped you to recover and live a really awesome life.

K: Yeah, well, I'm living the life I want to live. It's not ruled by social media.

T: So, on top of that, you've gone after some pretty big goals. Like you did XPD, Marathon des Sables, the Alps to Ocean cycle trail – you seem to like that crazy shit!* Why?

K: I used to do that stuff before my accident: I love pushing my boundaries, getting out of my comfort zone; it gives you resilience and empowerment. I think that's one of the reasons I've bounced back so well. And I think racing has helped me develop my mental toughness.

T: So how did you get or improve that mental toughness?

K: Hmm. Well, in a race you reach what you think is your limit, but then you keep going. And when you finish the race, you reflect on that moment, and I think that's

* Kate did XPD two years after our accident. XPD is the 'expedition adventure race' – a 500-kilometre race of mountain biking, trekking, kayaking and abseiling. Marathon des Sables is a 250-kilometre multi-day ultramarathon through the Sahara Desert. And the Alps to Ocean in New Zealand is a 300-kilometre cycling ultra.

what strengthens your mind. And after a while you realise it's just the human mind because you keep doing it.

T: So. You know how you're single . . .

K: Yes. Thanks for reminding me [both laughing].

T: Well, the research shows that if you are in a healthy relationship, it contributes to your happiness. A good, healthy relationship. Not a crap one. So d'you want to find someone to share your life with, or it's not a priority, or you think, if it happens it happens?

K: I've always been independent and individual. I've never been on a dating website, and I also wonder how much to reveal about myself. Like, do I say I've had an accident? Or do I not say anything in my profile and then when I see my date in real life, will they be annoyed? Do I disclose it, or do I not disclose it and risk getting berated by someone? But at the same time, I know myself and I'm not like, 'Oh, I wish I could find someone.'

T: No, definitely not. Your life at the moment is very rich and full and meaningful. I think even if you had a partner you'd still be doing all the stuff that you're doing.

Have you found the experience we've been through has made you spiritual or religious?

K: No. I think life's a random series of events. At the Coroner's Court I see really sad cases every day – people who are in a head-on collision on their way home . . . People just die.

T: I try to remember that nothing's permanent. So just enjoy what you have, while you have it.

K: That's the way I look at it: tomorrow's promised to no one.

What doesn't kill you makes you stronger

I really have a strong desire to punch people who say this to me. It's a massive over-simplification and also, um, some of the things that almost kill you profoundly affect you for the rest of your natural life.

However, some survivors of trauma acquire a better understanding of their own inner strength, a renewed appreciation for life and a strong focus on helping others.[2] The theory of post-traumatic growth explains this kind of transformation. The theory was developed by two clever psychologists (Richard Tedeschi and Lawrence Calhoun) in the mid-1990s. The basis of the theory is that people who endure adversity can often see positive growth afterwards. And so, rather than the blunt 'what doesn't kill you makes you stronger', I prefer Tedeschi and Calhoun: 'I am more vulnerable than I thought, but much stronger than I ever imagined.'[3]

According to these researchers, post-traumatic growth could take a number of different forms:

- finding personal strength
- gaining appreciation
- forming deeper relationships
- discovering more meaning in life
- seeing new possibilities

If I reflect on the hard times I've been through, I feel like I've definitely grown in these areas. And if you've been through traumatic growth, you can probably tick some of them too. Note: I am in no way saying that going through trauma is a good thing. Some people, yes, they grow as a result. Not all people do.

So how can you try to ensure that if you face trauma, you grow as a result? According to psychologist Jonathan Haidt, we must first be able to make sense of what we have gone through. Why did it happen to us, and what's the good in it?[4] It's not the challenge or trauma that causes growth. It's about our interpretation of it. We must be able to *rewrite our life story so that it's of benefit to us.*

I'll give you some examples. My life story goes a little like this: I was tragically injured in a bushfire . . . *and now I get to share my story with millions of people around the world, helping them to live happier and more confident lives.*

Paul de Gelder lost his arm and leg to a bull shark . . . *and now is one of the world's leading advocates for the conservation of sharks.*

Adam Goodes suffered terrible racial abuse from AFL fans and media commentators . . . *and was made Australian of the Year, and became one of the country's most respected campaigners and leaders.*

So, dear reader, if you've been through a traumatic event – a divorce, an amputation, an illness – anything – you can unlock post-traumatic growth by . . .

Writing your story down.

Seems almost too easy, doesn't it?

James Pennebaker invented what's called the 'expressive writing' method in the 1980s. He found that writing about traumatic experiences for as little as twenty minutes a day for three or four days produced positive changes in the writer's physical and mental health.[5] The people in Pennebaker's studies who used the time to vent got no benefit. It was the people who used the time to make sense of their experience and showed progress across the multiple days who benefited from the exercise.[6]

Pennebaker suggests writing about your situation for a maximum of fifteen minutes over four days, and not to worry about grammar, sentence structure, spelling or any of those other fiddly word things.

And, crucially, before you end your last session, in his book *The Happiness Hypothesis* Haidt recommends that you answer these two questions:

1. Why did this happen?
   and
2. What good might come out of it?[7]

This task is harder than it sounds. You're confronting reality. How can you make sense of your divorce? Of your business going bust? Of a parent's decline in health? And if you're not disposed to be an optimistic type, you'll find doing this even harder. After all, optimists have a higher happiness set-point: they see the silver lining when there are clouds of steel wool and have a disposition to look on the bright side.

One of my favourite go-to tools in this process is reframing. No, I'm not talking about reframing the pictures on your walls, I'm talking about reframing the way you view your challenges. In a nutshell, reframing means looking at the same situation in two frames – one negative, one positive.

I'll give you an example from my own life. Every year, I have about four operations. No one looks forward to surgery and, even after having had more than two hundred medical procedures, they're still not exactly a walk in the park for me. So, here's what I do. First, I look at the surgery through a negative frame. It's scary, it's painful, there are no guarantees as to what the outcome will look and feel like, I'll lose a lot of time in recovery and won't be able to do much. So, it's easy for me to feel down because I can't go outside for a run or to the ocean for a surf – the stuff I do to help me feel good. It can also be hard to keep working towards your goals when you've got to take a few weeks out.

If I looked at the operations like this, there's no way I'd want to do them!

The next thing I do is look at the procedure that's coming up through a positive frame. I get to catch up with all the medical staff who have worked with me over the years; it's a forced time-out and a break from work; I get to eat ice cream and watch as many movies as I want; I can spend all day in my pyjamas; I have a lot of visits from my friends and family; and if I want to improve myself this is part of the deal – plus, how lucky am I that I live in Australia and if I want an operation, I can afford to have one, and I can speak to my doctors and make it happen!

I use this same process whenever I face something challenging. I hope you won't mind me saying so, dear reader, but I even used it while writing this book. When I got stressed about the writing, I chose to think about you. The person reading my words. How grateful I am that I can write a book, and have people read it. That's a really incredible opportunity.

The thing about going through a hard time, recovering from a hard time and maybe even growing from a hard time, is that since we're all different, and we all have different experiences, there is not one super-size Band-Aid that can help. You might find expressive writing massively beneficial, you might find reframing to be an extremely helpful tool, and you might find my strategy of 'three wins' (we're coming to it) to be super-effective. Or, you might not. And so I'll return to my words at the beginning of the chapter – it might also be a good idea to consider seeing a trained professional to help you through.

Here's a list of some of my hardest experiences

- I was in a bus crash coming home from high school and one of my classmates died.
- My parents divorced when I was in high school.
- At university, I had a mean, controlling boyfriend who made my confidence hit rock bottom.
- I got catastrophically injured during an ultramarathon, and spent two years in recovery.
- I was made redundant from my job as a mining engineer.
- I had to endure a court case that went on for years.
- A friend and one of the surviving runners from the fire, Martin Van De Merwe, died while he was training for an adventure race.
- I've made a couple of big mistakes in my business, ones that have lost me a lot of money.

A lot of these experiences were shit.

Actually, all of these experiences were shit. Looking back on all of them, and reflecting on them, I'm able to pinpoint what they taught me, and thus be grateful for them. However, it is *not* imperative for you to 'find the lesson' the same day you're handed a cancer diagnosis. It's important and beneficial for your mental wellbeing to be able to say: 'What I'm going through right now is hard.' The lesson? It comes with hindsight, my friend. But trust that it is there.

I've got some final tips for how you might handle hard times, and then we'll move on. Deal?

Okay, first up . . .

Three wins

When I was still in hospital, every night before I went to sleep I'd make a little mental list of things that I'd done well. Part of me thought that my list was pathetic. *Walked two laps of the hallway.* Can someone give me a fucking medal? But this process of listing your 'wins' is not only scientifically valid, it's also a psychological leap forward in retraining your brain, because most of us, when we go to bed at night, rehash all the ways our day went wrong.[8]

So instead, I want you to try listing three wins. Doing so can also help you to practise reframing. Instead of allowing your thoughts to wander to observations such as, 'I said something really dumb in that meeting this afternoon,' you could recall, 'I learnt some really interesting stuff in our meeting today.' Or instead of dwelling on how rude your child was to you this morning, you could remember how kind he or she usually is.

These might not sound like things to focus on if you are in the middle of an ordeal that's blown open your life, but the evidence is that such approaches can help. In a study undertaken by a Catholic Family Services organisation, one of the key protective factors for their workers in traumatic environments was: 'It is imperative that a culture of celebrating wins and the elevation of clients' voices feature prominently in everyday workday practices. Strength-based narratives can contribute to enhancing and developing resilience in staff and directly contribute to a vicarious resilience-informed approach.'[9] And in one of the first research pieces about small wins, psychologist

Karl Wieck talked about breaking down serious problems into a set of small wins, which helps create an environment where change is not overwhelming.[10]

Use your strengths

All of us have strengths. And all of us have different strengths. Maybe you have a wicked sense of humour, you love learning, you have an incredible zest for life. Maybe you're gifted at teamwork or have a high degree of self-control or you're humble as fuck. Or maybe you know you must have *some* strengths but you have no idea what they are (and if this is you, please go to the Resources section for a great tool!).

You might believe that you can become more resilient and optimistic by weeding out your weaknesses, when in fact, the opposite is true.[11] By simply focusing on our strengths we feel good about ourselves, which is an inherently motivating way to feel, and hence we are more likely to believe in our capacity for recovery.[12] Just like the 'Three Wins', by focusing on your strengths, you're training your brain to focus on the positives.

•

Other people's hard times

Now I want to go through some tips to help you to help someone *else* through a hard time. I'm gonna keep this simple. Because, really, it is simple. When someone you know is going through a hard time, you just have to *be there* for them.

Yet that's not something we're taught how to do! It can feel awkward when a friend is having a tough time, or experiencing grief or loss. Like, what do you even say?

Well, here's my guide.

The Do's

1. Do say something

Sometimes people are so afraid of saying 'the wrong thing' that they don't say anything. At all. Don't do this. If you don't know what to say, here are some words to try:

> 'I'm so sorry. I don't know what to say, but what you're going through is hard/tough/shit and I'm here for you.'

> 'I'm here for you if you ever want to talk. Like now. Or later. Or in the middle of the night.'

> 'I know you don't know yet what will happen – and neither do I. But you won't go through this alone. I will be there with you every step of the way.'

2. Do be proactive

Don't ask, 'How can I help?' The person has just gone through something horrible. They might not want to ask for help, or know how you could help. By asking this question you're putting the need for help back on to them to deal with. Offer specific ways you can help. When you're at the shops or buying groceries, pick up extra toilet paper or food and drop it over. Call them and say, 'I've made an extra-large pot of chicken soup, I can drop it over tomorrow afternoon. Is that okay?'

3. Do tell stories

If someone has died, tell stories about them – share how they had an impact. Remember, the grieving person is thinking all the time about who they've lost. You're not going to upset someone more by bringing up that person, or by sharing a story about them.

4. Do encourage support

Encourage the person to find support from people who have been through the same situation, via support services (to which you could offer to accompany them); also, you could encourage them to seek help from a psychologist or counsellor. Make a list of local support groups or helplines they could look into.

5. Listen, be present, check in, follow up

One text or one call is not enough. Also, what does 'I'm here for you' look like to you? Don't let time/distance/money be an excuse – 'being there' can mean lots of different things. If you can't physically be there, find another way to show up. You can call and leave a voicemail or a text message – but don't do this just once, do it regularly. 'Hey, mate, was thinking of you, love you. Give me a call back if you're up to it, otherwise I'll try again next week.'

Remember, you can support the person in the way that you feel the most comfortable. Just work to your strengths, and be consistent.

Here's what 'being there' looked like for different people during my recovery:

- My nan sent me a letter and a box of chocolates every week for a whole year. I got fifty-two letters that year!
- My mum cooked for me every day.
- My brother, who's into fitness, would come in to hospital and do a training session with me.
- My dad would have conversations about science with me.

If you're a movie buff or a big reader, send a movie recommendation or a book you think they would enjoy.

Make them a playlist on Spotify. Cook them your signature dishes.

Whatever 'being there' looks like to you, do it and do it consistently.

6. Do draw a circle

Let me fill you in on a theory created by psychologist Susan Silk and writer Barry Goldman. Here's how it works: draw a circle. In this circle, write the name of the person who is going through a hard experience. Now draw a larger circle around the first one. In this ring, put the name of the person closest to that person. In each larger ring, put the next closest people. Partners first. Parents and children before other relatives. Intimate friends in smaller rings, less intimate friends in larger ones.[13]

The person in the middle can say anything she wants to anyone, anywhere. She can complain and moan and curse and say, 'Life is unfair' and 'Why me?' Others can say those things too, but only to people in larger rings. Make sense? So if you're talking to someone in a ring smaller than yours, don't bitch and moan about how the situation is affecting you. Instead, listen, be supportive, offer help. And, if you do want to vent, or rail against the unfairness of the situation, go ahead: but only to someone in a bigger ring.

The Don'ts

1. Don't say 'It's going to be okay.'

You don't know that. It's easy to feel like you want to make things better for the person experiencing pain or grief. But don't sweep their pain under the rug. Be real with them.

2. Don't offer up platitudes

Stuff like, 'Everything happens for a reason,' 'God only gives you what you can handle,' 'They're in a better place.'

3. Be particularly careful with statements about faith and spirituality.

Your faith might be an important part of your life and how you deal with hard times, but don't assume to know the beliefs of others, especially when they are experiencing major loss or grief.

4. Don't say 'at least'

'At least you didn't lose your whole house in the flood.' You're forcing gratitude on someone during a time that is really tough to handle. Also, don't share stories about other people who've been through a similar experience with a worse outcome. If your friend's partner has just died, she doesn't need to know about your other friend whose partner and sister died the same week.

5. Don't expect acknowledgement for nice things you've done straight away, or ever.

When I was in recovery, someone sent me flowers and then rang me up to check that I'd received them, and then reminded me to water them because they cost $60! Not cool. People appreciate your efforts to be there for them, even if they don't have the capacity to thank you. Normal rules of society don't apply. It's not rude that someone in trouble hasn't been in touch. Just keep being there for them.

Adversity. Hard times. Wading through shit.

However you want to splice it and dice it, all of us are going to go through periods in life that aren't particularly comfortable and that we'd rather not take part in, thank you very much. I like what Mark Manson said to me about hard times: 'Adversity is inevitable. Our minds delude us into hoping if we just do X, Y and Z, we'll never have to deal with adversity, and it's not true. Adversity is the constant of life. Therefore, you might as well look for the struggles and problems that feel meaningful and important. That's really all happiness is – being satisfied with one's problems.'

My opinion? I totally agree with Mark: hard times are inevitable, so my perspective is to accept that in moving through them, we can learn as much as possible about ourselves and others. Hard times are, eventually, critical to measuring happiness. They give us a baseline from which to compare our life, and see just another ordinary day for the glorious magic it is.

Dear reader, if a hard time befalls you, please know that it's not permanent. That things can and will change. That things can and will get better. Crises come in many forms, but remember that you have the inner resources to cope with whatever life throws your way.

Mick Fanning aka White Lightning

Mick, you've had your fair share of adversity in your life. Do you think going through those tough experiences has helped you to be happier? Or has it made you unhappier? Or do you not look into them that deeply?

I do look at those experiences. I think when you hit the bottom of the barrel, you know what to expect and you don't want to feel that again. Coming off my 2015 year, which was a hell of a year – I got a divorce, I got attacked by a shark and then I lost my brother – and I got to the end of that and I was spent. I had nothing. I didn't have anything to give myself; I didn't have anything to give other people; I was just empty. So I made a conscious decision that for the next year, I was just going to concentrate on filling up my personal goals and filling up my personal fun tank. And it's definitely made me better and, I think, happier. I look at other people and my situation and I think that there are people out there who have nothing and they're still smiling and having fun. I think my life is pretty bloody good so just suck it up and get over it.

What sort of stuff makes you happy?

Being active. If that's surfing or going to the gym or going for a walk with my dog. Being active gets everything moving. I feel like if I sit still for too long I can't get enjoyment out of things. It's almost like the hamster on the wheel. Spinning the wheel is fun, and spinning the wheel creates more fun.

And so if you've gone through some sort of injury that means you can't be active as much, I would assume then that would affect your happiness?

Yeah . . . and for me it's been goals. So it's been setting weekly goals and checking in and asking, 'How am I compared to last week?' or 'How did I go with this task or this program?' I haven't been looking too far ahead at the long term. Obviously not surfing for six months is straight hell, but it's been awesome for me to reflect on where I started with this and where I am at every week. Reflection is key. When I reflect I can see that I have made progress. But I need to be able to trust the process too. It is a bit of a mind-fuck sometimes!

•

TL;DR

- Hard times happen to us all.
- When you're having a bad day, it's okay to accept it and say, 'Today's crap.' Remember, all your emotions are valid. And it's okay to not feel 'happy' all the time!
- If you've gone through (or, are going through) a hard time, reframing can be a useful tool.
- If you know someone who's going through a hard time, and you have no idea what to say, you can say this: 'I'm so sorry. I don't know what to say, but what you're going through is tough and I'm here for you.'
- Be proactive if you know someone is going through a hard time. Don't ask open-ended questions like, 'Is there anything I can do?' Be specific: 'I've made a pot of chicken soup – is it okay for me to drop it over tomorrow afternoon?'

11
Fun

I don't know about you, but on days when I've had some fun (we'll come back to what that might look like and how you can make it happen), I feel more light-hearted, I have more energy, I'm in a better mood, I'm more productive; I'm *happier*. Typically, you look forward to fun, even though not all parts of fun *are* fun. Case in point: I find spending time with Michael and my children fun. What I don't find fun is arranging with Michael who's taking Hakavai to swimming and who'll be home in time to read him bedtime stories. And spending time with Hakavai: some parts are sheer euphoria. But not all parts (like shepherding him into the car for said swimming outing and him having a meltdown because I won't let him get an ice cream).

Surfing can be fun. But it can also be hard work and frustrating. Travelling can be fun. But airport delays and realising you've booked accommodation in the wrong city isn't. Shopping online can be fun, but blowing your budget less so. And shopping IRL can be fun, but sometimes the hover mode of assistants can be stressful. *I'm just browsing! Let me have a look! If I need help of course I will ask BUT AS I'M JUST BROWSING I DON'T NEED HELP JUST YET, DO I?*

The things we find fun can also be hard work. And the things we find fun aren't necessarily fun in every moment.

How do I get fun into my life? Well, to take it back to the time straight after I got injured, was my life fun? Fuck, no. I had to endure agonising bandage changes every day. I was dealing with the emotional toll of my life being so changed. I was severely limited in what I could do. I was living with my in-laws (love 'em, but still) and the dynamics of Michael and my relationship turned upside down: suddenly we weren't young lovers; it was a patient–carer situation.

BUT. When I did have the occasional fun moment (laughing at Mum when she imitated the doctors, watching an episode of *SeaChange*, escaping into a book) I would try to hold on to it and enjoy it.

As gradually I recovered, both physically and emotionally, I found that the work I'd discovered for myself, my business as I built it up from the ground, was for the most part for me fun. I work with fabulous, funny, smart colleagues and I'm proud that in my business fun is *central* to how we operate – in fact, having a sense of humour is one of our values.

Having said all of this, it's *very* easy – for me, and I'm sure for a lot of you out there, too, in this crazy world we live in now – to stifle fun in favour of being *more productive*. We're all guilty of this. Even though we know we'd find half an hour doing *insert your brand of fun* far more enjoyable than doing the laundry, we feel *more productive* by getting shit done. And so, unfortunately, the laundry often/usually/always wins.

Some time back, when I reflected on how I was spending my days, I felt sad to realise that often I was being a bit of a killjoy. If I was struggling on a work project, I found it hard not to let that negativity spill into my home life. But even when I was having genuine fun – jumping on the trampoline with Hakavai, say – I found it hard to turn off the 'I must be *productive!*' soundtrack that blared like a megaphone in my head; hard not to think of other ways I could be using my time effectively.

The easiest and best way for me to squash my inner killjoy?

Two things. Number one, staying mindful (see page 67). I try not to get too caught up in the future, and all the things that need doing, and focus on what is happening right here and right now. Staying in the moment is hard, for adults anyway. Young kids have a knack for it, a completely devil-may-care attitude to life in general, and there's plenty of evidence to suggest that we should do everything we can to encourage their spontaneity and their ability to play.[1]

And number two, if I was naturally interested in something, I would allow myself to see where the path would take me. Case in point, I recently decided that bush foods were fantastic and it would be fun to know more about them. I signed up for and went on several bushwalks – informative and interesting and fun. I purchased a variety of books about bush foods. I went on walks with Hakavai to look for certain bush foods. After that, I decided to better organise the photos and notes I had on bush foods. So I started up a spreadsheet. I was happily copy and pasting, inserting and changing fonts, when I had a deflating thought: *Where does this road lead? Will I be asked to speak at bush-food panels? Will I write a treatise on bush foods? Will I ever be an expert on bush foods? No, of course I won't. So why bother?* (Gah! Us adults can be so . . . boring.)

I've had to teach myself that it is precisely *doing* the fun thing that is the point. Not where it will end, or whether it will contribute to a 'productive' day – whatever that means, since a productive day could just as well be about enjoying yourself as it could be about producing lots of Excel spreadsheets.

I'm a novice with bush foods. There's lots of walks and guides on bushwalks that I'm interested in, and I have done a few, but there's also a whole heap that I haven't got around to. That's okay. If I enjoy an activity, if it allows me to switch off, if it allows me to be mindful, to be in flow, to spend quality time with my family . . . then it's okay with me.

Fun as a job

Although we all need to make time for cool activities that give us pleasure, and often we have to make time for them – not just let them magically unfold – when you lead a full life, seeing friends, going out, sitting down to plan or do a nice activity, can, at worst, be just another thing to add to your to-do list. Fun stuff isn't supposed to be a chore, though. And feeling rushed every second of your day, constantly checking your watch and wishing the person you're having coffee with would ask for the bill because you have to get to the butchers before they shut so you can buy the sausages your mother-in-law asked you to get before you go pick up your child and have to deal with your own mother telling you that your son needs three spare pairs of shoes and why didn't you remember to pack a hat before fielding phone calls from a colleague who wants to know if you saw her email about the content piece she was editing that afternoon . . . is not fun at all. In an already overscheduled life, organising 'fun' can be a drain.

Case in point: a while ago Michael, Hakavai and I had tickets to go see The Wiggles. I'd been eagerly looking forward to the concert for months. (I'm not sure if Hakavai realised what was going on.) The concert was in Sydney, where we do not live, so I booked a hotel. That's fun, staying in a hotel, I thought. Luxury fun, even! I booked the deluxe room. $380 a night.

We got to Sydney and went to the beach, because we're a beach family and going to the beach is fun. Michael and I had a fight at the beach. We parked at the hotel, $25, and retreated, grumpily, to our (overpriced) deluxe suite.

To put us in a more fun mood, Michael went off to find a bottle shop to get some beers and I ordered takeaway. $78.

Our takeaway arrived and I took Hakavai downstairs to pick it up. On the way back to our room we got out at the wrong floor and had to wait for another lift. As we waited, ten debutantes and their partners came out of their rooms. The lift arrived and they filled it.

We got the next lift – to the right floor. I opened up our Vietnamese takeaway. It looked suspiciously Chinese. The spring rolls were odd, the fried rice soggy, the chicken stir-fry gluggy.

We went to bed. At 1 am I was woken up by the debutantes partying on the floor above. Electronic beats were pulsing their way through the ceiling, high heels clattered above us. Hakavai woke up. He was not happy.

In the morning we went back to the beach and had breakfast. Hakavai didn't eat; Michael and I argued about how much he wasn't eating.

We decided to go shopping. It took us an hour to park; we had approximately ten minutes to shop before we had to head to the concert. ($6 for parking.)

We went to The Wiggles. On entry we were accosted by a woman selling balloons and stars. I bought a star for Hakavai. $25. Hakavai started crying and pointing at the over-priced food. I gave him the healthy snacks I had packed and he promptly threw them on the floor. Because I desperately wanted to redeem the day, I lined up for twenty minutes and bought a cookie and a chocolate milk for Hakavai. He didn't want them. So I glumly chomped my way through his snacks, thinking what a dismal disappointment the weekend was.

Forty minutes into the show, Hakavai fell asleep. Michael said, 'C'mon, darl, let's go.' He tucked Hakavai under his arm and started making his way out. I picked up all our shit and, seething, followed Michael out. *That's it!* I screamed (in my head. I didn't want anyone at The Wiggles to know just how batshit crazy I can be). *That's the last bloody time I organise anything fun for my family. They're a bunch of whingers.*

We piled into the car and started the long drive home. Hakavai started singing 'Big Red Car'. And Michael and I looked at each other and smiled.

So, did we have fun? Overall, this weekend, which I'd been looking forward to for a long time, didn't turn out to be that much fun at all *in the moment.* Sometimes high expectations don't translate into a brilliant experience. And even though, while it was happening, the weekend wasn't super-fun, it was definitely memorable, unlike a lot of my weekends, which, although nice enough, are sometimes as bland as mashed potato with no butter, salt or pepper. And reflecting on and savouring the weekend, drawing on that memory bank, has amplified its 'fun' factor.

I'll give you another example. When I was seventeen, I went to New Zealand to work at the ski fields. As the snow season came to a close, I started travelling around the South Island with some friends. We ended up staying in a backpacker hostel in Christchurch. There was a Govinda's vegetarian restaurant around the corner, with all-you-can-eat soup, rice and curry for $5. In other words, heaven for a broke little Turia.

But in Christchurch, slowly but surely, my friends started to leave me. One by one, they jetted off to far-flung destinations . . . leaving the curry and me. One day, friendless and bored, I went down to the hostel's front desk to see if there were any day trips I could go on.

There was a line of people waiting at reception, so I plonked myself down on the couch, next to a rosy-faced, curly-haired German girl. I said hello and we got talking, swapping stories and regaling each other with our travels so far.

German chick: 'Ah yes, you must go to Iceland, it's exquisite, I spent two weeks sleeping at the foot of a volcano, and every night I'd watch the Northern Lights while I played my *Schäferpfeife*.'

Me: 'There's a really good vegetarian restaurant around the corner.'

When the line had cleared, the hostel receptionist (who looked exactly like Jemaine from *Flight of the Conchords* – tall, square-ish head, rectangular glasses) waved hello to us and asked 'Who's next?'

Wanting to showcase the manners of Antipodean folk, I motioned for my new German friend to go first. They got discussing the various glaciers and fjords she could visit, and once she'd decided on a tour, she went to pull out her credit card. But she couldn't find it. And with a flush of panicked rage, she turned around, looked at me, and accused *me* of taking it. She started screeching, 'What have you done with it? Why did you sit down next to me? That's why you were being so nice, you wanted to distract me! Search her!'

And the next thing I knew, Jemaine's doppelgänger had got up from behind his desk, asked me to stand up and started to pat me down – looking for her credit card. Even though I knew I hadn't taken it, I started to shake. I went bright red and stammered over and over that I hadn't taken it, before finally running up to my dorm room in tears.

Point of this story? Was it fun being accused of being a common thief? No. Would I have preferred to have been accused of pulling off a multi-million-dollar diamond heist armed with only a pocket knife and a box of matches? Of course. But has this interaction provided me a lot of fodder and dareisayit – fun – rehashing it with various friends? Nah. Not really. But I try. And one day I'll visit Iceland. Which does sound fun.

Actual fun

In lots of ways what I talk about in this chapter is connected to my chapter 'Zest'. Enjoying ourselves, having an appetite for pleasure and joy, are such important contributors to our mental wellbeing; and that kind of good energy almost always translates into a feeling of lightheartedness; at its best into delight.

As we touched on earlier, children are great role models where fun's concerned, and the younger the better. (Although maybe not a newborn young. Those neonatals, lovely as they are, aren't up to very much apart from the ol' eat-sleep-poo-repeat.) When you watch a group of kids playing with a ball, or building Lego, or immersed in a game of hide and seek, or tag, or in a fantasy world they've created, they are unself-conscious, most likely full of energy, contentment, excitement. They're focusing hard, calm and they're . . . happy.

Children have a sense of playfulness, adventure and curiosity that adults could learn a lot from. Hang on, though – we were once children, too, right? We've all experienced that immersion of jumping up and down on a trampoline over and over again to get a funny feeling in our tummies. And if you haven't experienced that stuff – you should try it *now*! But, um, maybe get your pelvic floor checked out first.

So, how can we channel a child's love of play, their endless interest and curiosity, when we've got rent to pay, bills piling up, mouths to feed and stacks of work to finish? Obviously it doesn't have to be Fun by Trampoline (though I highly recommend you try that once).

We all have a right to enjoy ourselves, to lose ourselves in something we enjoy, and the benefits of doing that are enormous. So before we delve into working out the fun activities that suit you and your life, I wanted to talk a bit about the power of play and its benefits.

Passion and play

There's a bloke in England called Ken Robinson, who did a TED talk on the power of creativity. It's been watched close to 65 million times. So, yeah, it's a pretty good one (see the Resources section). In his book *Finding Your Element* he describes your 'element' as being the intersection of your aptitudes and your passions – in other words, what you're good at and what you love to do.[2] Lots of people spend time doing things they're good at but they don't necessarily like. So if you can find something you love, even if you're not the best at it, that's a great step in the right direction towards fulfilment and fun. Robinson observes that if 'you're doing something you love, by the end of the day you may be physically tired but spiritually energised'.[3] When I relate this to my own life, and how euphoric I feel after a big trail run, or after a great day of writing, it feels true to me. It's about energy, says Robinson, and what stirs your energy. And, of course, energy = happiness.

So, how do we find stuff that can fill us with passion and enliven our days?

Write a fun list and make time for it

You may already know what you find fun. Or you may have no bloody idea. If you're not sure what you find fun, answer this question: what did you like to do for fun as a kid? Maybe you liked looking at rocks, reading, pretending to be Nancy Drew, listening to Mozart?

As a ten-year-old, I used to spend my pocket money buying *Archie* comics, and I'd record myself on an audio cassette reading from the comics, using different voices for different characters. And then? I'd make my whole family listen to the recording. So honestly, there's no judgement from me – whatever tickles you.

Whatever you find fun, I want you to write it down in a list that we're going to call – wait for it – a Fun List. And *then* I want you to write out how long each activity normally takes.

Why am I getting you to do this seemingly fruitless task? It's my opinion that most of us believe we don't have enough time for fun. And, granted, some of the activities on your fun list (partying in Ibiza?) might be difficult to squeeze into a Tuesday arvo. But, some of the activities (doing a Sudoku puzzle) might only take you fifteen minutes.

For example, I find going for a bushwalk highly enjoyable, but it's a two- to three-hour activity, minimum. Reading is an enjoyable activity, and is something I can do anywhere at any time. On my list, I've allowed twenty minutes for a spot of book reading.

Making a cup of tea to go with a homemade slice comes in at around ten minutes and can be done in between conference calls. Texting Michael or my family or friends makes me feel good, and takes less than five minutes.

For more activities that could be included, I asked my letter gang* what they did for fun:

- Fun to me is anything in the water – sitting in the bath tub, floating in the pool or in the lake. I just LOVE the feeling of the water and feeling sort of weightless :). – **Gena**
- I love riding a segway. Like flying on the ground. – **Debra**
- I make quilts for fun! I love the fabric selection, cutting it up to sew it back together and seeing the end result. But best of all is seeing the look on the face of the recipient. Fun comes in all guises. – **Caroline**
- My fun activity is cycling around the neighborhood on my unicycle. It's not only fun for me, but makes any adults I pass smile and kids are fascinated. – **John**
- Riding horses! – **Rebecca**
- Drinking gin and online shopping! – **Mel**

---

* My newsletter list, but saying 'letter gang' makes me feel heaps cooler.

- I get my kicks by roller skating. I did it when I was about 12 and loved it. So bought myself a pair of $800 skates (I know, right!) and am loving it. Brings a smile to me each time I do it. – **Charlotte**
- I love doing brain training exercises that make me think and are really enjoyable. Bonus: you are exercising the one muscle you can't really move when doing other exercises. – **Kimbo**
- A couple of years ago I bought one of those inflatable T-Rex suits. So far I've worn it at the beach, to the post office, the hairdresser, my local café and when I took my best friend's kids to see Santa. Sure, you get dogs barking at you, but it's pure random fun at no one's expense and everyone has a good laugh (and usually a selfie). Last weekend I was MC at the wedding of my friend's daughter. She asked if Rexy could put in an appearance, so after the formalities were done, the T-Rex appeared and started twerking on the dance floor. Is this the part where I mention I'm a forty-nine-year-old woman? You're NEVER too old for random fun! – **Sandra**
- Fun for me is lots of things:
  - sipping mimosas with my best friends on the couch while we laugh about the silly things we did ten years ago
  - going for a run by the sea
  - going to a HIIT class with new gym friends who make me laugh
  - eating food – duh!
  - preparing a healthy dinner while watching *Kath & Kim* on repeat
  - having a family dinner

- spending time with my partner doing the smallest things like a trip to Bunnings or having a dips platter on our patio!
- patting dogs at the beach. – **Alice**

Friends and fun

In my chapter 'Love', I talk about how precious our friends and close relationships are. They can be a big part of us having fun. I always considered myself to be a fun person who gets tons of energy and pleasure from enjoying the company of my good friends, but at the end of one year, when I looked back on how I'd actually spent my days, I realised I'd dedicated a major part of my time to working. On a Saturday night, when Hakavai was in bed and Michael was out with his mates, I found myself ecstatic about sitting down with my laptop, a glass of red, and writing. I often *didn't* make time for my friends. If other people had organised something, I'd happily go along, but I rarely took the initiative. Hopefully good friends, who understand you, forgive that. They know that you're there for them, and they for you, and that at some future point you will go back to having fun together.

When I was working on this chapter I got a text from a friend: 'We should go to this!' It was a link to buy tickets to *Harry Potter and the Cursed Child*, a play that went over two nights. In Melbourne. I was going to be in Melbourne for work, but I'd been looking forward to escaping my family so I could actually get other shit done without constant distractions. It seemed a rather complicated and arduous mission to get the tickets and organise logistics, and would this mean we would go out to dinner as well, and the theatre wasn't in the same suburb as the hotel I was staying in and it all just seemed too hard. Plus, surely my Harry Potter fan phase had ended a decade ago?

I'm a little embarrassed to say that I finally went along – *because I was writing this chapter.* I knew the excursion would give me more to write about.

Was it a brilliant use of time? YES! It was fantastic. I caught up with my best friend. We ate our way all over Melbourne. We bought official merch at the Harry Potter play. We laughed. We shrieked. We had a sleepover. We woke up the next day and had breakfast. We both did some work. We got ready for the second night. I wore my official merch again. We got ice creams. We had a fun-tastic time.

Make time for fun. Prioritise it. You'll enjoy it, and it'll make you enjoy your life a lot more, too. After all, we're only here once. We can't spend all our hours being *more productive.*

•

TL;DR

- It's easy to stifle fun in favour of being more productive. But it's important for your happiness to be able to lose yourself in something you enjoy.
- A fun list can be a good way to focus on what you like doing, and can help you to break out of your routine.
- Having fun is a great way to try and enjoy your life that little bit more, which in turn, will make you happier.

12
Goals

You're likely to know by now that I'm a big fan of goals and goal-setting. The idea of a goal on my horizon makes me very happy, and in this chapter I'm going to explain the effect that goal-setting (and, of course, achieving!) can have on your happy-ometer.

Righto. So, we can all divvy up our lives into separate components, right? You've got your personal relationships with friends and family. Your intimate relationships. Your work. Your physical health. Your emotional health. Your finances. How much fun you have in your life and how much you give back to the world. And these areas influence each other. For example, if you're going through a divorce, you're probably distracted at work, you might be spending a lot of money going through the legal system, and the most fun you're having is using the automatic stapler at your office. So every component of your life matters. And happiness, confidence and a deep-seated sense of self-assurance come with making progress in any part of your life.

So does making 'progress' (in other words, having a goal) make you happy? A *resounding yes*! But, don't take my word for it (just a tad upset that you don't trust me is all). Research has shown that people who are striving for something significant – whether that's learning something new, raising moral kids or changing careers – are *way* happier than those of us who don't have strong dreams or aspirations.[1] The process of working towards a goal is just as important to our sense of wellbeing as actually attaining the goal; in fact, working towards a meaningful life goal is one of the most *important* strategies for becoming lastingly happier.[2] In the words of our friend Ralph Waldo Emerson, 'It's not about the destination, it's about the journey.'

Goals are critical to our happiness. Why? Having a goal provides us with purpose (what am I up to at the moment? Oh, y'know. Training for a marathon). It gives us something to work towards (I need to go do my run today as part of my training program). And, it gives us something to look forward to (can't wait to eat my post-race meal of doughnuts!).

We have this idea that if something is challenging, then it's bad for us. But I don't buy that. If something is challenging you, it's fucking *fantastic*. It's stretching you, it's forcing you to grow, it's forcing you to become more. And honestly? If you're not growing, if you're not challenging yourself, if you're not learning, then by definition you are stagnating.

Mick Fanning is a fan of challenges and the effect they can have on your day-to-day life:

> Yeah, for sure you have goals, like, you want to win this, and you want to win that, but I always found that I performed better when I focused on performance and enjoyed the process of it

> all . . . and when I challenged myself without worrying too much about what the outcome would be. Easier said than done!
>
> I would set goals for my performance, so I wouldn't need to worry about my results. And if I was performing well, then results should come. I think if you don't grow, that's where you're going to get stuck. Being a really big goal-setter, I would try to challenge myself weekly, and I would write my goals out and stick them on the wall . . . I was always looking at ways of trying to improve myself, it was a process of constant refinement; I never let myself get stuck in a stagnant place where I was bored with what I was doing. Once you're stuck and feeling like your routine or what you're doing is boring, that's when the darkness starts to creep in.

Now we've got that sorted, let's dive into what a goal is. You may know that I have a course dedicated to helping people achieve their goals: my School of Champions. In the School of Champions, I call goals 'champies', short for Champion Quests. Maybe it's a bit silly, but I reckon you've gotta make these things fun, otherwise what's the point?

So, when I talk about goals, I'm talking about champies. And a champy is not just something on your to-do list. This ain't no 'change the hallway lightbulb' territory. A champy is a goal that sets the bar a little higher. It's a goal that will force you out of your comfort zone in order to achieve it.

How do you know if a champy is right for you and if it will make you happy? *You don't.* That's the bad news. You might think you want to become a world-class harpist. You spend thousands on a beautiful wooden harp, you get the lessons, and you practise morning, noon and night . . . and three months later you might realise that you fucking *hate* the harp.

There are no guarantees. But I do have some tools to help you out before you take the leap.

Firstly: the champy checklist

If your champy doesn't make you a little uncomfortable and nervous, it might not be a champy worthy of you. I use a checklist to make sure I've got a champy worthy of the title. It goes something like this:

- Is the champy something you actually want or desire?
- Does this champy scare you a little?
- Are you nervous about your capabilities to achieve it?
- Does it stretch you?
- Does it force you out of your comfort zone?
- Will you be really proud of yourself once you've achieved it?
- Will you be able to look back in five years' time and say with a smile on your face, 'I DID THAT!'?

And remember, it's all relative, right? If you haven't run for two decades, and you want to sign up for a four-kilometre fun run, I would think that would definitely be a champy for you. But if you pound the pavement four times a week, then a small fun run probably won't satisfy the champy criteria. Sure, it might still be enjoyable and a bit of a social event, but you won't get that sense of personal growth that makes achieving a goal so satisfying.

Secondly: the pain-point time machine

To explain this one, I'm going to use an example. Let's say you have a champy to make your side-hustle a full-time, serious 'quit your job and tell your boss to suck it' business. Cool.

Now, imagine fast-tracking five years into the future. You haven't made the leap, you're still in your current nine-to-five job at someone else's business – a player in someone else's dream. How do you feel?

Now, fast track ten years with the same conditions. Then fifteen years, then twenty years, and finally twenty-five years. Are you happy keeping everything exactly as it is? Or has not exploring this champy become a big regret?

If you go through that exercise, and you're accepting of the status quo, AWESOME! That's fantastic. But if it shows you certain outcomes you want to achieve, use that as a guide for setting new champies.

Thirdly: don't should on yourself

A champy is not something you think you 'should' do. Don't think you should start running because all your mates run. Forget that. If it doesn't resonate with you, if it doesn't compel you, if it doesn't motivate you – it's not a champy. A champy needs to be something you *want* to do. It needs to be yours and yours alone. The research shows that you will be happier, healthier and more hard-working if you are working towards a goal that you genuinely want and that aligns with *your* interests and *your* values.[3] Which leads me into the next point.

Fourthly: I have no idea what I'm into or what I value

Yes. This is kind of a big deal. Because if you don't know what you're interested in or even what you value, how do you know what champy to set? And if you don't have a champy, are you *doomed to a life of unhappiness*?

No. You're definitely not doomed, you alarmist, you. But, there's some simple questions you could ruminate on to figure out what kinds of things you like to do.

What are you really good at? Maybe you're a good listener, an organisational whizz, you speak another language?

What do you like doing just cos it's fun? (Go back and check the 'Fun' chapter if you're so focused right now on GOALS that you've forgotten what you find fun.) Making Spotify playlists? Going out to restaurants? Bushwalking? Going to the circus?

If you had all the money in the world, what would you do? Write a book? Start a not-for-profit? Try organic farming? Learn to fly a helicopter?

Answering these questions as honestly as possible will give you some guidance as to what your interests and values are.

So, for example, if as a kid you loved making muffins, as an adult you always get complimented on the delicious meals you make, when you have free time you enjoy making soufflés, and if you had all the money in the world you'd renovate your kitchen . . . maybe something to do with cooking might be a good champy for you? Such as writing or compiling a cookbook, starting a vegan cooking blog, doing a Twenty-one-Day Muffin Invigoration challenge, undertaking a pickling course. You get the picture.

It's not the right time to start

Now you know what a champy is and should be, I'm gonna give you a red-hot tip.

It's not the right time to start. Yep. It's not the right time to train for that half-marathon, to read more, to get your driver's licence or start your own business.

It's never the right time! It's never the right time for *anything*, unless you're talking about sitting on the couch with a bowl of Ben & Jerry's watching Netflix. Here's the thing, dear reader: I don't want you to wait for some golden, flowers-falling-from-the-sky, magical moment when everything is perfectly aligned for you to start working on your champy. Because that moment, my friend, will never come. The only way to make progress is to stop waiting for the right time and *to get started right now*.

But wait! I hear you say, *I'm not ready*. Well, of course you're not, you delightful goose! You couldn't complete the goal today because you haven't done the work to achieve it. Is that as clear as mud? See, we need to start before we're ready. You might think, yes, well, when I lose those ten kilos, *then* I'll be a fit and active person and I'll be capable of trekking to the Everest Base Camp. NO! I stamp my feet like Hakavai throwing a tantrum. You've got it backwards.

Sign up to go on the Everest Base Camp trip in a year's time. Pay your deposit. Tell people you're going (research shows that making a public commitment to a goal dramatically increases the likelihood of achieving it[4]). Start fundraising. Six months out you'll remember all too clearly that you are doing Everest Base Camp in six bloody months and people have given you money for the blind dogs – oh nooooooooooo. This will do wonders to incentivise you to start training; next thing you know you're walking the ten kilometres to work every morning with your headphones on listening to gangsta AF music and feeling like a BOSS. You go to Nepal, do the trek, make it to camp, and come home with an incredible sense of confidence and self-belief. YOU DID IT, YOU LEGEND, YOU!

The white bear

If I ask you *not* to think of a white bear, what's the first thing you think of? Um, a white bear?

Our brains can't picture something that's not there. So if your champy is to *eat fewer Tim Tams*, you all of a sudden start thinking: TIM TAMS! YUMMY CHOCOLATEY TIM TAMS! Caramel Tim Tams! Tim Tam straws with a cup of tea!

My tip? Try to reframe your champy in the positive. So, instead of, 'I want to lose twenty kilograms', your champy could be 'I want to do a half-marathon.'

How to set a champy properly

What

The first thing you need in your champy-chasing journey is pretty obvious, really. (Aren't you glad you saved yourself that cash?) You need to know what you're chasing. You'd be surprised how many people don't know what it is they want. And if you're in this camp, dear reader, and are having difficulty defining what you're going after, here's a hint: write a list of what you don't want from your champy. And that will help you with what you do want. *Comprende, padre?*

The more specific you are about your goal, the more likely it is that you're gonna commit to it. Because being specific makes us accountable, it makes the goal measurable *and* it makes it tangible. So if your champy is to get fit, think about what it means to you. Is getting fit going to one yoga class a week? Or is it being the CrossFit World Champion? If your champy is to write more – does that mean you want to start a blog, or publish a *New York Times* bestseller? You might want to lose weight so you have more energy for your kids; you might want to raise money for a cause close to your heart; you might want to launch a start-up because you think you've got an idea that can make a difference in the world.

Here's an example of a very specific, very clear champy that I set out to achieve. What I wanted: I wanted to complete an Ironman within eighteen months (of deciding this was my champy). I wanted to finish the day with good form and enjoy it.

Why

The next thing you need? You need to know *why* you want to achieve your champy. Having a strong *why* keeps you motivated, and the stronger your *why*, the more likely you are to achieve your goal.

Don't believe me? Smarty pants. Let me ask you a question. Could you run 100 kilometres, right now?

For sure, most people would find the idea very un-fun, they would say no, and even people who do enjoy running long distances would most likely say something like, 'I can't right now as I haven't been carbo loading, but give me a week.'

So my next question is . . . If the person you loved the most in the world said, 'The only way you'll see me again is if you run 100 kilometres right now . . .'

There couldn't be a stronger *why* than that, right? So d'ya reckon you'd do it, or at the very least die trying?

Here's the thing: if our *why* is strong enough, we can motivate ourselves to do anything. *Anything!* Now you might be tempted to pick a *why* that's unselfish or that 'sounds good'. But the goal-getting process is harder than that. It needs you to be unflinchingly honest with yourself.

The reason I wanted to do an Ironman? I wanted to prove to everyone who doubted me that I was fitter, faster and stronger than I ever had been before the fire. That really fuelled me. I had something to prove, something to keep me going when the going got, inevitably, rocky.

I'll give you another example of why figuring out your *why* is so crucial. After the fire, I spent six months in hospital surrounded by surgeons and nurses and doctors who had literally saved my life. I was in such awe of them and for months afterwards, having realised I wasn't going back to engineering, I considered retraining to become a doctor. But when I went through the champy process – asking myself what exactly I wanted from retraining and qualifying as a medical professional, and why I wanted to do it, I realised my 'why' was quite simple: really, I wanted to help people. And there's heaps of different ways to help people! In the end, I decided there were ways to help people that were more aligned with my skills and temperament – so I started the business I have today.

As you can see, going through this two-part process (identifying *what* your champy is specifically, and *why* you want it) is critical.

Break those barriers

Let's start with a rhetorical question: wanna know what everyone has in common? Well, it's something they *don't* have. Am I talking in riddles again? Maybe. Here's what I mean: you might feel like the reason you're not getting ahead, or the reason you can't start a business, or the reason you can't develop an idea is because you *don't have* something. You don't have the time, or the money, or the support, or the contacts, or the experience, or whatever it is, to do it.

I call these, quite unimaginatively, the *don't haves*, and everyone's got them. If you're lucky, you'll have several!

Some of your *don't haves* might sound like this: 'I'm working full time so I just *don't have* the time to write my book.' 'I'm a single parent and I *don't have* any support.' 'I didn't go to the right university so I *don't have* the right networking contacts.' 'My family is stretched financially, and we *don't have* the money.'

It doesn't matter what you *don't have*, it doesn't matter what limitations you *do have*. At the end of the day they're all barriers between where you are now, and where you want to be.

But here's the good news (finally!). I have a great strategy for you that'll help you work through this. I call it: my 'barrier bulldozer'. So, put ya hard hat on, roll up your sleeves and let's get started.

I want you to list all the barriers standing between you and where you want to be. To help you, here are some that were on my list when I decided on one of my goals: running my own business.

At the time, I didn't have:

- Any media or public-speaking experience.
- A day job to tide me over financially – I'd been made redundant, I was living at my in-laws' place and Michael was my full-time carer.
- A convenient location – I lived in a regional town three hours from the closest city so when someone did agree to meet with me for a coffee, I had to ask a family member to drive the six-hour return trip.
- Any business experience – I had an engineering background so I was great with maths formulas and spreadsheets but

not so great at things like web development and social media and marketing.

- My health – I was still physically extremely vulnerable. I was still wearing my mask to help heal my skin. I had to have operations every couple of months, which meant I was missing big chunks of time that could've been spent working on my business. So to me, it really felt like I was taking one step forward and two steps back.

They were *some* of my barriers. I had heaps more. And every time I made progress, another few would crop up, *as they always do*.

So, once you have your champy firmly in mind, I want you to write down your list of barriers. And then I want you to make sure you've been really specific about your barriers. Let's say your goal is to start up a business of edible stickers. Instead of saying 'I don't have time', be really clear about what you don't have time to do. For example, 'I don't have time to cook dinner every night and also work on my new business idea.' Instead of saying 'I don't have money,' say 'I don't have enough in my savings account to pay rent this month and invest in a new camera for the photos on my blog.'

The more specific you are, the easier it will be to find specific solutions. Because saying 'I don't have time' is too arbitrary. How do you fix not 'having time'? But not having time to cook dinner and work on your business idea? There's plenty of solutions for that. You could get a slow cooker. You could ask your friends to do meal swaps, you could order a few weeks of a meal-delivery service. Don't be arbitrary. *Be specific.*

If you're a super-positive, happy person, this exercise might not sit well with you. It can feel really confronting to see all those barriers and limitations and reasons why you can't do something you want to do. That's okay! We're not going to wallow in this uncomfortable space. Instead, we're going to bulldoze through every one of your pesky barriers. And that, my friend, is going to feel really empowering.

So, now to the fun part. For each barrier on your list, I want you to find a solution: what I call a 'breakthrough'. Without knowing your exact personal circumstances and life experiences, I'm sorry, I can't figure out your breakthroughs for you. But I do have a tool that will help you. It's an acronym: S-P-A-R.

SPAR

The S stands for . . . support

This is crucial. To figure out your breakthrough, you need support! Is there a coach who helps people to do what you want to do? Is there an expert in your field who's written books or who keeps a blog about the subject you're interested in? Is there a community group or an online community of people who want to do something similar? Are there friends or acquaintances who are interested in the same goal, who can give you advice or point you to others who might support you?

For example, if you've got an incredible idea for a book, but one of your barriers is not knowing how to structure the material, well, you could get a writing mentor. You could read books on how to write a book. You could join a Facebook group for budding writers. You could join an actual writing group. How far you take this is up to you, but in short – *get support.*

The P stands for . . . perspective

Think about your barrier logically. If a friend came to you with the same issue, what advice would you give them?

What solutions could you come up with? Sometimes we get so stuck in our own heads that we can't see the solutions right in front of us. With barrier-breaking, it's all about looking at things with a new perspective. So, pretend you're looking at your situation for the first time with fresh eyes.

The A stands for . . . ask someone!

Ask a trusted friend or family member what they would do. Get them to help you brainstorm solutions, and remember, you need to try to be open to their ideas, no matter how silly you think it might be! I also want to preface this by saying you've gotta ask the *right people*. For instance, asking your Uncle Barry, who has never left his small home town, how you could generate international media interest, isn't the best idea. Sorry, Uncle Baz! Asking your friend who works in PR for a global publishing firm? Better person to ask.

The R stands for . . . research!

In other words . . . research it! I know this sounds flippant. But your barriers aren't unique. I can guarantee you they've been faced before. There are millions – literally – of websites, books, articles, magazines, journals at your fingertips in the twenty-first century. It has never been easier to research something. Yes, you can use Google to help you figure out your breakthrough; you can also visit a library, ask an expert (on or offline), check out relevant writing on the subject – however you research, though, make sure you stick with reputable sources. I wouldn't recommend gleaning all your facts on a subject from internet chat forums or Tumblr!

Motivated?

Wanna know what most people say to me? They say, 'Turia, you are so beautiful and funny and wise. If Beyoncé and Rihanna had a baby, it would be you.' Wanna know what else they say? They say, 'You're always doing so much – you must be one of those naturally motivated people, right?'

Hell, no. I don't bounce out of bed every single morning, strike a superhero pose and yell, 'Bring forth this day!' Some days I'm tired, some days I'm stressed, some days I just don't *feel* like working out or writing or having that meeting or making that phone call.

There's this belief out there, especially when you're working on a business idea or a new project or a big goal, that magically you'll click into a motivated mindset in which you'll be overflowing with excitement and energy and enthusiasm and passion and just want to get stuck in. Always.

I'll concede, some days are like that. I'm sure you have days like that too. But most of the time life's not like that. I love what fitness expert Michelle Bridges says about motivation: 'Motivation is like a bad boyfriend – never around when you need it.'

So my advice is to forget motivation and focus on *consistency*! Consistency isn't sexy. It's not ground-breaking. But it's the word you need to hear, especially right now. And what does it mean to be consistent? Well, let's say you're working on a goal or a project within your business, and it needs an hour of your time at your desk every single day. Every time you go to sit down at your desk, I want you to say these words to yourself: 'Maybe today's session will be awesome, and I'll knock it out of the park, or maybe it will be crap and I'll be totally unproductive, or maybe it will just be mediocre. That's okay. I accept all of these scenarios. It doesn't matter what happens. I just need to show up.'

And here's the truth: if you show up day in and day out, if you focus on your consistency and not on the outcome, I'm telling you, in fact I guarantee you: you will make progress.

One final thing: as you're working on achieving your goal, and maybe interacting with other people with similar goals, look out for thoughts like this: 'Oh well, it's easy for her. She's doing so well because she [*insert something you think this person has that you don't*].'

Comparing yourself to others is normal but it's also toxic (see pages 120–22). You can't make progress if you're constantly distracted by what everyone else, or even one other person, is doing. And you know what? Saying someone is, for example, 'doing so well in their business because they have a lot of money to invest' implies that you *don't have* a lot of money to invest.

Saying someone 'has a supportive partner who cooks every night' implies that you *don't have* a supportive partner who cooks every night.

Saying someone 'sold out her online course because she already has a huge list to sell to' implies that you *don't have* a list.

And what, my friend, are these? *Don't haves!*

We covered it already. A *don't have* is a barrier. These barriers are ones you've created through comparison. So, you know what to do! We've covered the steps for breaking through your barriers.

Remember, comparing yourself to others will inevitably make you feel like shit. Plus, it's a zero-sum game. Practise gratitude, use the SPAR method, and remember: the best person in the world to live your life is . . . You!

I've achieved a goal and I'm not feeling as happy as I expected

Ah yes. That deflated-helium-balloon feeling. Yes, sure, you were ecstatic about achieving your goal, and you gained more confidence and self-belief in the process of attaining the goal, and blah blah blah, but why did no one warn you that you would feel like shit not too long afterwards?

Olympic athletes suffer something called an 'under-recovery' due to the physiological and psychological onslaught that the Games entails.[5] In track and triathlons, this phenomenon is called the 'post-race blues'. You, dear reader, might have even felt like this after a major life milestone like getting married or getting a job promotion you worked so hard for.

First of all, if you're experiencing this deflated-helium-balloon feeling, congratulate yourself. Only a true champy instigates this feeling. Second of all, cut yourself some slack. You did it! You worked your ass off for your champy! Thirdly, have a brief list of things you're looking forward to that are completely unrelated to your champy. Like, y'know, sleeping in past 6 am. Eating chocolate cake with friends. Having a glass of wine, visiting a new national park, going to a salsa class.

Allow yourself to savour your successes. (Go back to the start of the book and review the section on savouring.) And remember that this 'depletion' period is very normal.

•

TL;DR

- Goals are instrumental for our happiness. Goals = progress, and making progress in our lives helps us to be happy.
- I call goals Champion Quests. Or, champies for short. It feels more fun to me.
- A champy is not something like 'change all lightbulbs in the house'. It's something that stretches you, forces you to grow and, YES, helps you make progress.
- Make sure you know *what* you're after, specifically, and more important, *why* you want it.
- Forget motivation, focus on consistency.

The End

I had this lovely little book pretty much wrapped up. The introduction sizzled, the content was weighty, the conclusion did a good job of concluding. I had even started thinking about what outfits I would wear on my book tour (yellow was an obvious colour choice, but was it too obvious? And a hair bow would indicate I was young and fun, but was it perhaps a tad too frivolous?).

And then?

The bushfires happened.

And in February 2020, when the majority of Australians took a collective sigh of relief that fire season was coming to the end, coronavirus happened.

The reality is: hard times happen to us all. You dear reader, will experience these hard times and your life won't be perfect. There are times when you'll feel hopeless, and rejected and sad.

Our emotions vary. As does our happiness. What I hope this book and these stories have taught you is that, rather than having the singular destination of happiness in our minds, it's far more important to be able to notice and appreciate the happy moments in our lives.

Happiness is made of lots of little things. Being grateful for your cup of coffee, going for a bike ride with your kids, dropping off spare lemons to your neighbours, having goals that you're working towards.

The idea that 'happy' is a sole destination is, quite frankly, a ridiculous aspiration. Because maybe 'happy' doesn't exist. But 'happier' does. I hope this book helps to set you on that journey.

Lots of love,

Turia

Oops, read this too: @spendwiththem

Fires were raging down the south coast of New South Wales and obliterating some of the most beautiful parts of our land, decimating wildlife, destroying houses and businesses in their path. Australia and the rest of the world looked on in horror at the devastation.

For me, it felt a little too close to home – literally. My idyllic coastal town was surrounded by blazes; smoke blanketed the horizon; ash was raining on our houses and in our backyards. To be honest with you, I felt extremely useless. I wasn't out fighting any fires, I wasn't jumping in a boat rescuing residents from neighbouring towns, or organising food drops. I was heavily pregnant, had a toddler at home, and I had done literally nothing to help other people affected by these fires. It was hard for me to keep a lid on my emotions; not to panic.

One Monday morning, my colleague Grace (who also lives in this area) and I were trying to get back to 'normal' and get some work done. We couldn't. We felt shit; we just couldn't focus. I showed her some stuff I'd written over the weekend and we both cried and then my mum made us an omelette.

Mum: Why don't you girls have a fundraiser?

Me: Nahhhh.

Mum: Why don't you have a soirée!?

Me: That's the same thing, Mum.

Mum: Why don't you have a ball?

Me: Mum!!!!!!

Grace: I feel really bad for small businesses. Like, the town is dead at the moment.

Me: Yeah, I know. Me too. I love that gowithemptyeskies campaign. But it's hard here, cos I don't want to be encouraging people to come down the south coast right now.

Grace: Hmm. Well, you loved that buyfromthebush campaign too, yeah? Why don't we do something like that?

Me: Jump on their Insta and buy something?

Grace: No. Like, why don't we create a platform that supports small businesses in fire-affected communities?

Me: So, we visit fire-affected communities? Or we buy stuff? I'm confused.

Grace [with accompanying eye roll]: We *start* an Insta page. Let's say, for example, we profile a homewares shop in Milton. Then anyone in Australia or even in the world can find out about the homewares shop, buy something, support the business, put money back into the local economy, and boost morale – all at the same time.

Me: *Yeah.* That sounds really awesome! Fantastic idea! And it'll be relatively easy to do. We'll just post whichever businesses contact us.

From there, things moved real quick (as in, four hours).

We needed a name! Spend With Them seemed fun and apt.

Shit, we needed a logo! Thank you, Canva.

We needed some businesses. Cue phone calls to local businesses to get them on board.

As soon as we'd done all that, we posted this to my personal Instagram account:

> Fires had been raging up and down the South Coast for close to a month. People were evacuated from Bawley Point and Tabourie Lake. Milton was hit. Michael did food and supply runs in his boat. We watched as the sky went red and black days before Christmas.
>
> More fires broke out on New Year's Eve. I watched, my mouth agape, as two angry plumes from the fires north and south of us joined together over Mollymook Beach.
>
> And then the power went out. Mobile reception became spotty. Internet was down. Rumours swirled around town like the ashes that rained down on us. Embers in our backyards. Homes had been lost. Whole streets obliterated. A girlfriend's panicked text about her dad being trapped.
>
> I packed my go bag and filled the bath with water.
>
> Michael cooked bacon and eggs on the barbecue outside. Hakavai and I read books on the balcony. We watched as the fine grey smoke settled in on our beloved Mollymook Beach.
>
> At a quarter to eight, the evening was quiet. Not a peaceful and serene quiet, but an eerie quiet. An apocalyptic quiet. No one on their balconies drinking beers. No music blaring from our neighbours next door, or from the houses across the street. No revellers preparing to celebrate the New Year. And it was dark. No power. No lights.
>
> First of all: I'm sorry that I haven't been more proactive in this time.

It's been a tough few weeks for me emotionally. I've had to focus on not letting my emotions and own experiences get the better of me. I've tried to not let the panic genie out of the bottle (because once that genie's out, you've got zero chance of squashing it back in). And, I'm exhausted. I feel like I've done ten marathons. And we can't relax because it's only the start of summer, and it's not over yet. So just like in a marathon, I've realised I have to pace myself.

A lot of things have been tough. Being eight months pregnant, with a toddler, I've felt as useful as tits on a bull. I've had recurring nightmares about running through flames with my son in my arms. It's been difficult to sleep, eat or think and all I've really wanted to do is tap out, put my head in the sand and pretend that nothing is going on.

I thought about leaving our small town of Ulladulla multiple times. Why didn't I? People were stuck in their cars for hours. I saw terrifying footage of 30 metre high flames on the side of the highway at Sussex Inlet (a town just north of us and blocking the way out). And travelling south was like travelling into the jaws of the dragon.

When I found out friends were planning on defending their property I felt like shaking them. 'You have no idea!!!' I wanted to scream. You have no idea that a fire sounds like a thousand road trains coming towards you. You have no idea how hot it feels, and that you will watch your skin bubble before your very eyes. You have no idea that the smoke will feel like it's invading every single one of your pores. And you have no idea that in those last few seconds where it's almost upon you that you will KNOW that you are about to die.

At the same time, I've felt like it's not my place to flip out when people all around me have lost everything. I'm lucky – my family and I are safe and we haven't lost anything.

Friends have lost homes, precious belongings. Lives have been lost.

And once 'this' is all over, it won't be all over for many of the local businesses in fire-ravaged towns. A lot of these places (like my home town in Mollymook, and Kangaroo Island, Mallacoota, Eden etc.) rely on the tourist dollar for their very survival. I've been motivated by Tegan Webber's #gowithemptyeskies campaign and by the legends at @buyfromthebush.

And so this is what I'm doing. If you want to buy something (now, or in the future), check out @spendwiththem. Spend your money with the businesses in fire affected communities who need it. They need you. We need you.

This is a way to put money directly in the pockets of the people and communities who need it the most, and need it NOW.

Long after the threat is over and the choppers stop flying overhead. Long after summer ends and the wail of sirens ceases in the streets.

Help them rebuild. Make them feel heard. Spend with them.

And, if you're a business in a fire-affected town, hit us up at @spendwiththem to be featured.

Much love to all of you, donating, spending, and doing everything you can. I'm blown away.

Turia xx

And then . . .

Within an hour, we had over 10,000 followers. Grace was fielding phone calls from TV stations.

(I was still working out how to switch between my personal Instagram account and the @spendwiththem Instagram account.)

With a couple of hours we had over 40,000 followers. Grace and I spent the rest of the day and evening answering calls, emails and fielding DMs. We tried to share the stories of the businesses we were featuring as soon as we could, while also allowing each enough airtime of their own. So, for example, one of our posts went like this:

> Aaliyah of @earth.air.fire.water.organics grows and sells her own herbal tea. She normally spends Monday to Thursday harvesting, drying and packaging the teas. Then, over the weekend, she sells her herbal teas at the markets. The Green Wattle Creek fire tore through her village of Buxton twice. She was trapped in Buxton with no power, food supplies or water for five days. To #spendwiththem, go check out her Instagram account and click on the link in bio to shop.

The response to Aaliyah was phenomenal. She sent us an email a couple of days after being featured, which we shared on the @spendwiththem page:

Oops, read this too: @spendwiththem

8:26
SPENDWITHTHEM
Posts
spendwiththem
1/2
I have no words to express the gratitude I have!
I could hear my phone going crazy in another room, went to investigate and saw your post and a screen full of orders!
I have missed a month of markets and your post enabled me to get that months lost income in 2 hours!!
I save sat on my floor sobbing in happiness for the last hour.
You have lifted a weight off my shoulders.
90% of the orders have beautiful words of encouragement in the delivery notes
You guys are amazing!!
Aaliyah
View Insights
Promote
Liked by staywiththemau and others
spendwiththem Two updates from Aaliyah at @earth.air.fire.water.organics. Swipe to see them both... more
View all 275 comments
megankgale

A farmer from Nowra who made goat's milk soap received thousands of orders within a few hours. A Kangaroo Islander made a year's worth of wages after one of our posts. A paddock-to-plate farmer in northern New South Wales, battling the drought as well as the fires, was overrun with orders.

At close to midnight we had finally answered every single email, and responded to every single DM.

At five the next morning we had close to 100,000 followers. We had interviews all day, we received hundreds of emails, thousands of DMs. Kelly Rowland gave @spendwiththem a shout-out. I went to bed at three in the morning. I didn't get through all the emails. And I didn't get through any of the DMs.

The third morning, I woke up to find we had 170,000 followers. I was drained, emotionally and physically, and very very tired. I realised it wasn't sustainable or realistic for Grace and me to manage the workload ourselves. (Also, my baby was due in three weeks. And, um, I was due to submit my book manuscript in two weeks.)

We started saying yes to anyone who offered to help. I roped in my sister-in-law. Mates from the surf. A friend's mum. A copywriter in Sydney. Within three days, @spendwiththem had taken on a life of its own.

•

The @spendwiththem campaign was an awesome experience. It taught me a lot of things. Like:

People want to help

If people offer, let them help. We needed the help, and offering it made others feel good. When I thanked my sister-in-law, she thanked me. Particularly in times of crisis, people want to feel as though they're making a valued contribution. I rang my publishers and had to explain that I wouldn't be able to send them the manuscript when I'd said I would. And y'know what? They understood. We came up with a plan.

Start before you're ready

You'll never be 'ready'. You'll never have all the boxes ticked and all the i's dotted and the t's crossed. You can't anticipate all of the challenges that you'll face. If Grace and I had actually fleshed out our entire plan, yes, we definitely would have done stuff differently. But then we probably would never have launched.

Let go of being perfect and focus on the positives

I'm a pretty pedantic person. If I've got a spreadsheet, I want every damn cell filled in perfectly. If you're working with a bunch of vollies from all over Australia, people who are donating time whenever they have it, things won't always be perfect and exactly as if you'd done it yourself. That's okay. Some businesses took advantage of the @spendwiththem account. We shared some businesses that were in Sydney. People screamed at us and told us we needed a PA. People's emails were lost and we had to ask them to send them again. We shared photos without crediting the photographers; we sent people to incorrect websites. I gave out the wrong email address (including spendwithme@turiapitt.com) and once I posted the @spendwiththem content to my personal Instagram page.

When we made a mistake it was hard not to beat ourselves up and question what we were doing and were we doing it well enough? But then we'd focus on the small-business owner. For example, we received this DM from Guerilla Roasters, a speciality coffee roaster on the south coast of New South Wales. They were so overrun with orders after being featured on the @spendwiththem page that they hired additional staff. It was messages and emails like these that kept us going:

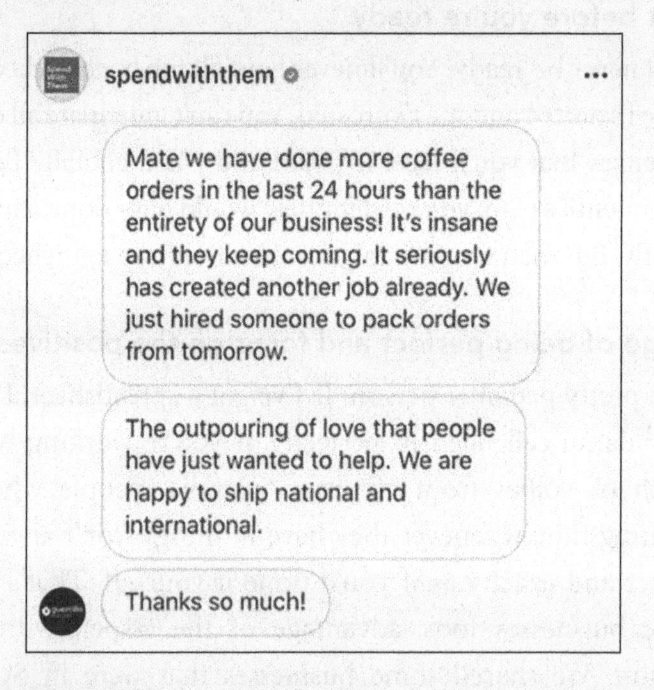

spendwiththem
Mate we have done more coffee orders in the last 24 hours than the entirety of our business! It's insane and they keep coming. It seriously has created another job already. We just hired someone to pack orders from tomorrow.
The outpouring of love that people have just wanted to help. We are happy to ship national and international.
Thanks so much!

The thing is: times of crisis shine a light on everything this book is about.

Choosing how you spend your money, checking in on your neighbour to make sure they're okay, wanting to help and then actually getting off your arse to help, taking stock of the small things – like how good a cup of tea tastes the morning after a panicked night of 'fire watch' (literally looking out the window, watching for embers, and monitoring the changing wind conditions, convinced your place is next to go . . . because it could be).

Your values come into sharp, crystalline focus in a crisis. What matters and more importantly – who matters.

I saw a man on the news during those weeks. He'd lost everything: his house, his garden. His belongings. The reporter asked, 'What have you noticed since the fire came through?' and he said, 'People hug me, and they really mean it.'

I think that's what a crisis does. A crisis cuts through the bullshit. It makes you present. It strips away the pretending. In a crisis, it's not just okay to be frank about how you feel, it's part of the deal. It demands us to step up, it betters us and among all the grief and anxiety and deep, immense loss, it helps us tap into what it really means to be 'Happy'.

your values come into sharp, crystalline focus in a crisis. What matters—and more importantly, who matters.

I saw a man on the news during those weeks. He'd lost everything: his house, his garden. His belongings. The reporter asked, 'What have you noticed since the fire came through?' And he said, 'People hug me, and they really mean it.'

I think that's what a crisis does. A crisis cuts through the bullshit. It makes you present. It strips away the pretending. In a crisis, it's not just okay to be frank about how you feel, it's part of the deal. It demands it of us, in depth. It reflects us, and among all the grief and agony and deep, extreme loss, it helps us tap into what it really means to be human.

A series of questions that lots of people ask me lots of the time (otherwise known as FAQs)

How do you define happiness?

Well, it's a bit of a long story. Sonja Lyubomirsky, who's a happiness researcher, reckons the 'concept of "happiness" refers to the experience of joy, contentment or positive well-being, combined with a sense that one's life is good, meaningful and worthwhile'.

I personally reckon it's feeling good most of the time, and feeling good about yourself and your life (again, most of the time). And I reckon that *we know* when we're happy. If work is going great and we're about to go on a date with a nice person, we feel good about ourselves. If we've finally got enough money together for a deposit on a house, we feel proud. Or, if we're volunteering with our local Landcare club, it gives us a sense of purpose and perspective about our own lives.

On top of that? Happiness is mutable *and* it's subjective.

Things that make me happy (bushwalking! Spending time with my family! Reading!) might be different to the things that make someone else happy (ice sculptures! Sand sculptures! Ice and sand sculpting!).

(For more, see 'Kindness'.)

How do you know when you're truly happy?

Hmmm. I don't think we can ever say, 'Yep. I've reached the final destination of Truly Happy Station.' Often, we think we'll be happy when we get a promotion/get married/lose ten kilograms/teach our Shetland pony how to roller skate. That's the arrival fallacy, yeah?

In my opinion, happiness is more of a continuum, a spectrum, a wiggle line. Sometimes we feel really happy, other times we don't, but that doesn't mean we're not content with our lives. I think we need to let go of this idea of 'One day I'll be happy', and focus on doing small things every day that make us happier.

(For more, see 'Self-talk'.)

How can I stop comparing myself to others, and learn to be grateful for my own life?

Well, cowgirl, looks like you answered your own question. Gratitude for your own life is the best way to stop comparing your life to other lives. I practise gratitude by thinking of three things I'm genuinely grateful for in my life, every morning. The smaller the better. Maybe you've got a knee injury and you're grateful that your boss has been understanding about it. Maybe you're grateful for your friend who you get a pedicure with every fortnight. Or maybe you're grateful for your fire on cold winter nights.

Remember, comparing yourself to others is a zero-sum game. You can do anything, but you can't do *everything*. Your energy, money and time are finite resources. So if you spend them on becoming the world champion of chess, that most likely means you can't simultaneously be the world champion of surfing. Comparing yourself to someone else doesn't make a whole heap of sense because we've got no idea what they've decided to focus their finite resources on.

(For more, see 'Self-love'.)

How to be happy if you're single?

A good, healthy relationship can be fantastic. It can be enriching to build a life with someone. But you can feel unhappy no matter your relationship status. Because, yes, you can be happy in a relationship, but you can also be unhappy in a relationship. An intimate relationship isn't vital for your happiness.

My advice is this: focus on all the moments in your life that make you feel good. Maybe you feel good when you tick off a task on your to do-list at work, or get stuck in to a DIY project at home. Maybe you feel good when you sit and enjoy a coffee in the sunshine, or go for a run, or jump into the ocean on a cold day, or when you go for a bushwalk. Focus on creating more of those moments, and being grateful for the moments you've had.

And in regards to finding a partner – one who adds happiness and companionship to your life? Well, I don't have a failsafe strategy for this (if I did, I'd be making millions as the female Hitch). There's no doubt that luck is a component of finding the right partner, but it's not the only component. Focus on being the person *you* want to spend time with. Do the activities you enjoy doing, hang out with people who make you feel confident, and (don't hate me saying this), put yourself out there. Go on dates, ask people out. Easier said than done, I know, but the platitudes are true: all the best stuff happens outside your comfort zone. And you'll learn more about what kind of relationship will make you happier if you do the work (dating, actively trying to meet someone) than you will by reading about it in this book. Even though I appreciate you reading my words!

(For more, see 'Love'.)

As a mum, how do you not forget about you?

It's so, so, so easy to put our kids first. It's our instinct: we're wired to do everything in our power to help them survive and thrive. But our instinct isn't designed to optimise our happiness! Everyone's different, but since you're asking *moi*, I'll tell you. Every day, I try to do something for . . . me! On a good day that's a surf, on a bad day with sick kids and a partner who's away, it might be writing a page or two of my book with a glass of red wine at night. I know that on the days where I do prioritise myself, and prioritise spending time with myself, I'm far less likely to be shitty and resentful with my family, and I'm a way better mum and partner.

(For more, see 'Morning routine'.)

Should we feel guilty or sad or bad for feeling happy?

Look, feeling guilty about feeling happy when others aren't is like not eating your dinner because there are kids starving in the world. It's a show of solidarity, for sure, but it doesn't put food on someone else's plate. Having said that, if you are privileged enough to be living a good life, and a happy life, why not shake some of that happiness around? Get out of your head and shift your attention and energy and focus on to others. Volunteer at your local homeless shelter, sign up to weed local bushland in your area, make a meal for someone you know who's lonely.

(For more, see 'Kindness'.)

Is having children a key part of being happy as we get older? Well, friend, here's some potentially disheartening (or heartening, depending on which way you're leaning) info. Kids are a major cause of marital conflict. They are a financial sinkhole. You have less sleep, less time, less money, and probably less sex.

Whereas a life without kids? It's potentially filled with career opportunities. Travel! Business-class travel! Travel to kid-free luxury island retreats.

Now, let me be perfectly clear: our sons bring Michael and me so much joy. They fill me with wonder, amazement and gratitude, and they have changed me for the better. And, despite everything I've just listed, I reckon I'd be hard-pressed to find a mum or dad who felt that, no matter how hard parenthood can be, their kids haven't brought them some happiness.

So, it's obviously a conflicting and highly personal arena we're entering with this question. Everyone you talk to will have a unique answer.

But you did ask for my advice, so here it is: if you genuinely don't want children, then own it! I don't think it's selfish to not want kids – it's far more selfish to have kids without feeling you really want them. Kids need energy, your time, your commitment. So if you're unsure, that's okay. It's uncomfortable not to conform to society's expectations. But it's even more uncomfortable to make a life-long commitment to something that *you weren't even sure you wanted in the first place.*

And ultimately, making the decision to have kids should have nothing to do with *our* happiness and everything to do with our kids' happiness.

(For more, see 'Money' and 'Fun'.)

I don't know if I'm happy. I think I am happy, and I have certain moments in my week when I am overwhelmed with a sense of joy, but soon I'm back to being me.

Well, my friend, you have hit the proverbial nail on the head. You can be happy, but that doesn't mean you have to be happy all the time. All our emotions are valid – including the uncomfortable ones such as jealousy, envy, anger, resentment. And if you feel angry or bored or just *bleh* – acknowledge and accept it. Part of happiness is accepting that we're not going to be happy all the time. I don't call it a ridiculous aspiration for nothing.

References

Introduction

1 Probably my favourite study on augmenting our happiness levels is by Sonja Lyubomirsky, Kennon Sheldon, David Schkade, 'Pursuing Happiness: The Architecture of Sustainable Change', *Review of General Psychology*, 9(2):111–31, 2005. This study is summarised nicely in Sonja Lyubomirsky's book *The How of Happiness*, Piatkus, London, 2007.

Chapter 1: Gratitude, savouring, anticipation

1 Robert Emmons, *Thanks!: How the New Science of Gratitude Can Make You Happier*, Houghton Mifflin Harcourt, Boston, 2000; Janice Kaplan, *The Gratitude Diaries: How a Year of Living Gratefully Changed My Life*, Dutton, New York, 2016.

2 Articles that tell us this include: Robert Emmons, 'Why Gratitude Is Good', *Greater Good Magazine*, 16 November 2010, accessed 27 January 2019, greatergood.berkeley.edu/article/item/why_gratitude_is_good; B. L. Fredrickson, M. M. Tugade, C. E. Waugh, G. R. Larkin, 'What good are positive emotions in crises? A prospective study of resilience and emotions following the terrorist attacks on the United States on September 11th, 2001', *Journal of*

Personality and Social Psychology, 84(2), 365–76, 2003; A. M. Wood, J. Maltby, R. Gillett, P. A. Linley, S. Joseph, 'The role of gratitude in the development of social support, stress, and depression: Two longitudinal studies', *Journal of Research in Personality*, 42: 854–71, 2008.

3 Robert Emmons, M. E. McCullough, 'Counting blessings versus burdens: An experimental investigation of gratitude and subjective well-being in daily life', *Journal of Personality and Social Psychology*, 84:377–89, 2003.

4 This quote is from Kaplan, *The Gratitude Diaries: How a Year of Living Gratefully Changed My Life.*

5 John Kralik, *365 Thank Yous: The Year a Simple Act of Daily Gratitude Changed My Life*, Penguin Books, Melbourne, 2011.

6 Laurie Santos, 'The Science of Well-Being', Yale University, 2018, accessed 1 April 2019; coursera.org/learn/the-science-of-well-being

7 Sonja Lyubomirsky, 'Hedonic adaptation to positive and negative experiences', *Oxford Handbook of Stress, Health, and Coping*, Oxford University Press, 2010.

Chapter 2: The very best morning routine

1 Roy Baumeister and John Tierney, *Willpower: Rediscovering the Greatest Human Strength*, Penguin Books, New York, 2012, conclusion.

2 For example, in this article: Vivian Giang, 'Why Early Risers Are Happier', *Business Insider*, 13 September 2012, accessed 10 December 2019, businessinsider.com.au/why-early-risers-are-happier-2012-9?r=US&IR=T. The article was based off this study: R. Biss, L. Hasher, 'Happy as a lark: Morning-type Younger and Older Adults Are Higher in Positive Affect', *Emotion*, 12(3), 437–41, 2012.

3 Dr Rob Carter III, Kirte Salwe Carter, *The Morning Mind*, AMACOM, New York, 2019, Chapter 5.

4 Marc Wittmann, Jenny Dinich, Martha Merrow, Till Roenneberg, 'Social Jetlag: Misalignment of Biological and Social Time', *Chronobiology International*, 23(1–2):497–509, February 2006.

5 Till Roenneberg, Martha Merrow, 'Entrainment of the Human Circadian Clock', *Cold Spring Harbor Symposia on Quantitative Biology*, 72:293–99, 2007.
6 Say, for example, K. P. Wright, A. W. McHill, B. R. Birks, B. R. Griffin, T. Rusterholz, E. D. Chinoy in 'Entrainment of the Human Circadian Clock to the Natural Light–Dark Cycle', *Current Biology*, 23(16):1554–58, 2013.
7 One article of many pieces of research that says as much is by M. Boubekri, I. N. Cheung, K. J. Reid, C. Wang, P. Zee: 'Impact of Windows and Daylight Exposure on Overall Health and Sleep Quality of Office Workers: A Case-control Pilot Study', *Journal of Clinical Sleep Medicine*, 10(6):603–11, 2014.
8 Katy Bowman, *Move Your DNA: Restore Your Health through Natural Movement*, Propriometrics Press, Ventura, California, 2017, Chapter 2.
9 Leanna Garfield, 'Checking Your Phone First Thing in the Morning Could Be Making You Unhappy', *Business Insider*, May 2016, accessed 18 December 2019, businessinsider.com.au/why-you-shouldnt-check-your-phone-first-thing-in-the-morning-2016-5?r=US&IR=T. The article was based on this study: K. Kushlev, E. W. Dunn, 'Checking Email Less Frequently Reduces Stress', *Computers in Human Behaviour*, 43:220–28, 2016.
10 Admiral William McRaven, Commencement Speech, University of Texas, Austin, 2014; youtube.com/watch?v=pxBQLFLei70
11 Charles Duhigg, *The Power of Habit*, William Heinemann, New York, 2012, Chapter 4.
12 Daniel Levitin, *The Organized Mind*, Penguin Books, New York, 2014, Chapter 1.
13 Rachel Nall, 'Are There Any Benefits to a Cold Shower?' *Medical News Today*, 12 July 2019, accessed 14 December 2019; medicalnewstoday.com/articles/325725.php#stronger-immune-system. Based on this study: G. A. Buijze, I. N. Sierevelt, B. C. van der Heijden, M. C. Dijkgraaf, M. H. Frings-Dresen, 'The Effect of Cold Showering on Health and Work: A Randomized Controlled Trial', *PLOS ONE*, 11(9):e0161749, 2016.
14 N. A. Shevchuk, 'Adapted Cold Shower as a Potential Treatment for Depression', *Medical Hypotheses*, 70(5):995–1001, 2016.

Chapter 3: Zest (energy, not citrus)

1 Gretchen Rubin, *The Happiness Project*, HarperCollins Inc., New York, 2015, Chapter 1.

2 This claim is supported by substantive research, including B. A. White, C. C. Horwarth, T. S. Conner, 'Many apples a day keep the blues away – daily experiences of negative and positive affect and food consumption in young adults', *British Journal of Health Psychology*, 18:782–98, 2013, and N. Ocean, P. Howley, J. Ensor, 'Lettuce be happy: A longitudinal UK study on the relationship between fruit and vegetable consumption and well-being', *Social Science and Medicine*, 222:335–45, 2019. Also, Tom Rath mentions it in *Eat Move Sleep*, Missionday, New York, 2013.

3 There are many proponents of this philosophy of eating 'real food' – Michael Polllan, David Gillespie and Sarah Wilson to name a few.

4 A. Nehlig, 'The neuroprotective effects of cocoa flavanol and its influence on cognitive performance', *British Journal of Clinical Pharmacology*, 75(3):716-27, 2012.

5 Drew Ramsey, *Eat Complete*, Harper Wave, New York, 2016, Chapter 1.

6 One of the most well-known and widely read book that synthesises some of this research is by Giulia Enders: *Gut: The Inside Story of Our Body's Most Underrated Organ*, Scribe, Melbourne, 2014.

7 C. White, '10,000 Steps – Is It Enough?' ABC News, accessed 19 December 2019, abc.net.au/news/health/2017-05-17/10000-steps-is-it-enough/8532768

8 Jono Lineen, *Perfect Motion*, Penguin Random House Australia, Sydney, 2019, Chapter 7.

9 H. Adam, A. D. Galinsky, 'Enclothed Cognition', *Journal of Experimental Social Psychology*, 48(4):918–25, 2012.

10 D. Kahneman, A. B. Krueger, D. Schkade, N. Schwarz, A. Stone, 'A Survey Method for Characterizing Daily Life Experience: The Day Reconstruction Method', *Science*, 306:1776–80, 2012.

11 T. Schwartz, 'Sleep Is More Important Than Food', *Harvard Business Review*, 2011, accessed 16 December 2019, hbr.org/2011/03/sleep-is-more-important-than-f.

12 N. A. Coles, J. T. Larsen, H. C. Lench, 'A Meta-Analysis of the Facial Feedback Literature: Effects of Facial Feedback on Emotional

Experience Are Small and Variable', *Psychological Bulletin*, 145(6):610–651. This journal article was summarised by *Science Daily* in 2019, accessed 16 December 2019, sciencedaily.com/releases/2019/04/190412094728.htm.

13 For example, M. Mortillaro, D. Dukes, 'Jumping for Joy: The Importance of the Body and of Dynamics in the Expression and Recognition of Positive Emotions', *Frontiers in Psychology*, 9:763, 2018.

14 Martin Seligman and John Tierney, 'We Aren't Built to Live in the Moment', *New York Times*, 19 May 2017, nytimes.com/2017/05/19/opinion/sunday/why-the-future-is-always-on-your-mind.html.

Chapter 4: Kindness

1 Sonja Lyubomirsky, *The How of Happiness*, Piatkus, London, 2007. The book referred to this journal article: S. Lyubomirsky, L. King, E. Diener, 'The Benefits of Frequent Positive Affect: Does Happiness Lead To Success?', *Psychological Bulletin*, 131(6):803–55, 2005.

2 Lyubomirsky, *The How of Happiness*. The experiment described is given in this journal article: S. Lyubomirsky, K. M. Sheldon, D. Schkade, 'Pursuing Happiness: The Architecture of Sustainable Change', *Review of General Psychology*, 9(2):111–31, 2007.

3 Ibid.

4 Lyubomirsky, *The How of Happiness*, Chapter 5.

5 Meik Wiking, *The Little Book of Lykke*, Penguin Books, London, 2017, p. 245.

6 Robert Cialdini, *Influence: Science and Practice*, HarperCollins, New York, 1984, Chapter 2.

7 S. Lyubomirsky, K. M. Sheldon, D. Schkade, 'Pursuing Happiness: The Architecture of Sustainable Change', *Review of General Psychology*, 9(2):111–31, 2007.

8 Dylan Alcott, *Able*, ABC Books, Sydney, 2018, p. 26.

9 Kate Northrup, *Do Less*, Hay House, Sydney, 2019, Chapter 5.

10 Valerie Folkes, 'Mindlessness or Mindfulness: A Partial Replication and Extension of Langer, Blank, and Chanowitz', *Journal of Personality and Social Psychology* 48(3):600–4, 1985.

Chapter 5: Self-talk

1 G. Deutscher, *Through the Language Glass*, Random House, New York, 2011.

2 Dr Tim Lomas, 'The Positive Lexicography', 2013; accessed 20 December 2019, drtimlomas.com/lexicography.

3 Katy Steinmetz, 'How Learning New Words Could Make You Happier', *TIME*, 8 May 2018, accessed 20 January 2019, time.com/5265277/learn-new-words-be-happy-translation/

4 L. Dye, 'Study: Negative Words Dominate Language', ABC News, 7 January 2006, accessed 2 February 2020, abcnews.go.com/Technology/DyeHard/story?id=460987&page=1

5 Ibid.

6 B. Fredrickson, *Positivity*, Oneworld Publications, London, 2009, Chapter 7. Original research from B. Fredrickson, M. F. Losada, 'Positive Affect and the Complex Dynamics of Human Flourishing, *American Psychologist*, 60(7), 678–86, 2005.

7 Brené Brown, *Gifts of Imperfection*, Hazelden Information and Educational Services, Center City, Minnesota, 2010.

Chapter 6: Self-love

1 B. J. Fogg, *Tiny Habits: The Small Changes That Change Everything*, Virgin Books, London, 2020.

2 C. Morewedge, D. Gilbert, K. Myrseth, K. Kassam, T. Wilson, 'Consuming experience: Why affective forecasters overestimate comparative value', *Journal of Experimental Social Psychology*, 46:986–92, 2010.

3 This was from Susan David, *Emotional Agility*, Penguin Books, New York, 2016, Chapter 4. The book references this study: Judith White, Ellen Langer, Leeat Yariv, John Welch, 'Frequent social comparisons and destructive emotions and behaviors: The dark side of social comparisons', *Journal of Adult Development*, 13(1): 36-44, 2006.

4 Zoë Foster Blake, *LOVE!*, Penguin Books, Melbourne, 2019.

5 Ibid.

Chapter 7: Love

1 Meik Wiking, *The Little Book of Hygge*, Penguin Life, London, 2016, Chapter 3.

2 Malcom Gladwell, *Talking to Strangers*, Penguin Books, New York, 2019.

3 Daniel Goleman, *Emotional Intelligence*, Bloomsbury Publishing, London, 1995, Chapter 13.

4 A good, scientifically and historically sound book about these phenomena is by Danielle Clode: *Killers in Eden*, Allen & Unwin, Sydney, 2002.

5 Steve Meacham, 'The king of the killers', *Sydney Morning Herald*, accessed 18 April 2010, smh.com.au/environment/conservation/the-king-of-the-killers-20100916-15er7.html.

6 Like this one: Julianne Holt-Lunstad, Timothy Smith, Mark Baker, Tyler Harris, David Stephenson, 'Loneliness and social isolation as risk factors for mortality: A meta-analytic review', *Perspectives on Psychological Science*, 10(2):227–37, 2015. Or you can literally google 'loneliness kills'.

7 Liz Mineo, 'Good genes are nice, but joy is better, *Harvard Gazette*, 11 April 2017, accessed 12 December 2019; news.harvard.edu/gazette/story/2017/04/over-nearly-80-years-harvard-study-has-been-showing-how-to-live-a-healthy-and-happy-life.

8 Ibid.

9 Robert Waldinger, 'What makes a good life? Lessons from the longest study on happiness', TED, 2010, viewed 10 October 2019; ted.com/talks/robert_waldinger_what_makes_a_good_life_lessons_from_the_longest_study_on_happiness.

10 Ellen Hendriksen, *How to Be Yourself*, St Martin's Press, New York, 2018; C. Wrzus, M. Hanel, J. Wagner, F. J. Neyer, 'Social network changes and life events across the life span: A meta-analysis', *Psychological Bulletin*, 139(1), 53–80, May 2012.

11 Read more in his book: Robin Dunbar, *How Many Friends Does One Person Need?: Dunbar's number and other evolutionary quirks*, Faber & Faber, London, 2010.

12 Esther Perel, *Mating in Captivity*, Harper, New York, 2017, introduction.

13 John Gottman, *The Seven Principles For Making Marriage Work*, Orion, London, 2004.
14 Gary Chapman, *The Five Love Languages*, Northfield Publishing, Chicago, 1992.

Chapter 8: Money

1 Peter Diamandis, 'Abundance is our future', TED, 2012, viewed 3 January 2020; ted.com/talks/peter_diamandis_abundance_is_our_future.
2 Clive Hamilton, *Affluenza: When Too Much Is Never Enough*, Allen & Unwin, Sydney, 2005.
3 Jeffrey Dew, 'Two Sides of the Same Coin? The Differing Roles of Assets and Consumer Debt in Marriage', *Journal of Family and Economic Issues*, 28(1):89–104, 2007.
4 Shelby Scott, Galena Rhoades, Scott Stanley, Elizabeth Allen, Howard Markman, 'Reasons for Divorce and Recollections of Premarital Intervention: Implications for Improving Relationship Education', *Couple Family Psychology*, 2(2): 131–45, 2013.
5 Hillary Hoffower, 'A woman who studied 600 millionaires says there's a misconception about wealth that just won't die', *Business Insider*, 20 January 2019, accessed 4 January 2020, businessinsider.com.au/difference-between-wealth-net-worth-income-2019-1?r=US&IR=T.
6 Daniel Kahneman, Angus Deaton, 'High income improves evaluation of life but not emotional well-being', *Proceedings of the National Academy of Sciences of the United States of America*, 107(38): 16489–93, 2010, pnas.org/content/107/38/16489.
7 Ian Sample, 'The Price of Happiness', *Guardian*, 7 September 2010.
8 Kahneman, Deaton, 'High income improves evaluation of life but not emotional well-being', *PNAS*, 2010.
9 Elizabeth Dunn, Lara Aknin, Michael Norton, 'Spending money on others promotes happiness', *Science*, 319(5870):1687–88, 2008.
10 The principles of this are given in this book: Elizabeth Dunn, Michael Norton, *Happy Money*, Oneworld Publications, London, 2013. Here is the original summary of the research: Dunn, Gilbert, Wilson, 'If money doesn't make you happy, then you probably

aren't spending it right', *Journal of Consumer Psychology*, 21:115–25, 2011.

11 Cassie Mogilner, Jennifer Aaker, 'The "time vs. money effect": shifting product attitudes and decisions through personal connection', *Journal of Consumer Research*, 36(2):277–91, 2009.

12 Dunn, Norton, *Happy Money.*

13 Daniel Kahneman, *Thinking Fast and Slow*, Penguin Books, London, 2011.

14 Matthew Killingsworth, Daniel Gilbert, 'A Wandering Mind Is an Unhappy Mind, *Science*, 330(6006):932, 2010.

15 Ibid.

16 Dunn, Gilbert, Wilson, 'If money doesn't make you happy, then you probably aren't spending it right', *Journal of Consumer Psychology.*

17 Timothy Wilson, Daniel Gilbert, 'Explaining Away: A Model of Affective Adaptation', *Perspectives on Psychological Science*, 3:370–86, 2008.

18 There is a difference between good debt and bad debt. If what you're buying won't go up in value or produce an income, it's bad.

19 Dunn, Aknin, Norton, 'Spending Money on Others Promotes Happiness', *Science.*

20 This was summarised in Dunn, Norton, *Happy Money*. This was the journal article: Dunn, Aknin, Norton, 'Spending Money on Others Promotes Happiness', *Science.*

21 Rob Nelissen, Marijn Meijers, 'Social benefits of luxury brands as costly signals of wealth and status', *Evolution and Human Behavior*, 32:343–55, 2011.

22 It was really hard to find an accurate figure for this. I got this figure from Ester Han, 'Big Stones and Bold Colours: How Celebrities Are Influencing Engagement Rings, *Sydney Morning Herald*, 6 February 2019, accessed 4 January 2020; smh.com.au/business/small-business/big-stones-and-bold-colours-how-celebrities-are-influencing-engagement-rings-20160205-gmmclm.html.

Chapter 9: Purpose

1 Barry Schwartz, *The Paradox of Choice*, HarperCollins, New York, Chapter 11.

2 Barry Schwartz, 'The Paradox of Choice', TED, ted.com/talks/barry_schwartz_the_paradox_of_choice.
3 John Helliwell, Richard Layard, Jeffrey Sach, World Happiness Report, Sustainable Development Solutions Network, New York, 2019, accessed 10 October 2019; worldhappiness.report/ed/2019/.
4 Rodger Dean Duncan, 'The Why of Work: Purpose and Meaning Really Do Matter,' *Forbes*, 11 September 2018, accessed 5 February 2020; forbes.com/sites/rodgerdeanduncan/2018/09/11/the-why-of-work-purpose-and-meaning-really-do-matter/#570911b368e1.
5 Ibid.
6 Ibid.
7 Sonja Lyubomirsky, *The How of Happiness*, p. 32.

Chapter 10: Hard times

1 Sheryl Sandberg, Adam Grant, *Option B*, Penguin, New York, 2017, Chapter 8.
2 Lorna Collier, 'Growth after Trauma', *American Psychological Association*, 47(10):48, November 2016; accessed 15 December 2019; apa.org/monitor/2016/11/growth-trauma.
3 I found out about these two researchers in Sheryl Sandberg and Adam Grant's *Option B*. Their work is in the *Handbook of Posttraumatic Growth: Research and Practice*, Routledge, New York, 2014.
4 Jonathan Haidt, *The Happiness Hypothesis*, Random House, New York, 2006, Chapter 7.
5 James Pennebaker, *Expressive Writing: Words That Heal*, Idyll Arbor, Washington, 2014.
6 There is a description of Pennebaker's studies in Haidt's book *The Happiness Hypothesis*.
7 Haidt, *The Happiness Hypothesis*, Chapter 7.
8 Karl Weick, 'Small Wins: Redefining the Scale of Social Problems', *American Psychologist* 39: 40–49, 1984; Teresa Amabile, Steven Kramer, 'The Progress Principle: Using Small Wins to Ignite Joy, Engagement, and Creativity at Work', *Harvard Business Review*, Boston, 2011; Martin Seligman, Tracy Steen, Nansook Park and Christopher Peterson, 'Positive Psychology Progress: Empirical

Validation of Interventions', *American Psychologist* 60, 410–21, 2005.
9 Jonathon Louth, Tanya Mackay, George Karpetis, Ian Goodwin-Smith, 'Understanding Vicarious Trauma', Australian Alliance for Social Enterprise, June 2019; centacare.org.au/new-study-understanding-vicarious-trauma/.
10 Karl Weick, 'Small Wins: Redefining the Scale of Social Problems', *American Psychologist.*
11 Lea Waters, *The Strength Switch*, Penguin Random House, Sydney, 2017.
12 Australian Health Ministers' Advisory Council 2013, 'A National Framework for Recovery-Oriented Mental Health Services', Australian Government Department of Health, Canberra; accessed June 2020, health.gov.au/internet/main/publishing.nsf/Content/67D17065514CF8E8CA257C1D00017A90/$File/recovgde.pdf.
13 The series of concentric circles is referred to as a Kvetching Order. For more: Susan Silk, Barry Goldman, 'How not to say the wrong thing,' *Los Angeles Times*, 7 April 2013, accessed 2 January 2020; latimes.com/opinion/op-ed/la-xpm-2013-apr-07-la-oe-0407-silk-ring-theory-20130407-story.html.

Chapter 11: Fun

1 Jane Hewes, 'Seeking Balance in Motion: The Role of Spontaneous Free Play in Promoting Social and Emotional Health in Early Childhood Care and Education', *Children*, National Center for Biotechnology Information, 1(3): 280–301, December 2014.
2 Ken Robinson, *Finding Your Element*, Penguin Books, London, 2014, Chapter 2.
3 Ibid., Chapter 4.

Chapter 12: Goals

1 Sonja Lyubomirsky, *The How of Happiness*, Piatkus, London, 2007. Also in Daniel Kahneman, E. Diener, N. Schwarz, *Well-Being*, Russell Sage Foundation, London, 1999; and Timothy Pychyl, 'Goal Progress and Happiness', *Psychology Today*, 7 June 2008.

2 Lyubomirsky, *The How of Happiness*.

3 Kennon Sheldon, Andrew Elliot, 'Goal striving, need satisfaction, and longitudinal well-being: The self-concordance model', *Journal of Personality and Social Psychology*, 76(3):482–97, 1999.

4 Lyubomirsky, *The How of Happiness*. The book referred to this research: Peter Bearman, Hannah Bruckner, 'Promising the future: virginity pledges and first intercourse', *American Journal of Sociology*, 106:859–912, 2001. And A. Greenwald, C. Carnot, R. Beach, P. Young, 'Increasing voting behaviour by asking people if they expect to vote', *Journal of Applied Psychology*, 72:315–18, 1987. And J. Norcross, M. Mrykalo, M. Blagys, 'Auld lang syne: Success predictors, change processes, and self-reported outcomes of New Year's resolvers and non-resolvers', *Journal of Clinical Psychology*, 58:397–405, 2002.

5 John Florio and Ouisie Shapiro, 'The Dark Side of Going For Gold', *Atlantic*, 18 August 2016, accessed 19 December 2019, theatlantic.com/health/archive/2016/08/post-olympic-depression/496244/.

Resources

For ease, I've gathered up most of the resources I've referred to in the book and put them in one spot: turiapitt.com/happy-resources. I've scoured the internet for the best stuff, like a life-changing TED talk and a playlist that's literally music to your ears.

As well, below is a list of exceptional resources that I'm 'positive' (haha) will contribute to you feeling good. I mean, I enjoyed them.

Digital courses

I've taught more than 40,000 people in my digital courses how to get happier and more confident. If you want to know more about them, check out turiapitt.com/happy-resources.

Books

These are the main books that I'd recommend if you're into this happiness stuff:

Zoë Foster Blake, *Love*, Penguin Books, Melbourne, 2019

John Kralik, *365 Thank Yous: The Year a Simple Act of Daily Gratitude Changed My Life*, Penguin Books, Melbourne, 2011

Sonja Lyubomirsky, *The How of Happiness*, Piatkus, London, 2007

Gretchen Rubin, *The Happiness Project*, HarperCollins, New York, 2015

Leigh Sales, *Any Ordinary Day*, Penguin Books, Melbourne, 2019

Sheryl Sandberg and Adam Grant, *Option B*, Penguin Books, New York, 2017

Food Books

Alyce Alexandra, *Thermo Cooker Fresh Favourites*, Viking, Sydney, 2019

Sarah Wilson, *I Quit Sugar*, Pan Macmillan, Sydney, 2013

Libby Weaver, *Dr Libby's Real Food Chef*, Little Green Frog Publishing, Sydney, 2012

Important services

If you're having a hard time or maybe feeling anxious, depressed or like you need some support, I would strongly suggest you seek the support of a psychologist, counsellor or other mental health professional. Here are some awesome organisations that can help you with that:

Lifeline

Lifeline is a national charity providing all Australians experiencing a personal crisis with access to 24-hour crisis support and suicide prevention services. Visit lifeline.org.au or call 13 11 14.

Beyondblue

Beyondblue works to address issues associated with depression, anxiety and related substance misuse disorders in Australia. Get support 24/7. Visit beyondblue.org.au or call 1300 22 4636.

Headspace

Headspace provides tailored and holistic mental health support to 12 to 25 year olds. Visit headspace.org.au.

Relationships Australia

A leading provider of relationship support services for individuals, families and communities. Visit relationships.org.au or call 1300 364 277.

1800RESPECT

This is the national sexual assault, domestic and family violence counselling service. Get support 24/7. Visit 1800respect.org.au or call 1800 737 732.

[illegible]

[illegible] Australia, [illegible] 2017. Viewed [illegible]

[illegible]

Headspace [illegible]

[illegible]

[illegible]

[illegible]

Acknowledgements

Ah! A long list of people I need, and want, to thank. You probably won't know any of them, though, so totally understandable if you want to skim it. I'm *really* just including it cos for some reason people like being acknowledged.

So! A big thanks to . . .

My letter gang! Thank you for allowing me to be in your inbox every week. It's a privilege to be able to write for you.

Grace McBride. A brilliant copywriter, marketing maven, and the co-founder of @spendwiththem. Thank you for your insights on this book, and for putting up with my incessant questioning and phone calls. You manage to understand exactly what I'm trying to say, and help me say it.

Catherine Hill, my editor. Thank you for your research recommendations, your input and your overall extremely judicious editing.

Ali Urquhart, my publisher. Thank you for your continued belief and support. I appreciate your guidance and your no-frills, upfront approach. Truly!

Pippa Mason, my agent. You get what I'm about, you get what I'm trying to do, you get me! Thank you. Oh, and thank you for enduring my flustered phone calls, my flurried emails, my panicked texts. Like, I said, you get me.

Mel, Kris and Amanda from Team Turia – thank you for being absolute legends while I wrote this book.

My friends and family, for demonstrating to me just how important good relationships really are.

My mum, for being the ultimate blueprint for what it means to live a happy life.

My beautiful man, for being the kind, compassionate, wholehearted and completely gung-ho human you are. Thank you for your support of everything I do.

And to my two beautiful sons, Hakavai and Rahiti. You have both enriched my life beyond measure. I love you infinitely.

Discover a new favourite

Visit penguin.com.au/readmore